# The New York Times

## COZY SUNDAY CROSSWORDS
### 75 Puzzles from the Pages of *The New York Times*

## Edited by Will Shortz

ST. MARTIN'S GRIFFIN ⚜ NEW YORK

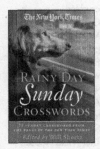

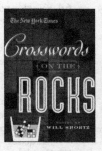
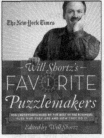

# BEST PICTURE ADAPTATIONS

## ACROSS

1 2013 Best Picture nominee in which a main character isn't human
4 Airplane part
9 "Hairspray" mom usually played by a man
13 Leg presses work them
18 60 minuti
19 Successors to Cutlasses
21 Best Picture adaptation about . . . a search for the perfect brew, with "The"?
23 Disney Channel's "___ and Maddie"
24 . . . inaudible metrical poetry, with "The"?
26 Northeast Corridor train
28 Like groaners
29 River islet
30 1988 chart-topping country album
32 Game for bankers?
33 Psychedelic
37 . . . a fat Eastern monarch?
43 One in a no-blinking contest
45 Second draft
46 Neighbor
48 Extended rental?
49 Sea urchin, at a sushi bar
50 . . . fools accompanying a pack of wild animals?
56 King's handful
59 Chance occurrence, old-style
60 Bad sound in a changing room
61 Vegas-to-Denver dir.
62 Part of a city network
63 "Relax"
64 Reusable part of a common thank-you gift
67 . . . a reed and percussion duet?
71 Group standing at the U.N.
74 Treat with a "Golden" variety
75 They rank below marquises
79 Words before and after "what"
80 O.T. book before Jeremiah
81 Chorus line?
82 Obstacle in road repairs, maybe
84 . . . an éclair or crème brûlée, with "The"?
90 Previously
91 Spork part
92 Daughter in E. M. Forster's "Howards End"
93 Neighbor of Irkutsk on a Risk board
96 Badger
99 . . . gorgeous fur?
103 Shred
105 Lit ___
106 Safari sight?
107 Singer DiFranco
108 Like a portrait that seems to be watching you
110 Winnower
113 . . . cooties from hugs and kisses?
121 Blender setting
122 . . . a salon woman I go to?
123 Tush
124 Set of anecdotes
125 A while, in hyperbole
126 Olympian with a bow
127 Jet similar to a 747
128 Benedictine title

## DOWN

1 Chihuahua greeting
2 Country singer Church
3 * * * *
4 Honeydew cousins
5 U.S. women's soccer star Krieger
6 Volume measure
7 Cause of boiling over
8 Sarge, e.g.
9 Jet
10 Stand up to
11 Bit of safari equipment
12 Enlightened Buddhist
13 "Enough is enough!"
14 "___ voce poco fa" (Rossini aria)
15 PIN point
16 One having a ball?
17 G.R.E. takers: Abbr.
20 Ice cream order
22 Juniors, maybe
25 Writer ___ Stanley Gardner
27 1880s–'90s veep ___ P. Morton
31 Step ___
32 Half of a Vegas show duo
34 Shroud
35 ___ Drive (street where Harry Potter grew up)
36 Dweller along the Mandeb Strait
37 Bridge support
38 "As such . . ."
39 College campus offering
40 Like carpaccio or crudités
41 Geisha's accessory
42 Metaphorical low point
44 Physicist Nathan who postulated wormholes
47 Attempt at a dunk tank
51 Spiced teas
52 The White House's ___ Room
53 Peeping Tom's spot
54 Modern encyclopedia platform
55 Muses
57 Simon of the "Mission: Impossible" films
58 It circles the globe
63 Merino mother
64 Stethoscope's place
65 War on Poverty agcy.
66 Main ingredient in queso relleno
68 Bite
69 Like candied apples
70 Gillette razor name
71 Liquor purchase
72 Ring around the collar?
73 Chief Theban god
76 Hightailed it
77 Peaceful protest
78 Apt anagram of SNAKE
82 Slip
83 Quash
85 Peachy

by Kevin G. Der

**86** Things zygotes come from

**87** Penpoint

**88** Commission, e.g.

**89** "You're stuck with me"

**94** What stars do

**95** Hilton alternative

**97** Equilibrium

**98** Sancho Panza, e.g.

**100** About ¾ of a football field

**101** ___ Heep (Dickens villain)

**102** Like some sponsorship packages

**104** One taking a long shot?

**108** Prefix with spore

**109** "Slow Churned" brand

**111** Antipasto pairing

**112** Reason for a class struggle?

**113** TV inits. since 1975

**114** Photographer's asset

**115** Certain fraternity chapter

**116** "Wowie!"

**117** Musician's asset

**118** Lapel attachment

**119** Suffix with subsist

**120** Never, in Nikolaus

## ACROSS

1 "Shucks!"
7 They might be covered on your first day of employment
13 Only a second ago
20 Ones with good poker faces?
21 Charm City ballplayer
22 With a leg on either side of
23 Where you can find . . . "jacket" or "yourself"?
25 "Yay!"
26 Lentil or coconut
27 Chinese philosophy
28 Student's saver
29 Plus
31 . . . "go" or "so"?
37 . . . "anybody" or "cooking"?
44 Dog holder
45 A.F.L.-___
46 "Over here!"
47 "Aww"-inspiring
49 Muhammad's birthplace
51 Lover boy
52 Like Fermat's last theorem, eventually
53 Much appreciated
54 They decide what's fair
55 Oteri of "S.N.L."
56 Material in mitochondria
59 Acclaims
60 Issuer of IDs: Abbr.
61 Shade
62 Its material is not hard
64 ___-gritty
65 . . . "got" or "tell"?

69 Result of hitting the bar?
71 "The price we pay for love," per Queen Elizabeth II
72 Goddess who gained immortality for her lover but forgot to ask for eternal youth (whoops!)
73 Flirtatious wife in "Of Mice and Men"
76 They stand up in their bed
77 Kind of gift
78 Sports team bigwig
81 Cash register
82 Like the installments of "A Tale of Two Cities"
83 "Ver-r-ry funny!"
85 Abu ___
86 Obliterate
87 Suspenseful sound
90 ___ Finnigan, friend of Harry Potter
91 Contraction missing a V
92 Kind of verb: Abbr.
93 . . . "two" or "face"?
95 . . . "building" or "hours"?
100 Flames that have gone out?
101 Assist in crime
102 Indian spice mix
107 Things you may dispense with?
110 Take over for
113 . . . "that's" or "special"?
116 "That much is clear"
117 Pays for the meal
118 Stay cheerful despite adversity

119 Back entrance
120 Jellyfish relatives named for a mythological monster
121 Private property?

## DOWN

1 Woof
2 "___ your daddy?"
3 River that flows south to north
4 Sets free into the world
5 "Ta-ta!"
6 Directional abbr.
7 "___ Nox" (Mozart title meaning "good night")
8 Greek vessel
9 Enthusiastic Spanish assent
10 Debt docs
11 Scale
12 Collection
13 Chin former
14 "DJ Got Us Fallin' in Love" singer, 2010
15 Women's retro accessory
16 Offensive poster
17 Small bite
18 Part of the classic Chinese work "Shih Ching"
19 Puny
24 "Was ___ hard on them?"
30 "___ Lat" (traditional Polish song)
32 Subside
33 Opposite of -less
34 Paranormal
35 Fine point
36 Provokes
37 Persian Empire founder
38 Impends

39 ___-Loompa (Willy Wonka employee)
40 Fictional braggart
41 The "O" of B.O.
42 Setting for a watch?
43 "We'll teach you to drink deep ___ you depart": Hamlet
48 Et cetera
49 Certain racy magazines
50 Lift
52 "Glad that's done!"
53 Street fair participant
55 "Aww"-inspiring
57 Empire State sch.
58 Org. with an emergency number
61 Razz, as a speaker
63 What the pros say
65 Hesitates
66 Default avatar for a new Twitter user
67 Reconstruction, for one
68 Contraction missing a V
69 From both sides, in a way
70 Songs of praise
73 City whose name looks like it could mean "my friend"
74 Track holder?
75 A Beethoven piece was für her
76 Win every game
79 Exhilarated cry
80 ___ cabbage
81 "End of discussion"
84 Botanist Gray
85 "A man can be destroyed but not ___": Hemingway
87 Age for a quinceañera
88 ". . . ___ quit!"

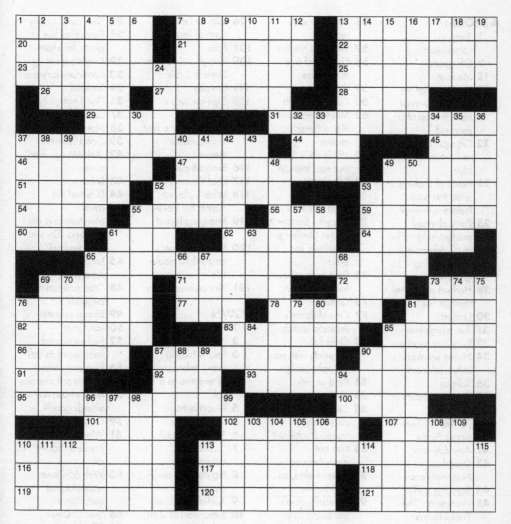

*by Tom McCoy*

**89** "The Silmarillion" creature
**90** Red ___
**94** Newspaper V.I.P. Baquet
**96** Pollute
**97** Too big for one's britches, say?
**98** Hotheadedness?

**99** Disposable board
**103** Let go
**104** Twinkler
**105** Lead-in to boy
**106** Something to mourn
**108** Red giant in Cetus
**109** Cozy

**110** Rend
**111** "The Name of the Rose" novelist
**112** "___ Meninas" (Velázquez painting)
**113** Highest degree
**114** ___-Wan Kenobi
**115** Family docs

## ACROSS

1 Jump to conclusions
7 Off-guard
12 Medium
19 Has reservations
20 It may be waved from the top of a pyramid
22 Olympic group in red, white and blue
23 Result of shaking a soda too hard before opening?
25 Parts of many modern addresses
26 In ___ (gestating)
27 Homecoming giveaways
28 Herbert of the Pink Panther films
30 Limited
31 5 is a high one
32 Busy Apr. workers
34 Noted sexologist, in her infancy?
36 Yahoos
38 Common tidbits in fried rice
40 "Is That All There Is" singer Peggy
41 Any day now
43 Daniel ___ National Forest
44 Stocking stuffer
45 Heroine of "The Rocky Horror Picture Show"
47 Strike caller
48 "The paternity results are in . . . it's the protagonist of a long-running BBC sci-fi show!"?
51 Bury
53 Masseuse's stock
54 Messages you don't want to send to your parents accidentally
55 Nosy person's request
57 Watson's creator
58 Element of one's inheritance
59 Go to ___
60 Cousins of gulls
62 Maiden name of Harry Potter's mother
64 1970s–'80s Sixers star and friends?
68 Take out to dinner
70 Area with R.N.s
72 Disorder that the Ice Bucket Challenge benefited, for short
73 Certain Facebook reaction button
75 Collar
77 One of Spain's Balearic Islands
79 Ones fully agreeing with you, metaphorically
81 Kind of pick
82 "P.U.!"
85 Controversial TV personality's magical sidekick?
88 "I'm not overwhelmed"
89 Overwhelms, as with humor
91 Ironically, small Starbucks size
92 "Two thumbs up!"
93 "Quién ___?" ("Who knows?": Sp.)
95 QB's try: Abbr.
96 "Primal Fear" star, 1996
97 Rimes of country
98 Hurt a Bond villain?
101 A little progress, idiomatically
102 Quick smoke?
105 Loving, as eyes
106 Inits. at Grand Central Terminal
107 Feds
109 Fanny ___, Barbra Streisand role
111 Quickly
113 Sign on Lucy's "Peanuts" booth . . . or a hint to this puzzle's theme
116 Broccoli pieces
117 Four Corners tribe
118 What's played mainly for kicks?
119 Mid-Long Island community
120 Rahm Emanuel's post-White House title
121 Not on board, say

## DOWN

1 Make sense
2 "Ish"
3 Sports bigwig every February
4 Alternative to a cab
5 Resort area in northeast Pa.
6 12-Across's skill
7 "___ moi le déluge"
8 Big name in audio equipment
9 Audio equipment
10 Jump-start of sorts, in brief
11 Eucalyptus lovers
12 Our Children magazine org.
13 Release
14 The P.L.O.'s Arafat
15 Just below average
16 Resolve a dispute in a modern way
17 Has the lights off, perhaps
18 Detective's assignment
21 "Butt out!," briefly
24 Certain airline alerts, for short
29 Knight's greeting
33 Continues forward
34 Topless?
35 Plead not guilty
37 ___ and aahs
38 Moue
39 Good listeners
42 "Ask Me Another" airer
43 Suborn
44 Directed the rowers
45 Matchmaking site that asks "Do you keep kosher?"
46 Land in South America
48 "You sure got me pegged!"
49 Strong appetite
50 Latin love
52 Bird so named because of its call
56 Frequent James Franco collaborator
58 Rock whose name sounds good?
59 Certain notebooks
61 Where "The Princess Diaries" is set
63 With 65-Down, technological escalations
65 See 63-Down
66 "The Hunger Games" star, in tabloids
67 Pattern for a forensic scientist
69 Future dealings?
71 Chip material
74 Financial ___
76 Dickens nom de plume
78 Beat
79 Department head
80 In fine shape

by Finn Vigeland

**81** Yemeni seaport
**82** Baseball V.I.P.s
**83** Like many uneditable files
**84** "Cry me a river!"
**86** Tabloid twosome
**87** Stereotypically rowdy dudes
**90** 1961 Michelangelo Antonioni drama
**94** Awards won by Stephen King and Agatha Christie
**96** Successor to South Carolina's Thurmond in the Senate
**97** Time to give up?
**99** Kentucky Derby winner's wreath
**100** Abbr. on a cover sheet
**101** Furnishings
**103** More dangerous in the winter, say
**104** Comedy, e.g.
**105** Loopy little films?
**107** Down Under greeting
**108** Bad thing to lose
**110** Rolling in it
**112** Superlative finish
**114** Longoria of "Telenovela"
**115** She-bear: Sp.

## ACROSS

1 It's accommodating
6 Comic cries of frustration
10 Grouped for threshing, say
17 Continuing story
18 Busybody
19 Sly one?
20 Many-time Indy 500 pace car
21 Pruritic
22 Goal on a first down
23 Handle letters
24 Boy who challenges stereotypes
26 Ruin
27 Hazel's love in "The Fault in Our Stars"
28 Musical with the songs "Santa Fe" and "I Should Tell You"
30 Blockheaded
31 Showing acute embarrassment, say
32 Anti-Communist fervor
34 1991 film with the tagline "The secret of life? The secret's in the sauce"
36 Symbols of audience disapproval
38 Feller in a forest?
39 ___'easter
41 Spinners
42 Most nail-biting
43 Fill-in-the-blanks diversion
46 The world, idiomatically
47 Soil
48 ___ lane
49 Poet who wrote "Jupiter from on high laughs at lovers' perjuries"
51 Like "E.T." and "Close Encounters of the Third Kind"
53 Finish ahead of
57 Summer, in much of West Africa
58 Former "Live" co-host with Kathie Lee
60 The Rolling Stones' "Get Yer ___ Out"
61 Sidekick in 1990s "S.N.L." skits
62 Trident piece?
64 Clog, with "up"
66 Call before reserving?
67 Stadium store souvenir
68 Stolas : women :: ___ : men
69 Distiller Walker
71 Affix, in a way
73 Bay, e.g.
74 First-year J.D. student
75 Use, as a dish
77 Save, with "away"
78 Top choice
79 Brand with two harnessed horses in its logo
81 Dolls' counterpart
83 Creepazoid
85 Trembling
88 Pilot
90 "Success-s-s!"
91 Meeting around lunchtime
92 Illegal action shown literally in this answer?
94 Not deep, as entertainment
98 Blushes
99 Cinnamon-flavored candy
100 Smarted
102 What spirits may do
103 Workplaces where gloves are worn, for short
104 Ordering option
105 Has a quiet evening, say
107 ___-Caps
108 "For real?"
111 On the double
112 Confront aggressively
114 Incident not worth talking about
115 Its capital is Whitehorse
116 Starting point for Pompeii tourism
117 Busy
118 Idyllic place
119 Part of a kite

## DOWN

1 Lab vessel
2 Noted name in suits
3 Long on screen
4 One going for a board position?
5 Like the moon during a total lunar eclipse
6 Designed to clear the air
7 Jerry Siegel or Joe Shuster, for Superman
8 Department store eponym
9 Busybody, maybe
10 Coronary ___
11 Detroit Tiger whose #5 is retired
12 Cambridgeshire city
13 Mobile home: Abbr.
14 Accepted an apology
15 Lasts
16 Calorie counter's temptation
17 Chow (down)
18 Turin title
19 Places to wallow
25 Crossed
26 Is angry
29 Keep, as a garden
31 Youth detention center in England
32 Over the moon
33 Feature of many a reception
35 ___ Umbridge, teacher of Dark Arts at Hogwarts
37 Now
38 Something that might fall off the shelf?
40 1948 John Wayne film
42 Chooses to lead
43 Legal maneuver
44 Requite
45 Cornell athletes
47 Tinder successes, say
48 Strictly follow
50 Limbs' ends
52 Trips in the dark?
54 Fake
55 Dual-channel
56 Stuffing herb
59 Sound heard at a beach
61 Decorous
63 Baltic capital
65 Pages have four of them
67 Frozen aisle icon
69 Ginger feature
70 Miss badly, say
72 Lived
75 Symbol of Washington State
76 "Oops!"
80 Cusps
82 Annual December pub crawl
84 Defects and all
85 Fats Domino's real first name
86 Grows sick of
87 Goofing (around)
88 Kind of body
89 Most common family name in Vietnam
92 Webster shelfmate
93 Key part: Abbr.
95 Break from a band, maybe
96 Crime writer Joseph
97 Brings (out)
99 Harass
101 Fairy tale figure
104 Evolutionary diagram
105 Pre-fries?

by David Woolf

**106** Org. with Divisions I-III
**109** Social gathering
**110** Like most children's programming
**111** Something said repeatedly on a ship
**113** Sgt.'s inferior

# SPORTS PAGE HEADLINES

## ACROSS

1 Foyer fixture
9 Paratroopers' gear
15 Building material for an 80-Across (in two different ways?)
20 Unsympathetic response to a complainer
21 Warhol's "Campbell's Tomato Juice Box," e.g.
22 Italian vessel?
23 Conflict at sea
26 Asia's ___ Sea
27 Geological flat top
28 Staple at a luau
29 Orange Pixar character
30 Main character in Kafka's "The Metamorphosis"
32 River ___ (tributary of the Thames)
34 Balls or fire preceder
37 Way off
40 Decides, in a way
44 Dura ___ (brain membrane)
46 "That's more than I want to know!"
47 Parenting problem at a zoo
52 Luke Skywalker's landspeeder, e.g.
53 Spill one's secrets
54 "The Governator"
55 Focus of study for Niels Bohr
56 Lead-in to dealer or dialer
59 Winter Palace resident
61 Particulars, in slang
62 Logician's word
63 Show weariness
65 Eight days after the nones
67 Choice word?
69 Cold War synopsis
74 Rimes with rhymes
75 Othello, for one
76 "Kewl!"
77 Catch
80 See 15-Across
83 It may be recounted
85 Be highly esteemed
87 Not mad
88 Roger Bannister, notably
89 Word repeated in James Brown's "It's a ___ ___ ___ World"
91 "Please show some compassion!"
94 Show of respect at the Vatican
99 Wood in Lucius Malfoy's wand
100 Dear one?
101 Rapt
102 Twosome
104 Incapacitate, in a way
105 "Inside the N.B.A." airer
106 Yemen, once
111 Subj. for a radio astronomer
113 One in a gray suit, for short
115 Most-applied-to sch. in the U.S.
119 Split pair
120 Overthrow of a monarchy
126 Smart ___
127 Only guest host in the 21 years of Leno's "The Tonight Show"
128 It requires a balancing act
129 City of Light, informally
130 Gives the old heave-ho
131 Faulty connections?

## DOWN

1 Food ___ (feelings after big meals)
2 John who wrote "Appointment in Samarra"
3 Hussein : Obama :: ___ : Garfield
4 "Through many dangers, ___ and snares I have already come" ("Amazing Grace" lyric)
5 Burgundy of "Anchorman"
6 "Pardon . . ."
7 Heart
8 Big name in headphones
9 Number cruncher, for short
10 Short shorts
11 Until
12 The Seal of Solomon and others
13 Before, poetically
14 Letters on many a racecar
15 Part of a plot
16 ___ queen
17 Pitched poorly
18 Queen ___
19 SAT org.
24 Raft material
25 Pentium creator
31 Profess
33 Long stretch
35 Supercontinent of 200 million years ago
36 "___ be my pleasure"
38 Scope
39 Climbs
41 World of Warcraft beast
42 Waver of a wand
43 Bathroom tile shade
45 Prepped
47 Cowardly Lion harasser
48 Bathroom bar
49 The Pink Panther, in "The Pink Panther"
50 Takes the place of, in batting
51 Seventh film in the "Rocky" series
52 ___ characters (basic means of writing Chinese)
57 "___ the season . . ."
58 Leftover
60 Hardly original works
63 Curled one's lip
64 Police blotter letters
66 Fair-hiring inits.
68 Org. with the Eddie Eagle safety program
70 Tree with catkins
71 Charms
72 Long stretch
73 Delicacy usually eaten as an appetizer
78 Marching band?
79 Queen ___ (pop music nickname)
80 Stoked
81 Deli roll
82 Rubens or Raphael
84 Gets fitted for a suit?
86 Drive-___
87 Pool site
90 Leave runny on the inside, say
92 Compete
93 Leftovers
95 Once-common campus event
96 Welcome to the fold?
97 Downside
98 Go haywire
103 Clear for takeoff?
107 OutKast chart-topper

*by Priscilla Clark and Jeff Chen*

108 On the button
109 Southern beauty
110 Low mounts?
112 Take a hit
114 Sein : German :: ___ :
    French
116 Cotton or country
    follower
117 Siberian river

118 Dry
120 Time out?
121 ___ russe
122 A card?
123 Deli offering
124 Alternatives to Macs
125 What a constant
    hand-washer prob-
    ably has, for short

## ACROSS

1 Carol opening
7 Unable to make a mess?
11 "Yeah, same here"
19 Crankcase base
20 Rib-eye alternative
21 "S.N.L." cast member, 1985–90
22 Emmerich who directed "Independence Day"
23 Portrayer of Buffett in "Too Big to Fail"
24 Doesn't cool down
25 What's involved in a tongue twister?
28 Alternative to "la"
29 School leader?
30 Good looks or a nice personality
31 Who said "If you even dream of beating me, you'd better wake up and apologize"
32 Very, very top of the earth's crust?
35 Outback baby
37 ___ Na Na
39 Subject of many an internet meme
40 Did some house-cleaning
41 Internet annoyances
44 Handler of many trays, for short
45 Unit of bricks, so to speak
47 Beryl and bornite
48 Mary Kay rival
49 First home of the three rich little pigs?
55 Sporty Spice of the Spice Girls
56 We all do it
57 Recently retired Laker great, to fans

58 Green Day drummer
63 Gussying up
66 Wally's bro, '50s–'60s TV
68 Raw footage?
69 Counting rhyme start
70 Bank window letters
72 Donald Duck's nephews, e.g.
74 ___ Barkley, Truman's vice president
75 Sing about?
76 Dixie term of address
78 Curt ___, 2001 World Series M.V.P.
80 Suffragist Elizabeth Cady ___
83 Polish site
85 Entrance requirements, informally
86 The first step
87 Two things the candy lover took to the beach?
90 Going ___
91 Still quite red
95 Abbr. on a copier tray
96 Every leader of North Korea so far
97 Like supermarkets, theaters and planes
99 Sci-fi-inspired toys of the 1980s
101 Suffix with Darwin
103 Point
104 Peer onstage
105 What an overbearing sergeant causes?
108 Green org.
110 Actress Hayek

114 . . . , to Samuel Morse
115 Spirits: Abbr.
116 What improved tire tread produces?
119 Something you might have a handle on
122 New Mexico natives
123 Ruin, as a parade
124 IMAX predecessor
125 Cousin of an impala
126 Seinfeld's "puffy shirt," e.g.
127 Painkillers
128 Spine part
129 Detects

## DOWN

1 It helps get the blood flowing
2 Some gowns
3 "American Psycho" author
4 The cantina in "Star Wars," e.g.?
5 Bit of summer wear
6 Onetime Expos/Mets outfielder Chávez
7 X-coordinate
8 Custom
9 New York native
10 "Vive ___!"
11 Response: Abbr.
12 Too tired for the task, say
13 Product that works, and is stored, under the sink
14 Mystery writer Dorothy
15 "___ bodkins!"
16 More run-down
17 Like some soap
18 Shifts to the right

20 Follow
26 Appointment book page
27 Fed. reactor monitor
33 Ink
34 Wee hour
36 Will work
38 Peddle
41 Coddles
42 Have thirds, say
43 Cornmeal dish
44 Hot
46 Winter Olympics powerhouse: Abbr.
50 "Glad the week's almost over!"
51 Pitchfork-wielding group
52 Help illegally
53 Narrows the gap with
54 Only country with a nonrectangular flag
59 Where they sell accessories at a pet shop?
60 Like a satellite's path
61 Unvarying in tone
62 Kind of truck
64 Red Cross setup
65 Humongous
67 Mark
71 Group sharing a tartan
73 Only state with a nonrectangular flag
77 Rap epithet
79 "Nope, huh-uh"
81 Night ___
82 Bottom-line figure
84 Villain in "The Avengers"
88 Historic blocks
89 Internet surfing, often

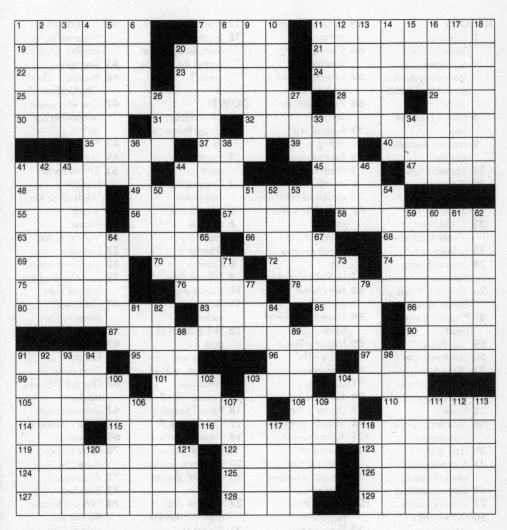

by Samuel A. Donaldson

**91** Daphne du Maurier novel made into a Best Picture
**92** Flooded with
**93** "South Pacific" star ___ Brazzi
**94** Squeak (by)
**98** Proportionate
**100** Like a clear night sky
**102** Quill tip
**103** Yearly tree growths
**104** Long-nosed fish
**106** Online finance firm
**107** Moved like sap
**109** Concern for vets
**111** "Peanuts" thumb-sucker
**112** North Woods denizen
**113** Queen ___ lace
**117** Some, to Spaniards
**118** Some Wall St. traders
**120** "Ideas worth spreading" grp.
**121** "Live ___" (Taco Bell slogan)

# DOUBLE QUOTE

## ACROSS

1 Onetime Scandinavian automaker (containing the first part of the "double quote")
5 Music's Prince of Soul
9 Precious Australian exports
14 Abandon détente
19 Victimizes
21 Like pets but not strays
22 2015 Oscar winner Morricone
23 Solitary sort
24 Dream of many Koreans
26 Youngest "Brady Bunch" daughter
27 "No, no, it's my treat!"
29 "___ Fideles"
30 Senatorial vote
31 "Key Largo" gangster Johnny
33 Church group
35 Break
36 Time periods in a polo match
39 U people?
41 Authoritarian announcements
44 Catch something
47 In the doldrums
50 Golden calf's maker
51 Birds with throat pouches
54 Comp-sci acronym
56 Steep
57 Sitcom whose title character was Fran Fine
59 Perfumery oils
60 ___-Cat
61 First secretary of homeland security
62 Tank tops?
64 Make noise while asleep
66 Corresponding expense?
67 First-chair violinist, perhaps
68 Person with an account
71 Political org. dating to 1854
74 Bear witness
75 Painkiller first sold in 1950
76 Unable to continue
77 Nameless network user
78 Some dumps
80 Image Awards org.
81 Hall of announcing
82 Pan's home, in myth
84 Minority branch of Islam
86 Longtime Texas politico Phil
87 Free throws, e.g.
91 ___ horn
94 Judges to be
97 Use as a bed
98 Mom-to-aunt term
101 Actress Mason
103 Journalist/ columnist Carl
105 France : madame :: Italy : ___
107 Request for permission
109 Showing few lights, as cities during W.W. II
112 Follow
113 Beeper from "a long time ago," informally
114 Speaker of this puzzle's "double quote"
115 Have another crack at
116 Long

64 Make noise while asleep
117 Humorist Bombeck
118 Spotted (containing the last part of the "double quote")

## DOWN

1 Like vindaloo
2 Golfer Palmer, to fans
3 Health care giant
4 Disputed North Pole visitor
5 Sir, in Surrey
6 Emulate
7 Head guy in "Hamlet"?
8 Draw in
9 Difficult duty
10 Market problem
11 Technology eschewers
12 Not secured, as a gate
13 Reagan-era program, in brief
14 Went over
15 Crosses the sill
16 Pernod flavoring
17 Crowd scenes?
18 "Woman With a Parasol" painter
20 Kikkoman product
25 "Oliver!" director Reed
28 "___ any drop to drink": Coleridge
31 Repent of
32 Consents to
34 "Bearded" flower
36 Celebrate gloatingly
37 Grown-up pullet
38 Deceptive police op
40 Freight train component
41 Delicately applies
42 Be deserving of
43 Treated with a preservative, as telephone poles
45 Teen spots
46 Michael's wife in "The Godfather"
47 One who seems responsible but isn't
48 Faux sophistication
49 Slam
51 Reform Party founder
52 "Idylls of the King" woman
53 Shaver
55 Without a date
57 Explicitly
58 Med. care options
59 ___ Villa (English football club)
61 Like major generals
62 Pushes
63 Nonhuman 1930s film star
65 Draft picks
66 Gun full of blanks, maybe
67 Shirt ornament
68 Fanta competitor
69 Quarters
70 Record label owned by Sony
72 As soon as
73 Fires (up)
74 "We are always the same ___ inside": Gertrude Stein
75 Nth degree?
76 Place for a throne
78 It's all downhill from here
79 "I feel that way, too"
80 Hairsplitter's objection
83 Storm shower?
84 "Homeland" network, for short

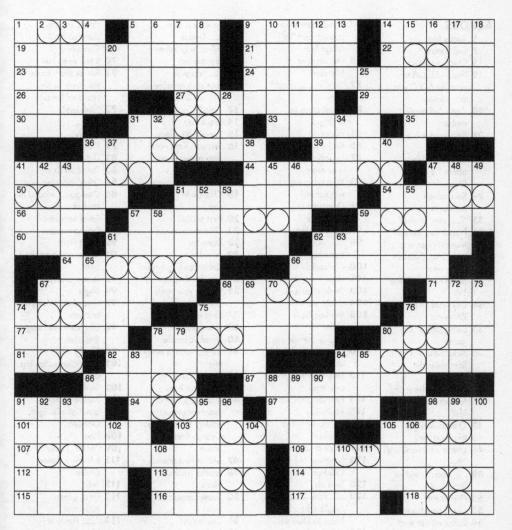

## by Patrick Berry

85 Darling
86 Take a turn for the worse
88 High rollers?
89 Add color to, in a way
90 Lead-in to -itis
91 It may contain bugs

92 Football Hall-of-Famer Bobby
93 Private meeting
95 Mazda two-seater
96 Fully enjoy
98 [Bo-o-oring!]
99 Harden
100 Underworld figure
102 Vietnam War copter

104 "___ Flux" (1990s animated series)
105 Cotillion attendee
106 Horatian collection
108 Put
110 "Gone With the Wind" studio
111 Verdi's "O patria ___"

## ACROSS

1 Really tiny
7 Deli fixture
15 Over yonder
19 First N.F.L. QB to pass for 5,000 yards in a season
20 Cathedral music maker
21 Best hand value in baccarat
22 Double feature about the Arctic Ocean?
24 Kardashian matriarch
25 "___ sow, so shall . . ."
26 French for "square"
27 Museumgoer, e.g.
29 Upholstery problem
30 Sealy rival
31 Some Korean-made TVs
34 City hard hit by the Zika virus
35 Didn't play in the game
36 Actor who was lionized in the 1930s?
38 . . . about the search for extraterrestrial life?
42 Chump change
45 Mustang rival
46 Unfair treatment, with "the"
49 . . . about baseball-sized hail?
52 First home?
53 Like a neat freak
54 Suffix with project
55 Actress Amanda of "Togetherness"
57 Additional, in adspeak
58 Got room service
64 Dope
66 Forget to carry the one, e.g.
67 . . . about Lee Harvey Oswald not being the lone gunman?
72 When doubled, something to beat
73 Bow

74 Bandleader who popularized the conga line
75 Like much of Namibia
77 "Within ___ a hell": Shak.
80 Number on un orologio
81 About
85 Kitchen counters?
87 . . . about attending a funeral?
93 Watchdog org., in two senses?
94 Occupant of a 52-Across
95 Stein relative
96 . . . about an insomniac?
100 Optimistic
101 Floor
103 Wide shoe spec
104 U.S.N. rank
105 Marked, as a ballot
107 Cap-and-trade org.
110 Basis of a political scandal, maybe
113 They lose their heads over time
114 Promising exchange
115 Really tiny
116 . . . about Pablo Escobar?
121 Manual component
122 Longtime "All My Children" role
123 Turn on
124 ___ Park (Chicago neighborhood once home to Obama)
125 Most geeky
126 Yak, yak, yak

## DOWN

1 H.I.V. research org.
2 Foot bones
3 Only U.S. state motto in Spanish
4 Hall-of-Fame slugger Johnny
5 Chemical suffix
6 Liszt wrote three for piano
7 Kind of heart valve

8 Tool for a duel
9 ___ Lingus
10 What may follow a breakdown
11 ___-Magnon
12 Tourist destination SSE of Delhi
13 Amalfi Coast city
14 Breaks up
15 Cross with a loop
16 Stephen King novel with a pyrokinetic character
17 Hill in Hill hearings
18 Change to all zeros, say
20 First section
23 "This means ___!"
28 Done for
30 Avoid
31 Canadian flag symbol
32 Fed. lending agency
33 Where your roots are
37 Kind of watch
39 Standoffish
40 Heraldic border
41 Cereal used in party mix
42 Open-house org.
43 A, on the Aare
44 It "never solves a problem without raising 10 more," per George Bernard Shaw
47 Like stuffed animals
48 Leader issuing a ukase
50 Some cameras, for short
51 Castle part
52 Pioneer Day celebrant
56 Address of the Boss's band
59 ___ Victor
60 Sides of a quadrangle, maybe
61 "___ not!"
62 High dudgeon
63 Nasty ___ (rap nickname)
65 Shade of green
67 ___ Johnson, former mayor of London

68 "Well, you've dazzled me!"
69 Commend
70 It has three feet
71 Range that's home to the Mark Twain National Forest
72 "Buh-bye!"
76 Art ___
78 Beliefs
79 Black
82 Didn't budge
83 Thrice, in Rx's
84 "Huh"-inducing, say
86 One going around in circles?
88 Small songbird
89 Sailing ropes
90 Short flight
91 Monet or Sartre, by birth
92 In due course
94 Blight
97 One of the Wayans brothers
98 Old-fashioned stage direction
99 Candy man
101 Electricity-eschewing group
102 Swift, in a way
106 Nickname for baseball's Dwight Gooden
108 Cool
109 "Roots" Emmy winner
111 Info for a dating profile
112 Ado
113 Drag queen's collection
114 "___ Plenty o' Nuttin' " ("Porgy and Bess" song)
117 Condition for a neat freak, in brief
118 Thor Heyerdahl craft
119 1950s pol
120 Body with many arms, for short

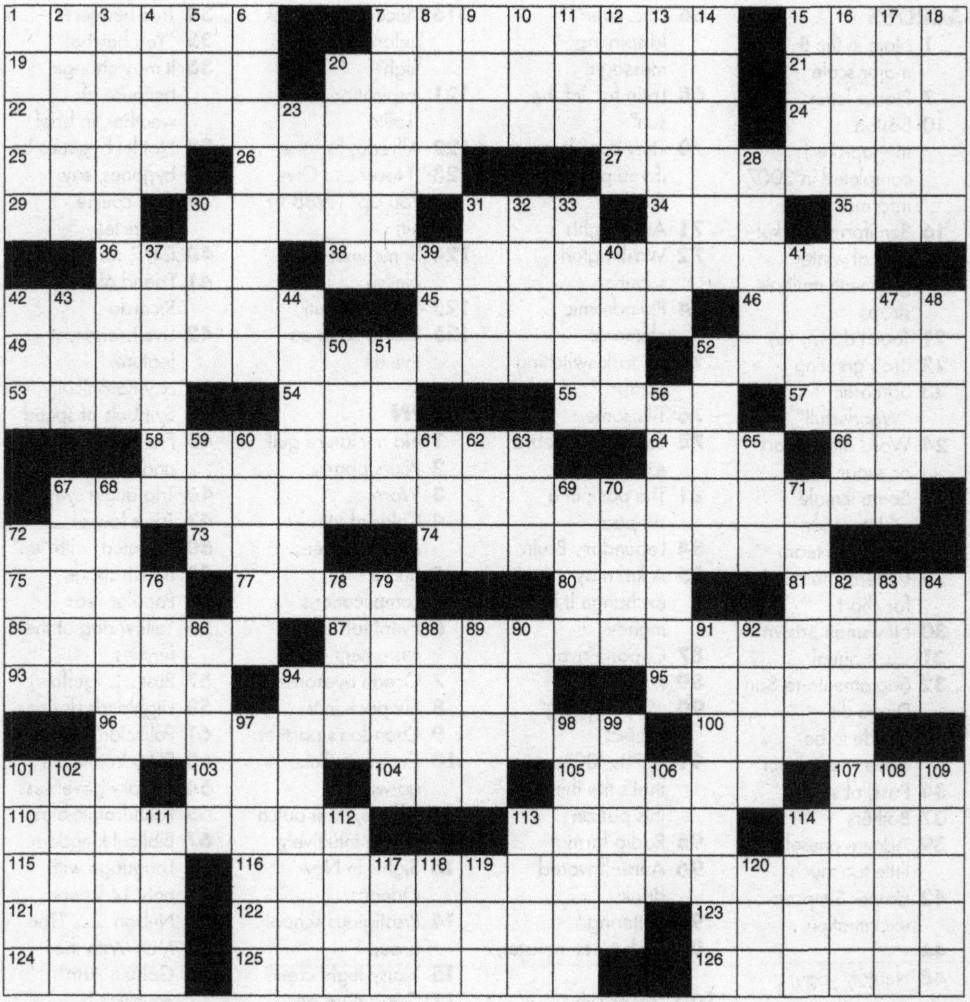


*by Jerry Miccolis*

# 9 OUT OF THIS WORLD

## ACROSS

1 Note in the B major scale
7 Platter letters
10 Boston megaproject completed in 2007, informally
16 Semiformal jacket
17 Item of winter gear with multiple straps
21 Touch down, say
22 Bro's greeting
23 Sarcastic "Wonderful!"
24 Word after smart or sugar
25 Some female athletic gear
27 Pinstriped team
29 Cybercrime target, for short
30 Newsman Brown
31 ___ manual
32 Sacramento-to-San Diego dir.
33 Grade to be concerned about
34 Pass, of sorts
37 Bothers
39 Admire oneself a little too much
42 Homer Simpson exclamation
44 -
48 Healthy yogurt mixins
49 One not looking for an expensive night on the town
52 Precollege
53 High degree in math?
54 Bris official
56 Approached aggressively
59 Scout group
60 Expired
62 Occupied, as a seat

66 "___ over" (dispiriting message)
68 Latin for "of the sun"
70 They can sleep if you play with them
71 Arctic lights
72 Washington suburb
74 Palindromic elemento
75 PC task-switching combo
76 Twosome
78 Stripe on a zebra, e.g.
81 The pack in a six-pack
84 Legendary Bruin
85 A kid may exchange it for money
87 Capone rival
89 P
90 "Silent Spring" subject
91 1970s–'80s craze that's the theme of this puzzle
95 Radio format
96 Anise-flavored drink
98 Bettering
99 Loch Ness monster, e.g.
100 Lat. or Lith., once
102 One who's been tapped on the shoulder?
103 Big name in electronics
106 Cry from the enlightened
108 Defunct spy org.
110 Response on un questionnaire
112 Mission requirement

116 Place to get drunk before getting high?
121 Inspiration for "Lolita"
122 Alfredo, for one
123 "Never ___ Give You Up" (1988 #1 hit)
124 Sometimes-sung pieces
125 Scraped (out)
126 Ball to keep an eye on

## DOWN

1 No miniature gulf
2 Pours poorly
3 Wore
4 Color of la Méditerranée
5 Some complications
6 Event for select customers
7 Ocean eyesores
8 Six-pack inits.
9 Chandon's partner
10 Common Coke go-with
11 Affixes, as a patch
12 Grasp intuitively
13 Sights in New Orleans
14 Prestigious school group
15 Noisy flight crew?
17 George on an annual Forbes list
18 ___ Academy (means of online education)
19 Iolani palace locale
20 Statistical tool for comparing means
26 It may start at 10
28 Buckingham Palace guards
33 Detoxing hurdle, for short

34 Tree hugger?
35 "You betcha!"
36 It may change because of weather, in brief
38 Not let bygones be bygones, say
39 Golf course obstacles
40 24/7, for instance
41 Friend of Lucy Ricardo
42 Live broadcast feature, oxymoronically
43 Symbols of speed
45 Fruit used in wines and syrups
46 Trig angle symbol
47 Trig's law of ___
50 Agitated, with "up"
51 Beach shade
54 Popular reds
55 Yellow dog of the funnies
57 Bust ___ (guffaw)
58 Highlands designs
61 Politician's asset
63 Palindromic nut
64 Literary governess
65 Palindromic blast
67 Biblical kingdom
69 Language with only 14 letters
71 Nelson ___, "The Man With the Golden Arm" novelist
73 "You betcha!"
75 Jumper cable connection
76 Dummy
77 Language that gave us "punch"
79 Sister of Cronus
80 Eastern ecclesiastic
82 Unnamed object
83 10th: Abbr.
86 Manage
88 Sketchy place?
92 Parts of sneakers

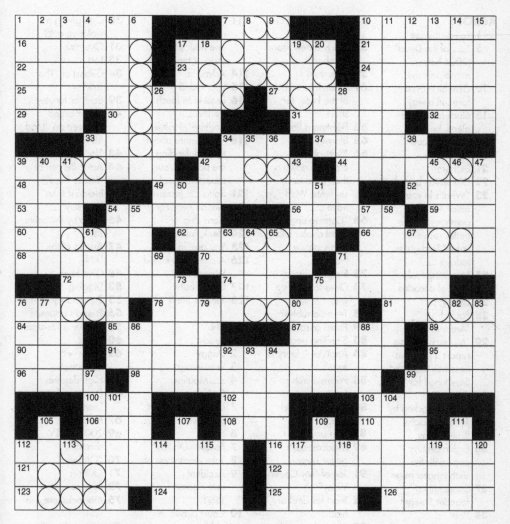

by David Steinberg

**93** Spinoff series with two spinoffs of its own
**94** Luxury Italian label
**97** Certain Honshu resident
**99** Umbrella holder, maybe
**101** Queen of ___

**104** Sleeping Beauty was under one
**105** OB/GYN's prefix with -gram
**107** "___ Lang Syne"
**109** Advertising buzzword
**111** Apiece
**112** It may collect dust

**113** Fareed Zakaria's channel
**114** ___-Jo ('80s track star)
**115** Specialty shoe spec
**117** Bother
**118** Digs
**119** Bother
**120** Not working anymore: Abbr.

### ACROSS

1 Fall birthstone
5 "___ of the Dead" (2004 horror movie parody)
10 Give birth on a farm, in a way
15 Black-and-white alerts, briefly
19 Wine bouquet
20 Big brewer
21 Starters
22 Old Italian bread
23 "What's in your attic? And do penthouses have better resale value? Find out in today's ___"
25 Menacing look
26 Parts of décadas
27 Duke grp.
28 Paul of "Ant-Man"
29 "Museum officials report a priceless vase has shattered. Stay tuned for the ___"
32 Group attacked by John the Baptist
35 Bruin Bobby
36 Eighth-century pope with the sixth-longest reign
37 Snapchat co-founder Spiegel
38 Past
40 Floor (it)
42 White-barked tree
43 "A courtroom artist has been arrested for fraud. ___"
49 Poet laureate Henry James ___
50 Coffee's draw
51 Epic poem section
52 Wye follower
53 Spots in la Seine
54 Obits, basically
55 Mixed martial arts org.
57 Many a new loan, for short
59 Blue state
61 Often-injured part of the knee, for short
62 Fighting a liar, e.g.
65 Blarney
66 "Schools are cracking down on their most tardy students. We'll have ___"
68 "Coming up, a pistol dueler tells us his stance. Now ___"
73 Ringing words?
74 Ones to keep up with
78 Tennis doubles?
79 Paces at races
83 Smelting waste
84 Anaïs of "Henry & June"
85 Princess with a twin
86 "Well, well, old chap"
87 Consumed
89 Mexican-born golfer Lorena
91 Joe of "My Cousin Vinny"
92 Start for deal or lead
93 "After the break, people are leaving the city during winter because of crime. Plus ___"
97 Mother: Prefix
99 Curator's deg.
100 Thurman of "Henry & June"
101 Come ___ surprise
102 Put on a jury
104 Clear the tables
106 Savor
111 "Our camera crew entered a one-hour photo shop at ten. ___"
114 Advance
115 Spa sound
116 Lead-in to much
117 "With ___ bodkin?": Hamlet
118 "With more about those defending the accused, our reporter is ___"
121 Sotto ___ (quietly)
122 Nation near Fiji
123 Corn chip
124 Sleek, informally
125 You are, in Spain
126 A comedian called Wanda
127 Grape nuts?
128 Tennis's Steffi

### DOWN

1 Ready
2 Doggy
3 Rescue org.
4 ___ Moulins, Québec
5 Like some support payments
6 Sets
7 Follow, with "by"
8 Take advantage of
9 Accident investigator, for short
10 Court player, in old lingo
11 Still on the loose
12 Not keep a secret
13 Special permits
14 Fix, as text
15 Singer Morissette
16 Pizza topping
17 About which it was asked "Why are you blue?," in a classic song
18 Spunk
24 Quiz show fodder
30 One giving a wake-up call?
31 Overcast
33 Lots
34 Gilbert of "The Talk"
39 Sci-fi or fantasy
41 Snack brand featured on "Mad Men"
43 Blot gently
44 Actor Bergen of "Jersey Boys"
45 Novelist John Kennedy ___
46 Grab by the collar, say
47 Annan of the U.N.
48 Give heed
53 Digging
55 Satisfactory
56 Friend's opposite
58 Fig. for a librarian
60 Points
62 Prefix with masochistic
63 High degrees
64 Devotee of Dionysus
67 Pond sight
69 2000–15 TV drama
70 "Oh jeez!"
71 Chilling
72 Bygone carrier
75 Morlocks' prey, in sci-fi
76 Historic headline of 1898
77 Old Irish character
79 "Up top!"
80 Anatolia, familiarly
81 Spot for the booby prize
82 Groom
85 Divulge
88 Start to fail?
90 Go ___ great length
91 Grilled sandwich

by Samuel A. Donaldson

**93** Daughter on the animated "Bob's Burgers"
**94** Egg-spensive jeweler?
**95** Saw through
**96** ___ Unidos
**98** Temple of Abu Simbel honoree

**103** ___-Unis
**105** Eye layers
**107** ___ Locke, the so-called "Dean of the Harlem Renaissance"
**108** Champing at the bit
**109** Native Israeli

**110** Below, as a goal
**112** Tall and thin
**113** Warning letters on some graphic videos
**119** Part of TNT
**120** Pester

## ACROSS

1 Southwestern cliff dwellers
5 Means of going down a 36-Down
9 Have a hole in one's heart
13 Meatheads
18 A Swiss army knife has a lot of them
19 Cream of the crop
21 Heads for Britain?
22 Thick-skinned grazer
23 Actress Streep playing a centenarian?
26 News show group
27 Soup accompaniers, often
28 Like the settings of typical Grant Wood paintings
29 Unruffled
30 ___ the top
31 Risky business for a compiler of quotations?
33 Good shot?
36 Counterparts of files
37 Smart
38 Not obvious to most
39 Evident worrywart
40 Done quickly
41 Protested from the stands
44 ___ Kitchen (frozen food brand)
45 Not wandering, say
46 Attorney general's investigation target
47 Like funk, now
51 Low-___
52 Alaskan beer container?
56 Beat the tar out of
57 Honorific for a colleague
59 Vetoes
60 Lies ahead
62 Co. captains?
63 Typographical no-no
64 SiriusXM star
65 Some fine wool
67 Charming group?
68 Some True Value purchases
71 Bad way to go?
72 Promote singer Crow's music?
75 P pronounced like an R
76 Pequod's co-owner
78 Meets with
79 James who sang "Good Rockin' Daddy"
80 Throat part
81 Shade in
83 Layers
85 Wilderness Road trailblazer
86 Fitness grp.
89 Nat ___ (channel)
90 Self-righteous types
91 Hung out
92 Debt for comedian Will?
96 Poet
97 Celsius of the Celsius scale
98 Safe place
99 "Hamilton" and "1776"
103 Beat
104 "I can't help you, but the Brady Bunch mom will be happy to assist"?
106 ___ Durkheim, so-called "father of sociology"
107 Nervous people are on it
108 Who wrote "A great flame follows a little spark"
109 Part of some small buildings
110 Gulf cash
111 Charges
112 Monopoly holding
113 Like a headlining act, typically

## DOWN

1 Preceder of snaps
2 Dept. of Labor branch
3 Lose a tan, say
4 Uranium 238 and strontium 90
5 Original "S.N.L." cast member
6 Rags-to-riches writer
7 January detritus
8 Body image grp.
9 Sirens, e.g.
10 Pinkish orange
11 According to ___ (by the rules)
12 Subj. for an au pair, maybe
13 Product possibly named after a real physician
14 One stop on Chicago's Blue Line
15 Greasy spoons
16 Common soccer score
17 100%
20 Caligula, e.g.
24 Gallbladder neighbor
25 Like dirty water
29 Ruckus
31 "Enough!," to a Roman
32 ___ park
33 "___ me!"
34 Focus of onomastics
35 Frost-covered biochemical solid?
36 See 5-Across
40 Hell of a location?
41 Banana Republic competitor
42 Good listeners
43 Big name in Scotch
45 "Love Actually," e.g.
46 Battle of Hastings participants
48 Like actor Flynn post-dieting?
49 A good thing to get out of
50 Black ___
52 Gung-ho
53 Cutting costs?
54 Bathroom fixture
55 One of the Jacksons
58 Banished
61 "I'm still waiting . . . ?"
63 Roused
64 Gets ready to do a load, say
65 Driving aid
66 65-Across producer, maybe
67 Plains dwellers
68 Arrondissement heads?
69 Macduff, for one
70 Disseminated
73 Request from
74 Katherine who co-starred in "27 Dresses"
77 It stops talking
80 Telemarketer's action
82 Notable whistle blowers
83 Green shampoo
84 Sang gracefully
85 ___ acid
86 Died down
87 Little fingers or toes
88 Buzz in space
90 Tut-tutters
91 Attacked, with "out"
93 One-eyed female on "Futurama"
94 Shake
95 The Cascades, e.g.

by Ian Livengood

96 Monument Valley sighting
99 "Gimme!"
100 Common calculus calculation
101 Signs (on)
102 Booking time
104 Bunny boss
105 Small lump of tobacco

# WONDER-FUL

## ACROSS

1 "It's a pity other cars aren't built this way" cars
6 Fischer, to Spassky, e.g.
11 "Stop!," at a port
16 Ring around a classical column
18 Verdi aria
19 Spots for auto logos
21 Rap's __ Boys
22 Flat-bottomed boat
23 Passionate kiss
24 Busy time for malls: Abbr.
25 Nascar unit
27 Row maker
29 Life force in Chinese philosophy
30 High-powered guns
32 Home to more than half the world's active geysers
37 Enigmatic one in "The Hobbit"
38 Dunham of "Girls"
39 Organized hikes
40 Follower of Joel
41 Approver of new meds
43 Snack brand whose name hints at its flavor
44 Zika monitoring org.
46 Alternative regimen to an 84-Down, informally
49 Surrender
51 Whacks
54 I C U, e.g.
58 Highly rated bond
59 Highly rated Bond?
61 Telenovela, e.g.
63 Fury
64 Result of many years of study, for short
65 Halley of Halley's comet

67 Like Serbs, but not Hungarians
68 What might replace you?
69 Subject of many Ansel Adams photos
71 Mortgage, often
73 "The Simpsons" character in a green jacket
74 Disney dwarf
75 Kind of treatment
77 Cousin of goth
78 Bethesda-based research agcy.
80 Federal agency established on August 25, 1916
85 Like some oaths
86 Region of ancient Greece
87 Insult, say
89 Election night graphic, for short
90 Annual N.Y.C. fund-raising event
92 Oprah's BFF
93 "Keep fighting the good fight!"
96 Like Sherpas
99 Very, very
102 Subatomic particle named for the weak force
104 "Mind . . . blown!"
108 House majority leader before DeLay
110 Good fact-checking types
115 "Three Coins in the Fountain" fountain
116 Light and breezy entertainment, informally
119 Dazzled
120 Portions
121 Concerted efforts
122 Break up with someone
123 Untethered

124 Nina Totenberg's milieu
125 Milk dispensers?

## DOWN

1 Blessed thing?
2 Painkiller containing caffeine
3 Neighbor of Ger.
4 Luncheonette order, for short
5 Six, in Italy
6 Dazzling
7 Annoy
8 The Henry who founded the House of Tudor
9 Raiders' org.
10 Erupter at 32-Across
11 Radio host Shapiro
12 Kind of pass
13 Nothing but
14 Henry W. __, Union major general during the Civil War
15 Disco relative
16 "So You Think You Can Dance" judge
17 Wire message
19 Harris's role in "The Right Stuff"
20 Jumps higher than, in sports slang
26 Gran Paradiso, e.g.
28 It's as good as XXX
31 Partner of sound
32 Word of support
33 Dog created by Jim Davis
34 Actor Wheaton
35 France's so-called "Capital of the Ruins"
36 Exit key
37 Sprint
42 Parts of a Jerusalem skyline
45 Harry's Hogwarts enemy
46 Drivel
47 "Man, that feels good!"

48 Indoor plants popular in waiting rooms
49 Like the name Nguyen in Vietnam
50 Beethoven's "Sinfonia __"
52 Purchase at an optometrist's
53 "Help!"
55 Feature of the Six Million Dollar Man
56 Samovar, e.g.
57 "Capeesh?"
60 Had too much of, briefly
62 Term of address for a noble
66 Tyrant
67 Islamic law
70 Defeat in a Nathan's Famous contest
72 Cracker shape
73 Win by __
76 Feeling of hunger
79 Mends
81 Not quite right
82 PolitiFact finding
83 Actor Penn
84 Regimen adopted by Bill Clinton in 2010
85 Clancy's Red October, e.g.
88 Born
90 Store head: Abbr.
91 Mayo container?
94 Egg: Prefix
95 "It's the __" ("I've changed")
97 Annual athletic honors
98 For whom the Edgar awards are named
100 Wall St. "500"
101 Drive-thru decision
102 Bob alternative . . . or partner
103 At this point
104 Webmaster's medium
105 Cookie with a Thins variety

**by Kathy Matheson and Jeff Chen**

106 Oscar winner for
   "Dallas Buyers Club"
107 Part of Y.S.L.
109 Thom ___ shoes
111 Virgin Mary's mother
112 Zippo
113 Ninny
114 Goes down
117 Tavern attachment
118 A.M.A. members

## ACROSS

1 Ditch
6 See-through clothing material
10 Listens to Shakespeare?
15 Taiping Rebellion general
18 Tourist's report
20 Ring or sphere
21 Mail
22 Reason to scream "Why won't this damn thing locate airplanes!"?
23 Honorary title in Wisconsin?
25 ___ Aduba of "Orange Is the New Black"
26 Insect that shorted out an early computer, spawning the term "computer bug"
27 "Ciao"
29 Surmise
30 Hamiltons
32 Domain of "Hamilton"
34 City with 500 attractions?
36 Takes in
38 Bay ___
39 Section of "Aida," e.g.
41 Letters after CD
42 "Hey, let's gather 100 people to enact laws and ratify treaties"?
46 Fired (up)
47 Glow
48 Get by
49 Super ___
50 Listen to violinist Itzhak's music?
52 Like blue moons
53 Norm: Abbr.
54 California missionary Junípero ___
55 "Ready to relieve 'em of a ___ or two" ("Les Misérables" lyric)
56 Stamp incorrectly, in a way
58 Group that appeared in the movie "Grease"
60 Oscars grp.
64 Out of gas, informally
65 Soft drink favored by the Marines?
68 Stephen of "Interview With the Vampire"
69 Sticky spots?
71 Cathedral feature
72 Blazing successes
74 "Oh, you're funny-y-y-y . . ."
76 Indian wear
77 Super ___
78 Setting for the beginning of "The Book of Mormon"
79 Church response that's taken as a given?
83 Lead-in to Pablo or Carlos
84 Like Navy SEALs
85 "Old MacDonald Had a Farm" sounds
86 "Got it"
87 Newspaper essay on why not to go outdoors?
89 Skit show, for short
90 E-cigarette output
91 Frat boy types
92 Assn.
93 Top of the agenda
95 Fastener with a ring-shaped head
97 Cries of approval
101 Tennis's King of Clay
102 Cry from comic book civilians
105 Futile
107 Meadow
108 Woody playing a medieval baron?
110 Books written entirely in chat rooms?
113 Robert of "Airplane!"
114 Singer LaBelle
115 TLC and Destiny's Child
116 Most "Doctor Who" characters, for short
117 "What if . . . ," informally
118 ___ cone
119 On edge

## DOWN

1 Walk with pride
2 Crosswords in 1924–25, e.g.
3 Home inspector's concern
4 "Selma" director DuVernay
5 Locks in place for a while?
6 What the "1" of "1/2" represents
7 Intellectual
8 Litigate
9 Home remedy drink
10 Bill of "Trainwreck"
11 Aladdin, e.g.
12 "Ratatouille" rat
13 Embroiled (in)
14 Biological pouch
15 Los Angeles Lakers' home until 1999
16 Assent to a married mujer
17 89-Across character played by Adam Sandler
19 "Tao Te Ching" philosopher
21 Mailed
24 "Howdy"
28 "___, verily"
31 Gray, say
33 Mythical father of Harmonia, strangely enough
35 Southern chain
37 Took in
39 America's Cup, e.g.
40 Rostand protagonist ___ de Bergerac
42 Sunday delivery
43 Bush labor secretary Chao
44 Sips
45 Puts under
46 Bits of truth
47 Name on many a college hall, informally
50 One easily bowled over?
51 Laugh-filled broadcast
53 Racer's brand
54 More see-through
57 Noted tea locale
58 The Titanic, e.g.
59 Gucci competitor
61 Bit of expert advice
62 Fill with gas
63 Like pageant contestants, typically
66 "Full speed ahead!"
67 Push-up muscle, informally
70 "That means . . ."
73 Passing remarks?
75 Showed over
77 Nisan observances
79 Green spirit
80 Something felt at Christmas
81 Post-Christmas events
82 Hit upside the head, in slang
83 Snoot
84 Eternally, to poets
87 Words of concession
88 Liable to spoil?
90 Cousin of a lemming
91 Sch. whose honor code includes chastity
94 Staffs
95 Start of a few choice words?
96 Big dipper
98 Native of Alaska
99 Goes "Ow, ow, ow!"
100 Like the response "Talk to the hand!"
103 Adele, voicewise
104 Spot checkers?
106 One of Asta's masters
109 College-level H.S. courses
111 "Dios ___!"
112 The "V" of fashion's "DVF"

by Paolo Pasco

## ACROSS

1 Flair
5 Indication of freshness
9 Weak
15 ___ bag (party giveaway)
19 Have a one-person apartment, say
21 "Old MacDonald" sounds
22 "Check and ___"
23 Neighbor of Illinois
24 Response to a flatterer
25 Subordinate: Abbr.
26 "That ___ part of our agreement!"
27 Short dagger
29 Flattened at the poles
31 Concorde, e.g.
32 Ball in a socket
34 24 in a caffeine molecule
35 Release from TLC or Alicia Keys
36 Tee seller
39 Like many a lad or lass
40 "Since you didn't hear me the first time . . ."
41 Actor Reeves
43 Start of a time capsule direction
45 Retired Steeler Taylor
46 Takes it easy
48 End-of-seminar feature
53 ___ letter (college app part)
54 Scads
55 Sources of mescaline
57 Prefix with parasite
58 School in Oxford, informally
60 ___-Atlantic
61 Burns's refusal
62 Where bees be
63 Slithy one, to Carroll
64 Diamond head?
66 ___ salad
67 Shout made while pointing
69 Cops, with "the"
70 ___ Alamos
71 Targeted
74 Spanish prefix with lineas
75 Begin a voyage
77 ___ Fresh (Tex-Mex chain)
78 Airport posting, for short
79 Multicolored candy in a yellow package
81 Noted index
84 Grp. sponsoring the Muzzle Loading Championship
85 Footnote material
86 Stemmed (from)
87 Transition
90 Go on
91 1997 film megahit
93 Site of the George Bush Presidential Library
94 Material in two states
96 Droop
97 The "e" of i.e.
100 Descend in a controlled fashion
101 Might be able to do it
104 Oscar-winning Berry
106 The "E" of HOMES
107 Like three men of rhyme
109 Beverage since 1922
111 Bareilles who sang "Love Song"
112 "Negotiations are off!"
113 Some fuel oils
114 Leave in
115 Gertrude ___, first woman to swim the English Channel
116 Meh
117 Lead-in to Victoria or Albert

## DOWN

1 Things aggressive people may throw
2 Turkish money
3 "Cease!" on the seas
4 Answer to "Is Bonn the capital of Deutschland?"
5 Kind of camera, for short
6 Releases
7 Bio course: Abbr.
8 Mani-___
9 "Ready!"
10 "It's all good"
11 They mind their manors
12 Foist (upon)
13 Most important piece in échecs
14 Relatives of scooters
15 One of two in the Adidas logo
16 Sushi go-with
17 Offered for breeding
18 "Don't let those guys escape!"
20 Choice
28 A U.S. flag is a common one
30 Ammonia and lye
33 Calvin Coolidge's reputed reply to a woman who bet she could get more than two words out of him
36 Old men
37 Red ___
38 Go (for)
41 Ocean bottom?
42 And more
44 "Going somewhere?"
45 "That makes sense"
46 Miracle-___
47 Electees
48 2022 World Cup host
49 Surrounder of la Grande Jatte
50 Martians, in "The War of the Worlds"
51 Wordsworth work
52 Negatives
56 Word often replaced with "your"
59 Ignoramus
60 Big mouths
62 United Nations concern
64 Tangles
65 Behemoths
66 City where Mexico's routes 1 and 2 meet
67 Word that becomes its own synonym when spelled backward
68 Giggle syllable
69 Basic form of a word
71 Spa sound
72 Do to ___
73 Bit
75 Simplify
76 Just like always
77 Big swig
80 Neglect
82 Number of hills in ancient Rome
83 Rx writer
85 Optometrist, at times
87 Pirate, in old slang
88 Breathe out
89 View in awe
90 Slightly
92 Noted philanthropic family
93 Lock
95 Relative of a weasel
97 Justice Kagan
98 Smooth and glossy
99 Like Calvin Coolidge
102 Neocons, e.g.
103 Ice cream flavor
105 Cain mutiny victim?
108 Positive sign
110 Game-winning line

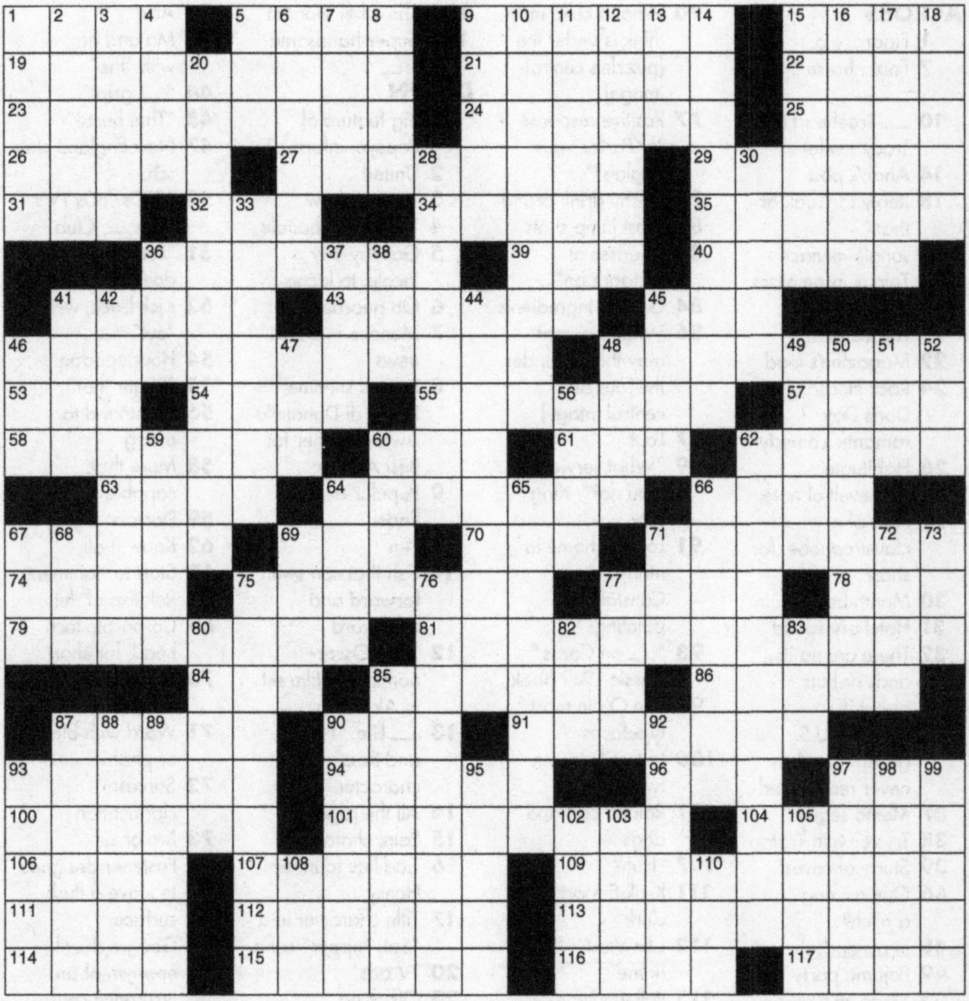

*by Tom McCoy*

# 15 SACK TIME

## ACROSS

1 Figaro, e.g.
7 Foal : horse :: calf : ___
10 ___ Trueheart (Dick Tracy's wife)
14 Ahab's post
18 Reply to "Look at that!"
19 Jungle menace
20 Things insomniacs count
21 Lollapalooza
22 Magazine's lead
24 Rock Hudson/Doris Day romantic comedy
26 Habituate
27 Roosevelt of note
29 Fear of a claustrophobe, for short
30 Month before juin
31 Hatchery sound
32 There are no ifs, ands or buts about it
35 Craft the U.S. government has never recognized
37 Memo segue
38 Tryster with Tristan
39 Study of caves
46 One making a pitch?
48 In a slapdash way
49 Pajama party
53 Stone, to Caesar
57 French Dadaist
58 Toss in
60 Buttonless garment
61 Cried over spilled milk, maybe
64 Snore loudly
65 Reddish-brown
67 One in front of a train
68 Prince Valiant's love
69 Cocktail sauce ingredient
70 What a child may think is under the [puzzle's central image]
77 Positive response to "Parlez-vous anglais?"
79 Slushy drink brand
80 Most jump shots
83 Charisse of "Brigadoon"
84 Gumbo ingredients
86 What a parent may think is under the [puzzle's central image]
87 Lout
89 "What services ___ thou do?": King Lear
91 London home to many John Constable paintings
93 "___ on Cards," classic 1949 book
96 Like O's in most typefaces
100 Letters between two names
101 Rained cats and dogs
107 "Huh?"
111 Kwik-E-Mart clerk
112 Like Verdi's "Caro nome"
113 Poll worker's request
114 Command to a dog
115 Item on a telephone stand
118 Line at the end of a day's diary
120 Choice: Abbr.
121 Speedily
122 Twist-___
123 Rang
124 "That ___ wrong"
125 "Auld Lang ___"
126 The other woman
127 Super-handsome

## DOWN

1 Big feature of Popeye, informally
2 United
3 Variety show
4 Tavern tap handle
5 Galway Bay locale, to locals
6 QB guarders
7 Menace in 2014 news
8 Record six-time David di Donatello Award winner for Best Actress
9 Popular airfare finder
10 Yen
11 Fish that can swim forward and backward
12 2014 Oscar-nominated film set in Alabama
13 ___ Life, "Porgy and Bess" character
14 All the rage
15 Paint choice
16 Cadillac founder Henry
17 Title character in a "Sgt. Pepper" song
20 TV ads
23 Office no.
25 Late author and Peace Nobelist
28 PBS supporter, for short
32 Relative of a raspberry
33 Tribal figures
34 Sloughs
36 Elflike
39 Dis
40 Trim
41 The world's largest is China
42 Acid
43 Ma and pa, with "the"
44 "___ grip!"
45 "That hurts!"
47 New England state sch.
50 1970s–'80s TV's "The ___ Club"
51 "I see what you're doing!"
52 Kick back, with "out"
54 Hodgepodge
55 "Roger that"
56 Command to a dog
58 More than capable
59 Doctors' orders
62 Know-it-all
63 Start to -tainment
66 Relative of -let
69 Corporate tech head, for short
70 Alternative to boeuf or poulet
71 Word with black or photo
72 Sarcasm clarification
73 Bro or sis
74 Fastener designed to leave a flush surface
75 Geographical eponym of an insurance company
76 The check that's in the mail, maybe
78 Former Laker Lamar
81 O.E.D. contents: Abbr.
82 Companion to whiskey in "American Pie"
85 New Mexico's ___ National Laboratories

by Ned White and George Barany

**87** Chortle
**88** All things considered
**90** Motel sign filler
**92** "No ___!" ("I give!")
**93** Shrimp ___
**94** Shenanigans
**95** Tickles

**97** Lively, on a score
**98** Battery part
**99** D-Day vessel: Abbr.
**102** Teary-eyed
**103** ___ bar (popular candy)
**104** Muppet with a "rubber duckie"

**105** Source of some quilt stuffing
**106** Pride of Lions, for short?
**108** "___ español?"
**109** Prince ___, Eddie Murphy's role in "Coming to America"

**110** Roosevelt of note
**114** Part of a rating
**116** Destination for some BART riders, for short
**117** Put down in writing?
**119** Cause of a tic, for short

# 16

## ACROSS

1 Pranks with a roll, briefly
4 Casualties of streaming services
7 Updated one's blog
13 Swap (out)
16 Navajo hogan, e.g.
17 Part of NATO
20 Forgo
21 Question from an owl?
22 Austin-to-Houston dir.
23 Chief
24 Actor Joaquin's complete bio?
26 Start of a legalese paragraph
28 Figs. in an author's acknowledgments section
30 "___ Wiedersehen!"
31 Hughes poem that mentions "the darker brother"
32 Troupe of lesser-known actors?
35 Reef-dwelling snapper
38 Unattractive fruit
39 2016 Olympics site
40 What swish shots miss
42 Word repeated in the postal creed
43 W.W. I battle locale
44 Schmaltz in kids' films?
50 "The meaning of life" once sold on it for $3.26
51 Throw together
53 Certainly not wish to repeat
54 Get by

56 "I don't mean to ___ . . ."
57 Like bibs and aprons
58 Sermon topics
59 Muhammad had 13
60 Birthplace of multiple saints
62 Slowly disengages (from)
64 Department store department
65 An airline now serves a Minute Maid beverage?
69 Whined like a baby
72 End of many a toast
73 Touch
76 Popular sans-serif font
77 Schools of thought
78 "Onward!," in Italy
81 Unfiltered
83 U.S. detainment site in Cuba, informally
84 Question posed with feigned shock
85 Ushers in
86 Joint action
87 Some apartments for scaredy-cats?
90 Drank to excess
91 R.V. camper's org.
92 [I'm devastated!]
93 Deli supply
95 Marauding group in Tolkien's "The Two Towers"
96 Game of tag, basically
100 Record half that stirs emotions?
104 Exerciser's target
105 "Shame on you!"
107 Dark force

108 European country slightly larger than Malta
109 Sandwich for a dieter?
113 Appear that way
115 Share
116 Volcano output
117 Slippery sort
118 Size up
119 Letters on some baggage to N.Y.C.
120 Word with sweet or sugar
121 Made damp
122 "Gangnam Style" singer
123 Winter D.C. hrs.

## DOWN

1 Channel that aired "Felicity" and "Smallville"
2 Curve-enhancing undergarment
3 Metallic shades
4 Certain Balkanite
5 Not as bright
6 ___ fly
7 Oomph
8 Factory watchdog grp.
9 Search far and wide
10 Home run territory, in lingo
11 Dark time, in poetry
12 Something that gets MADD mad
13 Smacks hard
14 "That is . . . not looking good"
15 Numbskull
17 Argument you may start in school
18 Cops, in slang
19 Sage swamp-dweller of film
25 The witching hour

27 Pat ___, three-time N.B.A. Coach of the Year
29 Discard
33 Inflexible
34 Handy take-along
36 Play-___
37 Modern airport amenity
41 Soft wool source
43 "Sure thing"
45 Parts of airports and fashion shows
46 Actress Kirsten
47 Display clearly
48 Goalie's goal
49 Locale painted on the Sistine Chapel ceiling
51 Caught on, with "up"
52 Junior, often
55 Something starting something?
57 Devices preventing off-hour openings of vaults
58 Image on the Arizona license plate
61 Deli supply
63 Brian of ambient music
64 Offerings to hitchhikers
66 "Challenge accepted!"
67 Common newspaper feature not seen in The New York Times
68 Chill, with "out"
69 E.W. or S.I.
70 One of the Trumps
71 "I'm ___ Her," 2016 political slogan
74 Work of extraterrestrials? - not!

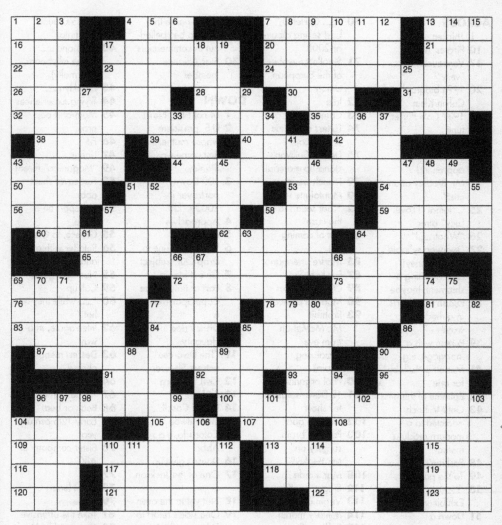

by Jeremy Newton

**75** Pops some pills, say
**77** "No joke!"
**79** Shortcuts into clubs
**80** Actor Williams of "Happy Days"
**82** Put together
**85** Guy into hip-hop
**86** Where the heart is

**88** Colorful pond swimmer
**89** ___-pah
**90** Kerfuffles
**94** Event for snocrossers
**96** "You're almost there"
**97** "So funny!"

**98** "World News Tonight" airer
**99** Talk show interviewee
**101** Aid for one going places?
**102** On edge
**103** Worry
**104** Kerfuffle

**106** Olive or avocado
**110** "How precious is that!"
**111** Actor ___ J. Cobb of "12 Angry Men"
**112** So last month
**114** You thinking what I'm thinking?

## ACROSS

1 Thicken
10 Pirates' home
17 Venezuelan's "very"
20 1994 biography of Calvin Klein
21 1937 Cole Porter tune
22 Serpent's tail?
23 Be willing to apprehend Mr. Bradley at any cost?
25 Original "I Love Lucy" airer
26 "What __!"
27 Doo-wop syllable
28 "Oh, baloney!"
30 One awaiting a shipment, maybe
31 Punish Mr. Harris in a medieval way?
39 Person with a mortgage, e.g.
41 Menotti's "Lullaby," for one
42 Epitome of thinness
43 Get Mr. Koch addicted to a modern reading method?
48 Fashion's Gucci
49 To the point
50 "Pictures __ Exhibition"
51 Down a submarine, say
53 Evade
57 Barrel in a bar
61 Kind of wave
65 Hungarian city known for its thermal baths
66 Preside over Mr. O'Neill's baptism?
69 __ Long, Union general in the Civil War
70 "__ Carter III," best-selling album of 2008
71 Smallest member of the European Union
72 Idle
73 Criminalize
74 Letters on Ozzie Smith's cap
75 Do Mr. Sullivan's stand-up material?
79 French weapon
80 Montaigne work
82 "That seems to be the case"
83 Act of coming out
85 Madre's hermano
87 Fur fighters?
89 Opinion pieces
90 Made in France?
93 Prohibit Mr. McMahon from ever socializing again?
100 Pool organism
101 12-Down soldiers, for short
102 Set as a goal
103 Perform brain surgery on Mr. Begley?
108 Mgr.'s aide
112 Singer __ Khan
113 Virginia __
114 Military march
115 Suffix with Ecuador or Euclid
116 Put Mr. Meese in an Armani suit?
125 Mauna __
126 Treater's phrase
127 Where the stars might be pointing?
128 Longtime 25-Across president Moonves
129 Brand name that used to be spelled out in commercials
130 Star Alliance member

## DOWN

1 Lee of NBC News
2 U.S. president whose mother's first name was Stanley
3 109-Down portrayer in 2003's "Elf"
4 Approaches
5 Purposes
6 "Turn On, Tune In, Drop Out" subject
7 Give a leg up
8 Part of Italy where Cape Spartivento is
9 Disney doe
10 Haughty
11 "The Divorcee" actress Shearer
12 Civil War org.
13 Bud
14 Noted Cosell interviewee
15 Colorado, e.g.: Abbr.
16 Doesn't give up
17 One of the Jackson 5
18 Not yet in the oven
19 One side's retort to "No, you don't!"
24 R.M.N. served under him
29 Some clouds
31 Apiphobiac's fear
32 Grand Forks sch.
33 Auto last made in 1936
34 "99 Luftballons" singer, 1984
35 Noted John Boehner feature
36 Prefix with Cities
37 Souse's sound
38 Slip (into)
40 Mike and __ (some jellybeans, informally)
43 Brooklyn __
44 Trying experiences
45 Mom-and-pop grps.
46 Fit
47 Linear
49 "Mogambo" threat
52 Fax cover sheet abbr.
54 Transport on a slope
55 Greece, to Greeks
56 Retailer with a cat and dog in its logo
58 Numbers game
59 Call up
60 "__ while they're hot!"
62 Interrogate, in a way
63 Dessert menu phrase
64 Sheets and such
67 "Esmé" writer
68 Beak or beat
71 Early 12th-century year
76 Sister company of ABC
77 Title
78 Ballet leap
79 Hope
81 Take the offensive
84 Caramel-filled treat
86 Figure in Tom Thumb tales
88 Wife of Esau
90 Adipocyte
91 Elvis sings it in "Blue Hawaii"
92 Household pets that need ultraviolet light in their cages
94 Buttons on the big screen

by David Levinson Wilk

95 Geisha's accessory
96 "Top Gun" org.
97 Disgusted cry
98 Medical suffix
99 "Mayberry ___"
104 Welcomed, as a guest at the door
105 Motif
106 Epitome of hotness

107 911 responder
109 See 3-Down
110 1994 action flick with the tagline "Get ready for rush hour"
111 "The Constant Gardener" heroine
114 Sicilian city

117 Way to go: Abbr.
118 Un-P.C. suffix
119 Souse
120 TV show filmed at 30 Rock
121 ___ sort
122 You: Fr.
123 Not vert.
124 And the rest: Abbr.

## ACROSS

1 Roast V.I.P.'s
4 Overall composition?
9 Military funeral concluder
13 Cars with floor-mounted ignitions
18 Density symbol, in physics
19 By itself
20 Kaaba visitor's faith
22 Say grudgingly
23 "I suppose it might seem odd that a reverend like myself would suddenly begin ___ . . ."
26 Top-___ (golf ball brand)
27 "Dirt cake" ingredients
28 Equine-related
29 Gun it
31 ". . . but I've always thought ___ had a more fun job than I do"
35 "For an avid philatelist like me, sorting envelopes is thrilling - I might spot a ___!"
37 Kind of ceremony
38 Show no modesty
39 Marvin of "Cat Ballou"
40 Friday's rank: Abbr.
43 Had
44 Poor writer's scribblings?
45 Indo-Europeans
48 "When a man is nervous about shipping breakables, I tell him, '___ carefully, sir' . . ."
52 Domino's order
53 Whirlybird
54 Actress Peeples
55 Big name in rum
59 Round-trippers, in sports lingo
60 ". . . and I write '___' on the box, which seems to reassure him"
64 Cambridgeshire's ___ Cathedral
65 Viking's destination
66 Don Juan's mother
67 "___ had enough"
68 "The best part of the job, of course, is when I'm out on the street ___"
73 Drawers of war?
76 Mesabi Range export
77 Tee-___
78 Remote place
79 Food label no.
80 "I'm a bit leery of dogs - it's unsettling to enter a yard and hear some ___ at me . . ."
84 From scratch
87 Lover of light
88 Distress
89 Old inits. in telecommunication
90 Vegas casino hotel, with "the"
91 The Bahamas' Great ___ Island
93 Novel for which Sartre declined the Nobel Prize
96 ". . . but dogs can't spoil how much I enjoy driving around in the ___"
99 "Homeowners get excited when they see me opening their ___ . . ."
104 Least bright
105 Eighty-eight
107 Dry out
108 "The Hot Zone" topic
109 ". . . and when I hand-deliver a package, the recipients are positively ___ - it's very satisfying!"
114 Fountain drinks
115 Berry of "Frankie and Alice"
116 Histrionics
117 Poetic preposition
118 Daisy variety
119 Ugly situation
120 Matches timewise, informally
121 Acid

## DOWN

1 1983 Michael Keaton comedy
2 Single-named "Hollywood Squares" regular
3 Results of chafing
4 Place to get a facial
5 Film director Roth
6 Tours turndown
7 Having one sharp
8 Manner
9 Ziggurat features
10 Interviews
11 Finishes
12 ___ ammoniac
13 More guarded
14 Onetime Freud collaborator
15 Queen in the "Star Wars" saga
16 Asphalt ingredient
17 Open terrain
21 Desert landforms
24 Flummery
25 ___ de combat
30 It comes from the heart
32 Comes to
33 Forest flutist
34 Palm phone
36 Hit with a charge
38 Flapper's wrap
40 Bookish type
41 Soviet foreign affairs minister during the Cuban missile crisis
42 Answering machine insert
44 2010 Apple release
46 Rolling in green
47 Triumphant cry
49 Revivalism?
50 Leave weaponless
51 Bygone Tide rival
53 French sweetie
55 Industry, slangily
56 Wardrobe items
57 Fork
58 Dunne of "My Favorite Wife"
60 Small island
61 It's closeted
62 Put the kibosh on
63 Film director Craven
65 Title for de Staël: Abbr.
69 On the subject of
70 Moves a head?
71 Golden ___ (General Mills product)
72 "Forget it!"
73 Striking player
74 Symbol of Athena
75 Lincoln while in Congress, e.g.
78 Babel
80 Car financing inits.
81 Where prisoners swing picks
82 Ear: Prefix
83 ___ monde
84 Like the GE Building

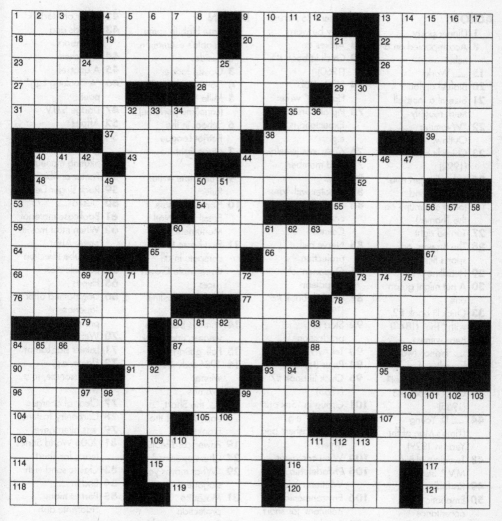

*by Patrick Berry*

85 Locomotive furnace
86 Lost Colony's island
92 Companion of Rex and Rover
93 Bird that may nest on volcanic ash

94 Unable to agree
95 Pack leaders
97 R&B's ___ Brothers
98 Car dealer's offering
99 Farmland rolls
100 Bungling fool
101 Fishing accoutrement

102 1980s–'90s Chrysler offerings
103 Iota
106 Woes
110 Mugger on stage
111 Not straight
112 Novelist McEwan
113 Station for cinephiles

# CHICK LIT

## ACROSS

**1** Dinner party
**8** Accompanied on a ticket
**15** ___ Works
**20** Biofuel option
**21** Size of a football field, roughly
**22** "Wyoming Outlaw," e.g.
**23** Chick lit book #1 (1992)
**25** Italy's longest river
**26** ___ Pie Island (artist commune on the Thames)
**27** Turned right
**28** The Browns, on sports tickers
**29** Headline
**30** A nut might go on one
**33** Chick lit book #2, with "The" (1843)
**36** Bear witness
**37** ___ Franco (watch brand)
**38** "Down with thee!"
**39** Chick lit book #3 (1965)
**44** ___ D. Young (Time's Man of the Year in 1929)
**48** Two-time N.B.A. M.V.P. Steve
**49** Kerfuffles
**50** Emphatic acceptance
**51** Italian city where pizza was invented
**53** Mich. neighbor
**54** Clumsy handler
**56** P.R. locale
**58** Brand introduced by Philip Morris in 1975
**59** Chick lit book #4 (1974)
**64** Iron Man co-creator
**67** Where 76-Across may be worn
**68** Affixes on
**69** Chick lit book #5 (1960)
**74** "A Dog of Flanders" writer
**75** Pip of "Great Expectations," e.g.
**76** 67-Across jewelry
**77** Fold member
**80** Says
**82** Theater with fans
**84** Political commentator Colmes
**85** Nerve cell projection
**86** Opponent of Napoleon
**87** Chick lit book #6 (1930)
**92** Start to production?
**93** Tel Aviv's ___ Park
**94** Refer (to)
**95** Chick lit book #7 (1985)
**101** Group in "Sex and the City," e.g.
**103** Some washers and dryers
**104** Wine container
**105** Philadelphia's ___ Whitman Bridge
**106** Environmental pollutant, for short
**108** Snarl
**109** Chick lit book #8 (1967)
**114** Bracelet attachment
**115** Christmas or Yom Kippur
**116** Spread, as rumors
**117** Some church overhead?
**118** Bony
**119** Game highlights shower

## DOWN

**1** Rose high in some people's estimation
**2** Besides
**3** Gossip fodder
**4** Down, with "up"?
**5** Mille & ___ Roses (Lancôme perfume)
**6** School in the Patriot League
**7** Stage light
**8** Artery
**9** True-crime writer Rule
**10** Home of Agate Fossil Beds Natl. Monument
**11** First horse to compete in all three Triple Crown races
**12** With cold feeling
**13** Stuck
**14** Famous bathrobe wearer, informally
**15** Folk guitarist Leo
**16** 1986 Indy 500 winner
**17** Wombs
**18** ___ the Short, early king of the Franks
**19** Power cord feature
**24** Chess opening?
**29** "What moves you" sloganeer
**31** Mosquito protection
**32** Reno setting: Abbr.
**33** 180s
**34** Vitamin and supplement chain
**35** Night light?
**36** ___ time (never)
**37** Old or morning follower
**40** Harsh treatment
**41** "If at first, the ___ is not absurd, then there is no hope for it": Einstein
**42** Ulster or Norfolk
**43** Friends and neighbors
**44** Broached
**45** A quarrel
**46** "A Cooking Egg" poet
**47** Dodge S.U.V.
**52** Affairs
**54** Part of a support group
**55** Skating maneuver
**57** Femur or tibia
**59** Rock singer Dee
**60** "Just a ___"
**61** Bookcase material
**62** When most movies open: Abbr.
**63** YouTube selection
**64** Bar selection
**65** Hypes
**66** Dog named after a Japanese prefecture
**70** Werewolf feature
**71** Lakers star Lamar
**72** Flame, e.g.
**73** Impersonate, in a way
**77** Clear of charges
**78** Carpentry fastener
**79** -ess alternative
**81** 2005 World Series team, for short
**83** Classic sandwich
**84** End in ___
**85** Part of many ristorante dish names
**88** Shift's end?
**89** Book before Num.
**90** Hesitates
**91** Locale for many a gondola
**92** Whence the phrase "I will both lay me down in peace, and sleep"
**95** Conifer with durable wood
**96** Home of ConAgra

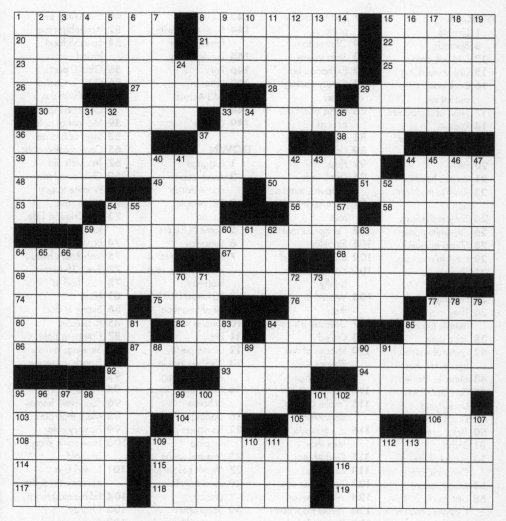

by Brendan Emmett Quigley

97 Seagoing
98 Día de los Reyes month
99 Group think?
100 Pacers' contests?
101 [blech!]
102 "Let's ___ There" (old NBC slogan)
105 Maze choices

107 Tanning salon fixtures
109 Doctor ___ from the planet Gallifrey
110 Samurai's home
111 Évian, e.g.
112 "Yo!"
113 Hue and cry

## ACROSS

1 Ornate
5 Spreads
12 Old pol. entity
15 Like some skiing
16 Dark patch on a distant sun
17 Niña accompanier
18 Roams
19 Century in Amer. politics
20 Pony
21 Yenta's habit
23 River to the North Sea
24 Bally enthusiasts
26 Off-white pottery
28 Sharp-tongued
29 Land in a stream
31 Thin as ___
32 Temper
34 Galumph
36 They may get people talking
38 Jazz style
42 General Assembly figure, for short
43 Mine, to Marie
45 Sun Devils' sch.
46 Underlying
47 Dutch brews
50 Ticket presenter
51 Shred
53 Period of the Cenozoic Era
55 Meditate (on)
58 Like much of New Orleans's French Quarter
60 Beaver's home
61 Shankar piece
62 ___ acid
63 Hoedown seating
64 Pooh's pal
66 What you used to be?
68 Bickering
72 "I like your thinking"
76 "Cat ___," 1965 film
77 Red-haired film princess
79 Olds sedan
80 Shot source
82 Exchange fig.
83 Citrusy cocktail mixer
86 Focus of a class action?
88 Novelist Hoag
89 Cancún, e.g.
92 Flap
94 Drink with tempura, maybe
97 "Howards End" role
98 Centipede maker
101 Singular
102 Balancing acts?
103 Kaplan course, briefly
105 Waited longer than
107 Drillmaster's call
108 Called
110 Rhodes of the Rhodes scholarships
114 M.P.G. watcher
115 "make believe" sloganeer
116 ___ guisada, Tex-Mex stew
117 Kind of gun
119 Continue
123 Twin Cities sch.
124 Waikiki wear
126 Yellow pool items
128 That, in Toledo
129 Sophocles title hero
131 Station line
134 ___ del Carmen, Mexico
135 Told stories
136 Norwegian king called "the 77-Down"
139 Clear
140 Station identification
143 Tie up
144 Pixar robot with a female voice
145 London daily
146 Rot
147 Letter in 145-Across
148 Cheat
149 Cheers

## DOWN

1 Luggage
2 Asian capital name starter
3 P.R. people
4 ___ no
5 Some N.F.L.'ers
6 Runaway
7 Make ready for a winter storm, as a highway
8 Ed heard in "Up"
9 Bit of free time
10 Onesie wearer
11 Enter
12 Game piece
13 "Go" square in Monopoly, e.g.
14 Cinderella's wear, at home
16 Darling
22 Hawaiian pizza topping
25 Minstrel songs
27 Month before juin
29 Swift's "A Tale of ___"
30 Soap opera creator Phillips
33 "___ Mio"
35 Ambulance, slangily
37 One in a maze
39 Schemed together
40 For ___ (cheaply)
41 Alexander, to Aristotle
44 Sardegna, e.g.
47 Asia's ___ Sea
48 What writer's block may block
49 5-4 ruling, e.g.
52 Assembly area
54 Spanish food brand
55 Old PC part
56 O.K., in Osaka
57 Ones with the Christmas spirit?
59 Mariner of note
63 Steel or bronze
65 Card catalog abbr.
67 Tracker's aid
69 Child-sized mitt
70 Promise to pay
71 Large cask
73 The Crimson Tide, for short
74 Bass lover?
75 Irish Rose's beau
77 See 136-Across
78 "___ had it!"
81 Nine
84 Skater Midori
85 Exsiccates
87 Campsite sight
90 Slowing, in mus.
91 French possessive
93 Highlands daggers
95 Water color
96 "Survivor" homes
98 More than pale
99 Hosiery color
100 How some shares are sold
101 Suited to a person's strengths
104 Edible mushroom
106 Charge
109 Fork
111 Said "No fair!"
112 They have rates and ratings
113 Jay who jests
118 Tongue-lash
120 Engage in a 1920s fad
121 One way to turn
122 Cornhusker St.
125 Draws out
127 Clowns' toys
129 Still in the game

by Kevin G. Der

**130** Spent
**132** Merry-go-round music
**133** Sly type?
**134** W. or Bam
**137** Actress Skye
**138** Nettles
**141** Sound at a spa
**142** Neth. neighbor

## ACROSS

1 Henry II player in "Becket"
7 Something that might get a rise out of people?
13 Clinch
16 Clinch, with "up"
19 Arrange again
20 Suburb of San Diego
21 "Livin' on a Prayer" band
23 Chinese restaurant offering / Wonderland affair / Group on the left?
25 Indigenous
26 Neo, for one
27 Baltimore specialty / Effortless task / Move on all fours with the belly up
29 Admit
31 Skins, e.g.
32 Ancient city NW of Carthage
36 Most red, maybe
39 Firmly fixed
43 Plunging / Play hooky / Vulgar
47 Scrunchies
51 Tip reducer?
52 Northern flier / Mixer maker / Put on the line
55 Buffoon
56 Lure
58 Idiots
59 "Up to ___," 1952 game show
60 ___ Hunt, Tom Cruise's character in "Mission: Impossible"
63 Sénat vote
64 God of shepherds
65 Dials

67 Yellowish brown / Bit of "dumb" humor / Many a forwarded e-mail
72 Hot cider server
74 Seat for toddlers
75 Time, in Torino
76 Indo-___
80 Item for a mason
81 Previous
84 Idiotic
86 Wonderment
87 Cause of congestion / Detective's challenge / Loony
90 Style of chicken
93 "Naturally!"
94 Winnie-the-Pooh possession / Baked entree / Sweetie
96 Grow together
97 Best to follow, as advice
100 Attention getters
101 It's no good when it's flat
102 Hero
106 Fancy Feast product / Cafeteria outburst / "Mean Girls" event
114 Hooded jackets
118 ___ sunglasses
119 Democratic territory / Cardinal, e.g. / "Over the Rainbow" flier
122 Biracial Latin American
123 "Ditto!"
124 1966 best seller set in Hong Kong
125 See 126-Across
126 Half a 125-Across year: Abbr.

127 They might be crossed
128 "The Battleship Potemkin" setting

## DOWN

1 Alternative to gov
2 Trillion: Prefix
3 Word with French or U.S.
4 Olive genus
5 Cross-country skiing
6 ___ deux âges (middle-aged: Fr.)
7 John Wayne western, with "The"
8 Toddler's need
9 Nickname for a seven-time N.B.A. All-Star
10 Frau's partner
11 Billionaire's home, maybe
12 Halfhearted R.S.V.P.'s
13 Letter-shaped support
14 Bean
15 German finale
16 "Brave New World" drug
17 ___ eye
18 Lit part
22 Ashkenazi, for one
24 Take in
28 Polo locale
30 New Deal inits.
32 They turn on hinges
33 A goner
34 "If only!"
35 Third-century year
37 "This ___ outrage!"
38 Reciprocal Fibonacci constant
39 Bomb

40 Suffix with drunk
41 Desk item
42 Kind of wave
44 "___ the season . . ."
45 Black in a cowboy hat
46 "Sleigh Ride" composer Anderson
48 Enero starts it
49 Times to remember
50 Med. land
53 Cornelius who wrote "A Bridge Too Far"
54 Creature worshiped by the Incas
57 As one
61 Appended
62 Zip
64 101-Across, e.g.
66 Alias initials
68 Bit of homework
69 Actress ___ Flynn Boyle
70 Rub out
71 Stimulating
72 Gladly
73 Old cry of dismay
77 Barks
78 Anticipate
79 Yucatán youth
80 Howe'er
82 "Treasure Island" inits.
83 Words before any month's name
84 Fortune profilees, for short
85 "Uh-huh"
88 ___ bono (for whose benefit?: Lat.)
89 "___ Bangs" (Ricky Martin hit)
91 Check, as text
92 Bklyn. ___

by Oliver Hill and Eliza Bagg

**95** Kind of power, in math
**98** Outs
**99** Speech blocker
**101** One going into a drive
**103** Hall's partner
**104** Santa ___
**105** Bugged
**106** They take vids
**107** ___ plaisir
**108** "Oh, pooh!"
**109** Butcher's trimmings
**110** Soulful Redding
**111** Slime
**112** Venezuela's Chávez
**113** Colonial land: Abbr.
**115** Rose's beau
**116** ___ Bay (Manhattan area)
**117** Sp. titles
**120** But: Lat.
**121** Some evidence

## ACROSS

1 Reduces to pulp
7 Betray, in a way
15 They're unoriginal
20 Haitian ___
21 Haiti's first democratically elected president
22 Iconoclast
23 Skip Thanksgiving leftovers?
25 Early spring bloomers
26 Operagoer's accessory
27 Broke bread
28 Longfellow's words before "O Ship of State!"
29 Singer Sumac
30 Say "No," "Never" and "Uh-uh"?
34 Mrs. Robert ___ (Mary Custis)
36 Make a big stink
37 Chacon of the 1960s Mets
38 Put up with
41 One may be original
43 Hopelessly lost
47 Plea for immediate absolution?
52 Abbr. on a cover letter
53 Wind in front of a stage
54 Kin of fairies
55 Not
56 Crested ___, Colo.
58 Chairlift alternative
60 Shake
62 Blot with a paper towel, maybe
63 Like food that's acceptable to cattle?
67 Inuit relatives
69 Checked, say
70 Italian sportswear name
73 They come with turndown service
74 Soviet ___
75 Burial site of early Scottish kings
77 Rents
78 Pipe material, for short
79 Memorable theatrical performance?
83 Shell, e.g.
86 Warning from a driver
87 Extremely, in 1970s slang
88 Joyce's land
89 Bottom-line bigwigs, in brief
91 Head-turning sound
93 Abstain happily?
99 Fairy
102 Steven who co-wrote "Freakonomics"
103 New Guinea port
104 Life-threatening
107 Blow away
108 Is well-endowed?
111 One giving an order
112 Declared
113 Dammed river in North Carolina
114 Maurice of Nixon's cabinet
115 Region conquered by Philip II of Macedon
116 Mounts

## DOWN

1 "Back to the Future" family name
2 "Get ___!"
3 California missions founder Junípero ___
4 Scottish poet James known as "The Ettrick Shepherd"
5 Southern university that shares its name with a biblical judge
6 Form a splinter group
7 Sled dog with a statue in New York's Central Park
8 Elizabeth in the cosmetics department
9 Abbr. following op. and loc.
10 The Wildcats of the Big 12 Conf.
11 Attack from the air
12 2010 chart-topper for Ke$ha
13 Like ___ in the headlights
14 Old Ottoman governor
15 Rural setting, in poetry
16 Green gemstone
17 Place in a Carlo Levi memoir
18 Scout's mission
19 David's weapon
24 Western tribe
28 Preposterous
31 Once, a long time ago
32 "Family Guy" creator MacFarlane
33 Ignore, imperatively
34 Barely beat
35 Oahu offering
38 In ___ (confused)
39 Mr. Burns's teddy bear on "The Simpsons"
40 Typical cemetery enclosure
41 Driver's target
42 Balloonhead
43 Seller of space or time, for short
44 Showy craft?
45 ___'acte
46 ___-deucy
48 Tennis's 1977 U.S. Open champ
49 Salon, e.g., informally
50 Accustom
51 ___-masochism
56 False deity
57 Baloney and then some
59 Dinner scraps
60 Memorable time
61 Vintage platters
62 Kebab go-with
64 Bravura
65 Cry to a mate
66 City east of the Sierra Nevada
67 Concert stack
68 Unexploded
71 Made haste
72 "___ dignus" (Latin motto)
74 Sans pizazz
75 Chapel line
76 Giant of old
79 Gist
80 Basic first step
81 Mateus ___
82 Chant syllables
84 Bear vis-à-vis the woods, e.g.
85 Fails miserably
89 Like a hair shirt
90 Bordeaux brothers
91 La Môme ___ (The Little Sparrow)
92 Sharpening devices
93 Sword lilies, for short
94 Send, as a check
95 Trump who wrote "The Best Is Yet to Come"
96 Instant
97 Lensman Adams
98 Good to go
99 Dexterity exercise
100 Like an Interstate
101 Jumps bail, say
105 Say "What to do? What to do?," e.g.
106 To ___ (precisely)
108 Siamese, e.g.
109 Filing org.
110 H

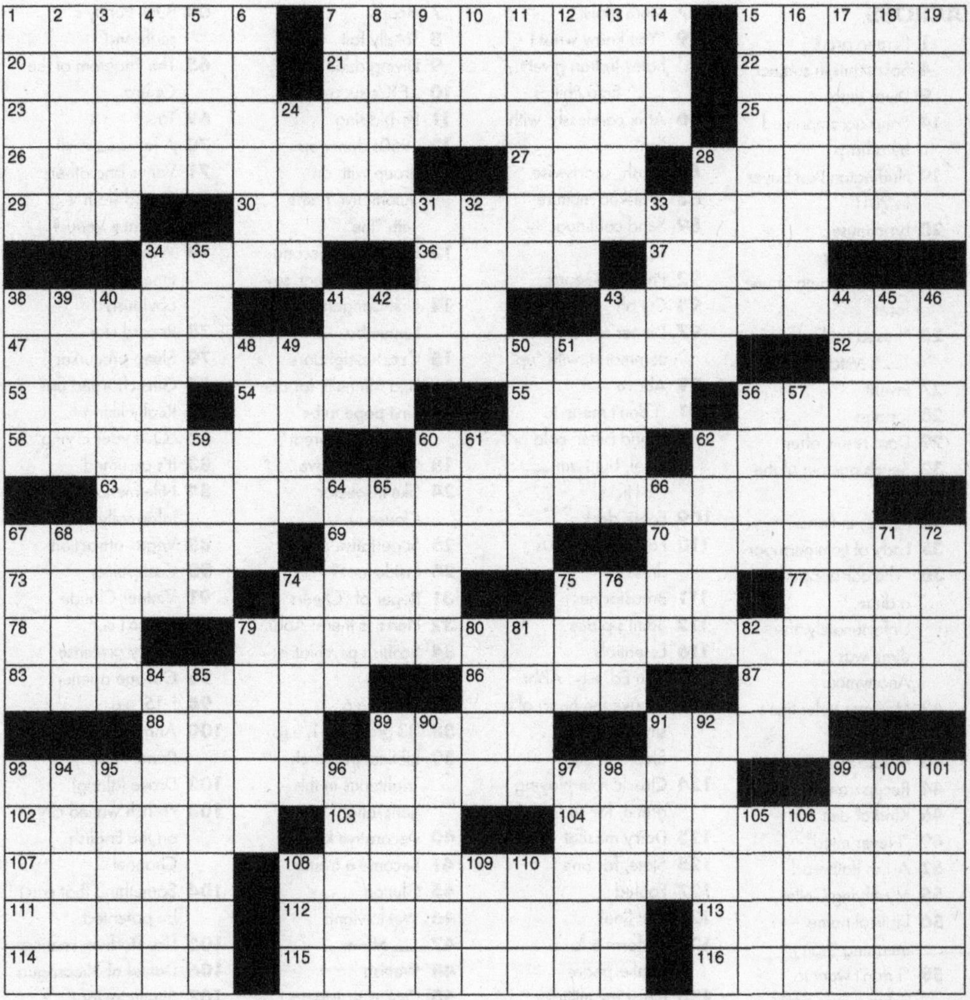

*by Paula Gamache*

## ACROSS

1 Screen grp.?
4 Solzhenitsyn subject
9 Dives (into)
14 Song accompanied by a harp
19 Huffington Post buyer in 2011
20 Lyric muse
21 Wear down
22 Tree-lined path in une forêt
23 "I used to do drugs. ___": Mitch Hedberg
27 Invent
28 Ignores
29 Dam result, often
30 Sends one out of the park
33 Alone, in Paris
35 Lady of Lammermoor
36 "The car stopped on a dime. Unfortunately, the dime was ___": Anonymous
42 Mexican Valentine's greeting
43 Madre's hermano
44 Recuperate
46 Kind of diet
49 "Never mind"
52 Asian flatbread
55 Mystifying Geller
56 Biblical name meaning "hairy"
58 "I don't want to achieve immortality through my work. I want to achieve it ___": Woody Allen
63 Like Jack, it's said
66 Some doors
67 Exploding stars
68 "Whoever named it necking was ___": Groucho Marx
75 Sci-fi film with a hatching egg on its poster
76 Cork's place: Abbr.

77 More moist
79 "You know what I hate? Indian givers. ___": Emo Philips
86 Affix carelessly, with "on"
87 Crush, sportswise
88 Whisked mixture
89 Send continuously, as video
92 Physicist Georg
93 Cut off
97 Dinner table command, with "up"
99 Above
101 "I don't mean to sound bitter, cold or cruel, but I am ___": Bill Hicks
109 Fool's deck
110 Fashionable '70s dress
111 Breastbones
112 Saint's place
116 Essentials
119 Con Ed, e.g.: Abbr.
120 "I have the heart of a small boy. It ___": Stephen King
124 Classic role-playing game, for short
125 Dairy mascot
126 Slate, for one
127 Fooled
128 Out-line?
129 Perform à la Shakespeare
130 Place for military supplies
131 Mayo container?

## DOWN

1 Feature of many a Jet Li film
2 "Already?"
3 Stanza successor
4 Get fixed?
5 19-Across has a much-used one
6 The Beatles during Beatlemania, e.g.

7 Heaps
8 Totally fail
9 Diving duds
10 J.F.K.'s successor
11 Forbidding
12 1960s doo-wop group with an automotive name, with "the"
13 Escorts to a second-floor apartment, say
14 First Congolese P.M. Lumumba
15 Czech neighbors
16 Liza Minnelli, for one
17 First pope to be called "the Great"
18 "Love ___ leave . . ."
24 Like Inspector Clouseau
25 Superlative prefix
26 Inside look?
31 Roger of "Cheers"
32 Pierre is there: Abbr.
34 Scottish psychiatrist R. D.
37 Squirt, e.g.
38 '13 grad in '11, e.g.
39 Biblical patriarch "righteous in this generation"
40 Decorative kit
41 Become a traitor
45 Glutton
46 Wet lowland
47 ___ Minor
48 Wettish
50 Crocus or freesia, botanically
51 Chinese gang
53 Eugene O'Neill's "___ Christie"
54 Palindromic time
57 Battle of the Atlantic vessel
59 Start of a fitness motto
60 Spot
61 Fruit that grows in a cluster
62 Cries of pain

64 Bugs Bunny's girlfriend
65 The Phantom of the Opera
69 Taunt
70 A law ___ itself
71 Venus and others
72 Grand slam, e.g.
73 Whence Venus?
74 When said three times, "Of course, obviously!"
78 Record stat
79 Sleep precursor
80 Gets charged up?
81 Really liking
82 "Quit your crying"
83 It's assumed
84 Nile menace, informally
85 Vegas attraction
90 Cashpoints
91 Vintner Claude
94 Doesn't cut
95 Empty pretense
96 Garage opener?
98 F-15, e.g.
100 Ann Landers or Ayn Rand: Abbr.
102 Drove (along)
103 French walled city on the English Channel
104 Something that can't be patented
105 Like stadium seating
106 Daniel of Nicaragua
107 Simultaneity
108 Admonish, as a child
112 Aspect
113 Org. for part-time soldiers
114 Colada fruit
115 Latin 101 verb
117 What you might do after retiring
118 Fabric scrap, say
121 Family girl
122 6 letters
123 Thus far

by Matt Ginsberg

## ACROSS

1 Fix, as a program
6 Water skimmers
10 Nickname for Baryshnikov
15 Gds.
19 Steve McQueen's ex-wife and co-star in "The Getaway"
21 Vogue's Wintour and others
22 Kind of torch
23 Electrical paths in New York City?
25 They're always charged
26 Flap
27 Poet's "before"
28 D preceder
29 Divert
31 Deux of these are better than un
33 Spill a Cuban drink?
36 Shelter that's often octagonal
39 Housing for the homeless: Abbr.
40 Pit crew's supply
41 One who says "Beg your pardon" after stepping on your toes?
47 Mordant Mort
49 "Exodus" hero
50 Father of Deimos and Phobos, in myth
51 Seedcase that inspired Velcro
52 Scot's "own"
53 Noblewoman
55 Dorm heads, for short
56 Mmes., in Iberia
57 Speak on C-Span, say
60 Burn cause
61 Gentleman's partner
63 Preachers' lies?
68 Get up?
69 Subj. of modern mapping
71 Bust planner, in brief
72 Sly sort?
73 What a mashed potato serving may have?
78 "Sock it to me!" show
80 Unbar, to the Bard
81 High-end camera
82 Superior body?
83 Abbr. unlikely to start of a sentence
84 Revolutionary?
88 Continuing plot in a TV series
89 "___ Did It" (2007 memoir)
90 Cookie first baked in Manhattan's Chelsea district
91 "Confiteor ___ omnipotenti" (Latin prayer starter)
92 "Understood, man"
94 Hairdresser's first do?
97 Luggage attachment
99 Cartoon exclamation
101 One way to serve café
102 Author Amy's family squabble?
107 Our sun's type
111 Baker or Loos
112 Pizza topping
113 FICA fig.
115 Prefix with metric
116 "It won't hurt ___"
117 The Miracles?
121 Ball boy?
122 Like a bagel
123 Homey's rep
124 Mtn. stats
125 Shakespeare's "spot"
126 Tofu sources
127 Spine-tingling

## DOWN

1 Blot with gauze, say
2 Pass over
3 One who sees everything in black and white?
4 Actress Thurman
5 Regards in wonderment
6 Rubberneck
7 Art, nowadays
8 Rocky of song
9 Tell, e.g.
10 Asian gambling mecca
11 Stores after cremation
12 Long-range shooters
13 Word after high or top
14 Source of Indian tea
15 Volcano near Aokigahara forest
16 Mass part
17 Bitin' things
18 ___ for elephant
20 Red Cross course, briefly
24 Line score inits.
30 Group with the 6x platinum album "Dr. Feelgood"
32 Backing: Var.
33 Bent beams
34 Some flakes
35 Suffix with psych-
37 Whistle-blower, in slang
38 Facebook co-founder Saverin
41 3.26 light-years
42 Sibyl, for one
43 Writer Eda
44 Chinese dynasty during the time of Confucius
45 Marquess's subordinate
46 Sow's counterpart
48 Prefix with port
54 Change the price on
56 Bedtime comment
58 Neaten
59 Season in le soleil?
62 First German emperor of Italy
63 Runner
64 Mideast nosh
65 Announcement upon arriving
66 ___ dictum (incidental remark)
67 Sarge, e.g.
70 CBS's "The ___ Today"
74 Audition (for)
75 100 Iranian dinars
76 Israeli seaport
77 Cow, in Cádiz
79 Director Kurosawa
82 Comics character who said "Big sisters are the crab grass in the lawn of life"
84 Keatsian, e.g.
85 Johnnie Walker variety
86 Plant manager?
87 Willingly
90 Chooses
93 Start to boil over?
95 Met by chance
96 Intaglio seals
98 If nothing changes
100 Base wear?
103 They have hops
104 Choose
105 Scotland's Firth of ___

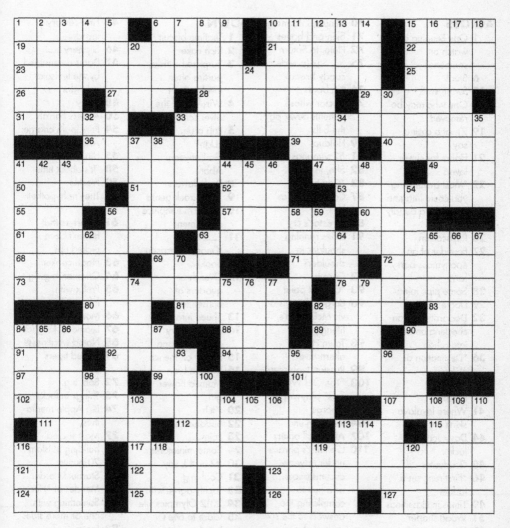

*by Caleb Madison and J.A.S.A. Crossword Class*

**106** Rake in
**108** Sash go-with
**109** "Rich Man, Poor
Man" Emmy
winner
**110** Actor McDowall
**113** Jeanne et
Julie, e.g.:
Abbr.

**114** Any boat
**116** ___ Lovelace,
computer
programming
pioneer
**118** ___ Szyslak of
"The Simpsons"
**119** Dull
**120** E-mail add-on

## ACROSS

1 One keeping a watch on someone?
6 Steal
13 Swine swill
17 One who may be removed
19 21, at a casino, say
21 Home for clover lovers
22 *Most awful thing you could imagine
25 One with a deadly tongue
26 Rapscallion
27 Founder of an eponymous berry farm
28 Some pipe joints
29 Dogie, e.g.
32 Declaration upon checking oneself into rehab
36 *Destination of 1911
40 "Does not compute"
41 Where lavalava skirts are worn
44 Davy Jones's locker
45 Graduates
46 *First rung on a ladder
49 Times in classifieds
51 Wood shaper
52 Hits and runs?
53 ___ Lingus
54 Hits or runs
55 Stub ___
56 "2001: A Space Odyssey" studio
57 Dost possess
59 A laser might read it
62 Brain-racked state
64 *Dunce's place
67 It may have a cross to bear

70 Minute, informally
71 Skin-and-bones
72 Pluto, to Saturn
75 ___ Stix (powdered candy brand)
76 Big boats
78 Doctor whose patients never pay the bills
79 Holdup
81 52 semanas
82 She, in Rome
83 *Destitution
87 Color again, as hair
89 Director's cry
91 Ones running shoulder to shoulder?
92 Corrupt
93 *Coldest point
96 Burger King vis-à-vis McDonald's, fittingly
98 Town House alternative
99 Russian legislature
103 "The Old Wives' Tale" playwright George
104 Years on end
107 Above all others
110 Optimist's phrase under adverse circumstances . . . or a hint to completing the answers to the six starred clues
115 Introductory drawing class
116 Like stars on a clear night
117 Luxury hotel along Manhattan's Central Park, with "the"
118 Unwelcome guest
119 Real softball
120 Baroque painter Hals

## DOWN

1 Teatime biscuit
2 Rich cake
3 Surprise birthday parties often involve them
4 Wirehair of the silver screen
5 Pub order
6 "Ugh!"
7 Go-between: Abbr.
8 Do followers
9 1970s rock genre
10 Scuba mouthpiece attachment
11 "___ Mine" (George Harrison book)
12 Over three-quarters of bunsenite
13 Sheer, informally
14 Almost every puppy has one
15 Bobby on the ice
16 Little, in Lyon
18 Many a flower girl
20 Pitch
22 Buddhist temple
23 Foie ___
24 Some miniatures
30 #2 or #3, say
31 Coal, e.g.
33 Tacitly agree with
34 2012 Olympics site
35 Close to one's heart
36 Place to get a yo-yo or choo-choo
37 Shakespearean prince
38 ___ Mahal
39 Cable inits.
41 Kiss, in 34-Down
42 One of three for $H_2O$
43 Mohawked muscleman

45 Fifth-century invader
46 Slippery ___
47 Dates determined by the lunisolar calendar
48 Ixnay
50 Actress Farrah
54 Principal's charge: Abbr.
55 Hinny's mother
58 "It's about time!"
59 Freckle
60 They're hypothetical
61 Quarters that haven't been picked up?
63 Naan cooker
64 Ottoman bigwig
65 Prefix with information
66 Monopoly util.
67 Leonidas' kingdom
68 Noted weakness?
69 Tamed tigers, say
72 Bob, e.g.
73 Things in locks
74 Big Apple media inits.
77 Most sacred building in Islam
78 20-ounce Starbucks order
80 Mendes of "Hitch"
82 Something with one or more sides
83 From ___ Z
84 "The Family Circus" cartoonist Keane
85 Plat du ___
86 Start to fix?
88 Come into
90 Creator of Aslan and the White Witch
93 Settle a score
94 Pennsylvanie, e.g.
95 "Legs" band, 1984

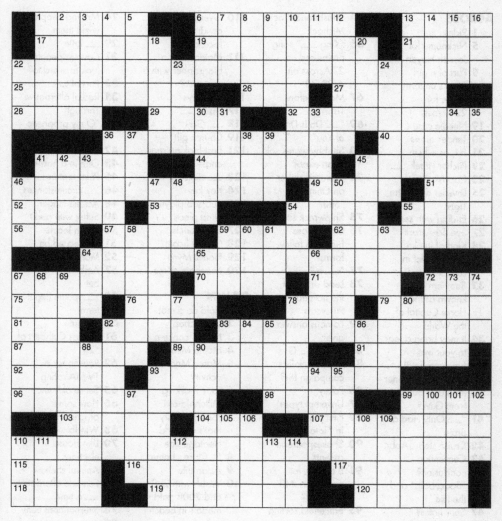

*by Xan Vongsathorn*

97 "Casablanca" role
99 Messing of "Will &
Grace"
100 Reversal
101 Specks of dust
102 Kwik-E-Mart
operator
105 "Goodness
gracious!"
106 Verne captain
108 Late-week cry
109 Gardener, at times
110 Pick
111 Charlemagne's
realm: Abbr.
112 Pay ending
113 Nickelodeon dog
114 Poet's "before"

## ACROSS

1 Rides
5 Nickname for Joseph Haydn
9 Part of a girl scout's uniform
14 Home for 22-Across
19 Needle case
20 Tender areas
21 Fix, as a hem
22 Pitcher Hideki ___
23 Capris?
25 Dweller along the Tigris
26 Ending with sea
27 See 66-Across
28 Kind of intake
30 Domes to let in London?
32 Southern city known as the Horse Capital of the World
34 It may bring a tear to your eye
36 Squeezes (out)
37 Verizon forerunner
38 Pre-2004 purchase from G.M.?
41 "___ Only Had a Brain"
42 Cruise stops: Abbr.
43 Convention conclusion?
44 "Spaceballs" and the like
47 Sour notes?
50 "___ Poetica"
53 Accustom
54 Toy rocket company since 1958
55 Verdi aria "___ tu"
56 Fractions of acres?
59 Boston Tea Party issue
60 He wrote "None but the brave deserves the fair"
63 Towers in the high country?
64 "Flashdance" actor Michael
66 "King ___," song premiered on 27-Across on 4/22/78
67 Month before Tishri
69 "___ Do Is Dream of You"
70 Shabby wares sold at an expo?
74 Featured singer on Eminem's "Stan"
75 Shipwreck site
76 Org. whose functions follow forms?
77 "___ evil . . ."
78 Lead singer of the fictional Pussycats
79 Famous answer giver
81 HBO's ___ G
83 What socialists campaign for?
86 Pokey
87 Unkempt types
89 First player listed in "Total Baseball"
90 Shakespearean assents
91 B and O, for presidents #43 and #44?
95 Battlefield sorting system
97 Spanish pot
98 Crucifix letters
99 Batter's need
101 Career criminals?
105 Eastern wrap
106 Actor Robert who played the villain in "Licence to Kill"
107 Rick who sang "Never Gonna Give You Up"
110 Overly air-conditioned room, facetiously
111 Material for a biographer with a recorder?
114 Monkeys
117 Disco ___
118 ___ Gay
119 Church gift
121 Best-looking rear ends?
123 ___-dink
124 Key key
125 Sub-sub-players
126 Blind piece
127 Some encls.
128 "Great Scott!"
129 Pianist Myra
130 Numbers game

## DOWN

1 Hold on a mat
2 Chop-chop
3 N.R.A. concern
4 Mr., in Milano
5 March Madness activity
6 Lane marking
7 Millennia-old Jordanian city that's a World Heritage Site
8 St. Clare's home
9 Asian title
10 Walsh with 2004 and 2008 gold medals in beach volleyball
11 Golf's Aoki
12 D.J.'s considerations
13 Like stars at night
14 Secs
15 Asia's ___ Sea
16 Ideal
17 Covered for, maybe
18 Baby bottles
20 Doo-wop syllable
24 Masked people wield them
29 ___ latte
31 Courses people look forward to?
33 Part of L.A.
35 Radial alternative
39 Through
40 "O my prophetic ___!": Hamlet
42 Genus of holly
43 One in a harness
45 Palm features
46 ___ circumstances
48 Actress Hagen
49 Suffix with audit
50 Union locale
51 Barbecued bit
52 More clichéd
57 Ambitious track bet
58 ___ sponte (legal term)
60 Fizzler
61 Actress Cuthbert of "24"
62 Reason for a TV-MA rating
65 Sense of humor
66 How some practical jokes go
68 Windblown soil
70 Like House elections
71 Animal shelter?
72 Pomade alternative
73 ___ a time
78 International bully
80 Actress ___ Ling of "The Crow"
81 Et ___
82 "Long," in Hawaii
84 Lead-in to -meter
85 Jet's noise
87 Giving it 110%, so to speak
88 Certain N.C.O.'s
91 Targets of martial law
92 Modern locale of ancient Illyria

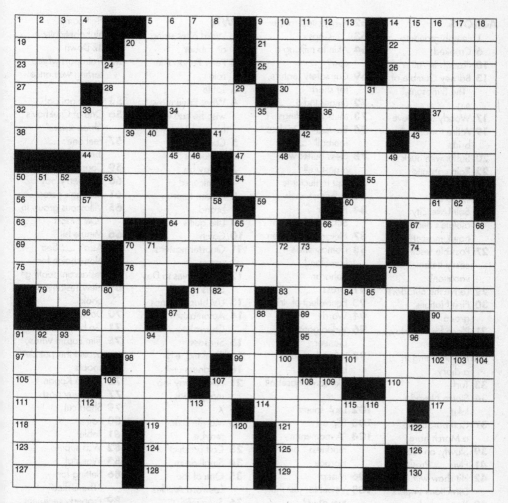

*by Daniel A. Finan*

**93** Loafers, e.g.
**94** One asked to R.S.V.P.
**96** Heart meas.
**100** Snag
**102** Fútbol cheer
**103** Oklahoma city
**104** In order that one might

**106** Pivotal times
**107** Incinerated
**108** Express shock or happiness, say
**109** "Great Scott!"
**112** Sommer in Southern California

**113** Jazzy James or Jones
**115** "___ le roi!"
**116** Athos, Porthos or Aramis
**120** Signs of ineloquence
**122** Utterance of a finger wagger

## ACROSS

1 Jewish grandma
6 Crooked
10 "Laugh-In" airer
13 Barney Gumble of "The Simpsons," e.g.
17 Woody and Steve
19 Attire for an Indian bride
20 Suffix with buck
22 Rain cats and dogs
23 Close by
24 Salt Lake City athlete's dear hawk mascot?
27 Possible result of a costly Italian vacation?
29 Leave the outdoors
30 First Nations group
31 Place for Wii play, say
32 Frank writing in a diary
33 Turf
34 Sierra Nevada lake
37 Comparable to a March hare
39 Slowly, on scores
41 Elvis ___ Presley
42 Hit show with New Directions singers
43 Some whiskeys
44 Gymnastics great Comaneci
48 Flurry of activity
50 Tribal healer
53 In pain
54 Shakespearean fairy king
55 Jokes in a campy 1960s TV locale?
58 Hazardous household gas
59 Marisa who played 75-Down's girlfriend

62 Kyrgyzstan range
63 ___-Caps
64 Akin to milking a cow?
69 Car safety feature, for short
72 Singer India.___
73 Musical endings
74 Baseball : Oriole :: football : ___
78 Bless butter with a gesture?
82 Apt to fluctuate
83 Bullying words
84 Former SoCal N.F.L. team
87 Never-before-seen
88 Damascene's homeland
89 Saharan
91 Gross
93 Equivalent of -trix
94 Wordy
96 Video game pioneer
98 What we may be?
99 Like some baseball teams
102 Leak sound
103 Slip up
104 "A momentary madness," per Horace
106 Misers
108 Vessel for just the two of us?
113 Role of a boxer's physician?
115 Tennis's Goolagong
116 Yank or Ray
117 Politico Gingrich
118 Concerning
119 Many a Bush military adviser
120 Org. in a big race of years past
121 That, in a bodega
122 Saxophonist Getz
123 Surgical tube

## DOWN

1 Word after string or rubber
2 Peter Fonda title role
3 Tattle
4 What Ernie may wish he had vis-à-vis his roommate?
5 Complete
6 Evaluates
7 It may be manicured
8 Frozen tater brand
9 Like quilts
10 Catch
11 Quartermaster's group
12 Alternatives to Dos Equis
13 UV blockage nos.
14 Automaker Chevrolet
15 Surpass
16 Shetland, e.g.
18 Loudness unit
21 Taking way too many meds
25 X
26 Margin size, maybe
28 Calf product
34 Small drum
35 One of the Leeward Antilles
36 Scammed
38 Interjection of disinterest
39 "The Fountainhead" author
40 Home of Punchbowl Crater
42 See 51-Down: Abbr.
43 Teller
45 Darkens
46 Hip to
47 Soil: Prefix
49 Actress Anderson

51 First name alphabetically in 42-Down
52 Train part where sorting was once done
53 Gallic gal pal
56 One of Chekhov's "three sisters"
57 Feel one's ___ (be confident)
59 Cousin of a gull
60 Mayberry boy
61 Kellogg's cereal
65 Villainous group in "Get Smart"
66 Minute bit
67 Asia's ___ Sea
68 Non-choice for restaurant seating?
69 New Testament book
70 Donkey's cry
71 Go bad
75 Film cousin whose accent this puzzle spoofs
76 Justice Kagan
77 Stairway post
79 Short cut
80 Fame
81 Tablet
82 Was supine
85 War stat
86 Setting for "The Office"
89 Property recipient, in law
90 They cut wood with the grain
92 Humane
95 Pipe holder
96 Restaurant lures
97 Most faithful
98 Actor Keanu
99 City on the Nile
100 Fleet Amtrak train
101 "Bedroom at ___" (classic painting)
103 Image on the back of a $1 bill

by Cathy Allis

105 Feds
107 Other: Sp.
109 Architectural
    pier
110 Formerly
111 Soon, poetically
112 Big top, e.g.
114 G.M. debut of
    1964

## ACROSS

1 Be bratty
6 Chaplin chapeau
11 Center of emotions
16 Long-range weapon, for short
20 Spa spot
21 It's got game, often
22 At just the right time
23 Pants, in brief
24 The Library's rare first-edition printing of "The Star-Spangled Banner" is, to its publisher's chagrin, ___
28 Pont Neuf's locale
29 Tractor-trailer
30 Betty of "Dizzy Dishes"
31 King at Karnak
32 Wingding
33 Unmanned vehicle that found the Titanic
35 "Yankee Doodle Dandy" Oscar winner
37 Piggish
38 Spanish treasure
39 Heavy cart
40 Very
41 Go out
43 Norbert Pearlroth spent 52 years of 60-hour weeks in the Library's Reading Room collecting material for ___
51 Fabulous writer?
52 "The Creation" composer
53 Ring site
54 Jagged chain
56 Lee, e.g.: Abbr.
58 Big name in country
59 This is not going anywhere
61 Cry of praise
65 Do some grilling
67 Rail org.
68 Amigo
69 The Library's Special Collections include one of George Washington's creations, ___
76 Uganda's Amin
77 Some chest-pounding, briefly
78 Have something
79 Boxes
80 Progresso offering
85 Take to a higher power
88 Plot thickener
89 Smooth as silk
90 Article used by Einstein
91 Grace in film
93 Fashionable beach resorts
97 The Library's Periodicals Room was the source of most of the excerpted material in the first issue of ___
101 Thermal opening?
102 A Lincoln
103 KFC side dish
104 Dye container
105 Hines of jazz
109 Pull-up pullers
112 Fret
113 Tease
114 Pinafores
116 Spot on the staff?
117 Neighbor of Swe.
118 Button ridge
120 The handle of Charles Dickens's ivory letter opener, in the Library's collection, is ___
125 Reddish purple
126 Without digressing
127 John who wrote "The Bastard"
128 Go-between
129 Goes on to say
130 Cartoonist Bil
131 Indolence
132 Irascible

## DOWN

1 Bozo
2 Informal talk
3 Stretchy garments
4 Disconnect
5 Hassle
6 Internet option, briefly
7 Vitamin-rich snack
8 Kind of wave
9 Crow
10 Short agreement
11 "Jabberwocky" birds
12 Lyonnaise sauce ingredient
13 With 14-Down, visually investigate
14 See 13-Down
15 Predecessor of Rabin
16 Caller ID?
17 Sign of the times?
18 Ulna and fibula
19 Cartoon criminal
25 Lachrymose
26 Humble
27 Wales, in medieval times
32 Roman squares
34 Torrent
35 Borneo borderer
36 Besides
39 Bank (on)
40 Hag
42 Pear variety
44 The Hub hub
45 Look on
46 Wonderland cake message
47 Inflamed
48 Hockey goal part
49 Small African antelopes
50 Barnstormers
55 Llullaillaco's locale
57 Shanghai-to-Beijing dir.
60 Easily handled, as a ship
61 Huzzahs
62 Words of worry
63 Hélène or Geneviève
64 Missile paths
66 You may get them in a bunch
70 Products with earbuds
71 Set straight
72 Melancholy, musically
73 Chart checkers, for short
74 Mandatory recycling, e.g.
75 Andalusian port
81 Andalusian aunt
82 Where "Parks and Recreation" is set
83 High-pH solutions
84 Heyday
86 Alphabetical order?
87 Setting of Johnny Depp's feature film debut
92 Noah Webster's alma mater
94 Splits
95 Tilted
96 Dickens's Mr. Pecksniff
98 Good name for a thief
99 Goggles

*by Bob Klahn*

**100** Goggles
**105** Mullah's edict
**106** Honeydew producer
**107** Drift
**108** They may be high
**110** ___ dignitatem
**111** Folkie Leonard
**112** Show-stopping

**113** Bench warmer?
**115** Love letters
**117** Actress Patricia
**119** Spruce
**121** Words of praise
**122** Spinmeisters?
**123** Can opener?
**124** Communication syst. for the deaf

## ACROSS

1 Herbert Hoover and Richard Nixon, e.g.
8 Go canvassing, say
12 Partner of whistles
17 Cop squad in "Monk": Abbr.
21 Surround
22 "Dies ___"
23 How olives may be packed
24 "Can't argue there"
25 Done for, finito, kaput
26 Execute perfectly
27 Auto security feature
28 Canal part
29 Knock off
30 Demander of special treatment
31 Suffix with exist
32 Univ., e.g.
35 Firmed up
36 Course after trig
40 Singer Redding
41 Is for you?
42 Pull in
46 Back on the ranch?
47 Backwoods
48 Drag wrap
49 Elands, to lions
50 Muse for Whitman
51 Sen. McCain's alma mater
55 Superlative suffix
56 "Hells Bells" band
57 Some fun in the sun
60 Petty manipulations
61 Spring (from)
62 Parade paths: Abbr.
64 W.W. II beach craft
65 ___-Magnon
66 Author R. L. ___
67 Hot
68 Mashed, e.g.
69 Dazed and confused
71 Cornerstone abbr.
72 What sgts. turn in at HQ's
73 Shrub used in dyeing
74 Some Nissan cars
75 Teaser on party fliers
76 Cherish
77 Light reflector
82 Diminish
86 Show a bit of courtesy (for)
88 Unwrap
89 Runs (around), informally
93 Nothin'
97 Under debate
98 Quite a tale
99 Bajillions
100 Turn away
102 Java
103 Mine blower
104 Creator of Genesis
105 Surfeit
106 Secretary of state under Carter
107 One of TV's Clampetts
108 Suffix with senior
110 Pre-sneeze sounds
111 Moolah
112 Parting of the Pacific?
113 It may be touch-screen
114 Diamond stat
115 Hilton or Westin welcomer
116 "Holy mackerel!"
119 Cusp
120 Bajillion
121 Rice pad
125 Linear, for short
126 I love, to Luis
127 Assn.
128 Funny Caroline
129 Sticks up
131 Off the shore
135 Opening letters
136 Conductor in a white turtleneck
141 Burrowing arthropods
142 Classic Alfa Romeo roadsters
146 Chrysler 300, e.g.
147 Chair toted on poles
148 It rarely has more than one part
149 Walloped
150 It rolls on a Rolls
151 "I'm outta here!"
152 Compatriot
153 [See blurb]

## DOWN

1 Argument ender
2 A, in Amiens
3 Actress Gardner
4 "The original sneaker" sloganeer
5 Carrier to Ben-Gurion
6 Parks in a bus
7 Neuter
8 Brie exterior
9 Hold 'em declaration
10 Less sophisticated
11 Treat in Torino
12 Repeating heart monitor sound
13 Musician Brian
14 Fan setting
15 Rewrite history, in a way
16 Photog's choice
17 Fifth-century pope
18 UPS drop-off site, often
19 Emilio of fashion
20 Hockey fake-outs
32 Portable cutter
33 Italian appetizer, literally "little toasts"
34 All-weather resort amenity
36 Run, as an exhibit
37 Literary duelist
38 Unexpressed
39 Hush-hush powwow
42 UV index monitor
43 Light in a floodlight
44 Macy's logo feature
45 One in a line at J.F.K. or La Guardia
47 Rules, quickly
51 Country that disappeared in '91
52 How-to unit
53 Seinfeld vis-à-vis Kramer
54 Author Tan and others
57 Noel starter
58 ___ Minor
59 Cast
63 Actress Ward
70 Gossipy Smith
77 Practiced actively
78 Some of them are turnoffs: Abbr.
79 "We've waited long enough!"
80 Pushed (aside)
81 Satisfying
82 Headaches
83 Do, by all accounts
84 Touch
85 Keeping under glass, e.g.
86 Muslim trek
87 Missouri River native
89 Involuntary extension of troop tours
90 Pueblo vessel
91 Its winner beats the loser with a stick
92 Lid problem
93 Bygone missile with a tribal name
94 Literary paradise
95 Mark
96 Colosseum entrance, e.g.
101 Blue-green

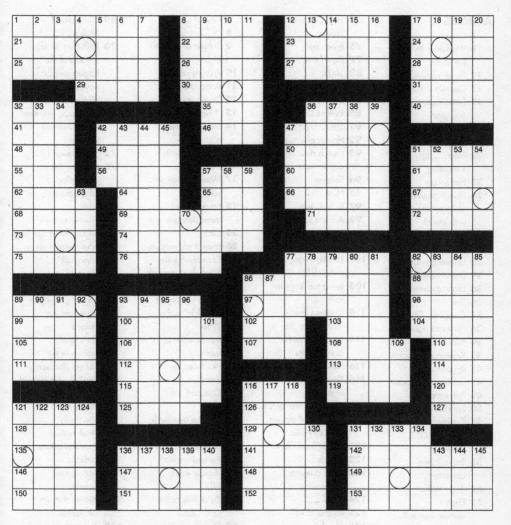

by Jeremy Newton and Tony Orbach

**109** Go after
**116** Daily talk show beginning in 2005
**117** Unprincipled
**118** Harsh pronouncement from a judge
**121** Pub order
**122** "Whoopee!"

**123** Happen again
**124** Niño producer
**130** Nimble
**131** Tennis's Arthur
**132** Filtered stuff
**133** Home to the sport of hurling
**134** P.O. box, e.g.
**136** Pre-C.I.A. grp.

**137** Capital of Zaire?
**138** Suffix on fruit names
**139** Exceptionally
**140** Santa ___
**143** Apathetic reactions
**144** Hit 2011 animated film
**145** Place to buy tkts.

## ACROSS

1 Chickens, e.g.
6 Workers with hammers
12 Punch relative
15 Captain of fiction
19 Enthusiastically accepted
20 Facing
21 Coffeehouse fixture
22 Take ___ (go swimming)
23 Not secure
24 How organized philosophers deal with ideas?
27 Like about 20% of the world's land area
28 Gillette product
29 Bronchodilator user
30 Highway S-curve?
34 Vex
35 Composer Charles
36 Playbook figures
39 Pulled off
42 Reinforcing bracket
45 Bygone copy
48 Suffix with Ecuador
49 Software basis
50 Spanish article
51 Countess bankrupts St. Louis N.H.L. team?
55 Some 35mm cameras
57 Actor Wilson
58 Digital communication?: Abbr.
59 Words on an "Animal House" cake float
60 Legendary Onondaga chief
63 Alien craft
66 Cackler
67 Warning before driving past the town dump?
73 Some Windows systems
74 Start of a selection process
75 Break up
77 Down time
80 100%
82 Marvel Comics hero
84 Denials
85 Wayne Gretzky?
91 Soph. and jr.
92 Holder of a runoff?
93 French river or department
94 Reliever
95 Must
97 Fr. holy title
98 Ancient Cretan writing system
100 ___ Pictures
101 Readily recite, with "off"
103 Being too large to fail?
110 Onetime Robin Williams co-star
114 So-called Mother of Presidents
115 "Shucks!"
116 Singles bar pickup strategy?
119 Flying monster of film
120 "Baywatch" actress ___ Lee Nolin
121 Rocket from China
122 Notice
123 Bit of Weather Channel news
124 By all ___
125 Kind of card
126 Chucks
127 Pick up

## DOWN

1 Israel's Ehud
2 Grammatically proper identification
3 Nail polish ingredient
4 Loser of 1988
5 "Casino Royale," for one
6 Animals with black-tipped tails
7 One of a dozen
8 "If ___ you . . ."
9 Subject of Genghis Khan
10 Princely abbr.
11 Arms race inits.
12 Diving seabirds
13 "Nuts!"
14 Make a queen, e.g.
15 Present at birth
16 Deleted
17 Maurice Chevalier song
18 Ecuador and Venezuela are in it
25 Zilch
26 Friends of François
31 Crumbly cheese
32 Symbols of strength
33 Dilbert co-worker
37 Safari equipment
38 "Matilda" author, 1988
40 As above, in a footnote
41 Not those, in Brooklyn
42 Ooh and aah
43 Dark
44 Hebrew matriarch
45 Classic song that begins "And now the end is near"
46 Vapour trail?
47 Jiffy
49 Ike or Billy at the O.K. Corral
52 Qatar's capital
53 Prince Albert's home: Abbr.
54 Root crop
56 Con
61 N.L. Central player
62 Co. ID's
64 Flipper
65 Biblical breastplate stones
66 Part of 10-Down, maybe
68 Mirror image?
69 Old ballad "Robin ___"
70 Philatelist George, founder of the largest weekly newspaper for stamp collectors
71 Frank ___, two-time Oscar-winning director
72 Turn outward
76 Onetime Texaco competitor
77 GPS options: Abbr.
78 Answer to the old riddle "What lies flat when empty, sits up when full?"
79 "Forget I said anything"
80 Score right before a win, maybe
81 Unique
83 G.I.'s food
86 Train systems
87 Actress Hatcher
88 Den ___, Nederland
89 Cluster
90 Wives in São Paulo
96 Mask feature
98 Puddle producer, perhaps
99 Incantation opener
100 Hybrid clothing for women
102 Actresses Best and Purviance
104 Marina sights
105 "Now I see"
106 Kathleen Kennedy Townsend, to J.F.K.
107 City south of Brigham City
108 Raises
109 "Fiddler on the Roof" role
110 When doubled, a Samoan port

*by Yaakov Bendavid*

111 Wowed
112 Start of some congregation names
113 Land in Genesis
117 Summer hours in L.A.
118 Auto monogram

## ACROSS

1 Bushed
5 Entrance to many a plaza
9 Rimsky-Korsakov's "The Tale of ___ Saltan"
13 Exactly right
19 Free
21 ___ avis
22 Attempted something
23 *Boardwalk offering
25 Thought out loud
26 It might make you snort
27 Home of the World Health Organization
28 Stickers?
30 ___ Day, May 1 celebration in Hawaii
31 Must-have
33 Soft ball brand
35 "___ mine!"
36 One on the way out
38 *Diamond substitute
44 1987 disaster movie?
46 Rest spot
47 Place for a pickup?
48 Word with exit or express
49 Something that's drawn
50 Whiz
51 Any hit by Little Richard
53 Many a Bob Marley fan
54 Mideast title
56 Seaport on the Adriatic
58 Turned away from sin
60 Earth
61 Outstanding
63 Lawn tools
64 *Handy things for a toy?
68 ###
72 Free
73 Itching
78 Took a corner on two wheels
81 Fix, as brakes
82 Vituperation, e.g.
83 Wake Island, e.g.
84 "Nothing ___!"
86 Transplant, in a way
87 "Up in the Air" actress Kendrick
88 Do followers
89 Navel buildup
90 Former flier, for short
91 Slugger
93 *Staple of "Candid Camera"
97 Xerox product
98 Baseball's Master Melvin
99 Loughlin of "Full House"
100 Nincompoop
101 Conditions
104 Killjoy
109 Comparatively statuesque
111 Point of view
113 Enfeeble
114 *Radio Flyer, e.g.
117 Like a winter wind
118 1997 Peter Fonda title role
119 Hoax
120 Old-fashioned
121 TV's Foxx
122 Brake
123 "Superman II" villainess

## DOWN

1 Kind of metabolism
2 Military camp
3 *Certain study session
4 Head of Haiti
5 ___ formality
6 Actor Hauer
7 Believe in it
8 Not his'n
9 Ad-packed Sunday newspaper section
10 A giraffe might be seen on one
11 Pound sound
12 You may catch them on a boat, in two different ways
13 Shrimp
14 Old Church of England foe
15 Role in 2011's "Thor"
16 Chinese dynasty of 1,200 years ago
17 Curved molding
18 Drops (off)
20 Start of a childish plaint
24 Believe in it
29 "Goody goody gumdrops!"
32 At any time, to a bard
34 Ward (off)
37 Survey choice, sometimes
38 Less cramped
39 Like some maidens
40 Trolley sound
41 Expedition
42 Keyboard key
43 Shows, as a thermometer does a temperature
44 "Uh-huh, sure it is"
45 The very ___
46 Hinder
50 Test ___
51 *Something to stand on
52 Piece over a door or window
53 It had a major part in the Bible
55 Descent of a sort
57 Many a summer worker
59 Solitaire puzzle piece
62 Wander
65 Blue Angels' org.
66 Ain't fixed?
67 Classic brand of hair remover
68 Line of cliffs
69 Intolerant sort
70 Bouquet
71 ___ of the past
74 Taper off
75 *It may be found near a barrel
76 Feudal serf
77 Fanny
79 Decrees
80 Lady of Spain
85 "___ do"
89 Service arrangement
90 Know-how
91 Boo follower
92 They're often acquired at a wedding
94 Drunk's activity
95 Scribbled
96 Got up on one's soapbox
97 One waving a red flag
100 Wild
102 Dentist's advice
103 Actress Berger
104 Bros, e.g.
105 Pass over
106 ___ no good
107 S. C. Johnson brand

by C. W. Stewart

**108** "Dirty rotten scoundrel," e.g.
**110** Old NASA landers
**112** Half of a sitcom farewell
**115** Project closing?
**116** It might get your feet wet

## 32

# SAY WHAT?!

## ACROSS

1 Nursery sounds
6 Bates's "Misery" co-star
10 Compadre
15 Having more than one band
19 Weapon, e.g., in military-speak
20 Regarding
21 Something well-preserved?
22 ___ avis
23 "I've heard enough, retail outlet!"
25 "I agree completely, dog-eared bit of paper!"
27 What you might get by moving a head?
28 "Stop right where you are, picture holder!"
30 "One if by land, two if by sea" and others
31 Extinguished, with "out"
33 Spots before your eyes?
34 Alaska Purchase negotiator
35 Symbol of royalty in old Egypt
36 Skunk, e.g.
38 Big-screen canine
40 Jeans brand
41 The majority
44 "You're in danger, tall hill!"
49 Surname in a Poe tale
51 Check out
52 Like racehorses
53 Objectivist Rand
54 "The chair doesn't recognize you, steakhouse and chophouse!"
59 Before, to Byron
60 Scorecard blemish
61 Lift provider
62 Vessels with spouts
65 Light TV fare
67 Sticky seedcase
68 Explorer Richard Byrd's plane
70 Writing surface
71 Make nonsensical notes?
73 Roast V.I.P.
75 Work in the field
76 "I'd be miserable without you, tapestry!"
80 D.C.-based news source
82 Australia's Lake ___ National Park
83 See 93-Across
84 Inasmuch as
85 "Goodbye, place I used to live!"
89 Philip with a 1975 best seller on C.I.A. secrets
90 Sistine Chapel ceiling figure
91 Like many sunscreens
92 Cessation
93 Is 83-Across
95 Big name in California wine
97 Endorser's need
99 Another name for Buddha
103 Speak for everyone in the room
104 "Just keep doing what you're doing, suitcases!"
109 One of the Bobbsey twins
110 "I read you loud and clear, breakfast meat!"
112 "It was all my fault, gun attachment!"
114 Over again
115 Pop singer Lopez
116 Addition to café
117 Keys in a chain
118 Amount that's settled for
119 Caddie's offering
120 "This looks like trouble!"
121 Manicurist's aid

## DOWN

1 Some nest builders
2 Lacking color
3 Diesel engine manufacturer
4 Rented out
5 Packs
6 Checked out before robbing
7 Athlete who wrote "Off the Court"
8 Complete
9 "You're mistaken"
10 Certificate on a wall, maybe
11 "___ Pearl" (Jackson 5 hit)
12 Gossip subject
13 One that's passed along
14 Brute of fantasy
15 Sign symbol
16 Kipling poem about Burma
17 Lack of constraints
18 James of "X-Men" films
24 Lay the groundwork
26 Great body
29 Old West gambling game
32 Inevitable
34 "Rugrats" father
36 ___ artist (film crew member)
37 Soprano pineapple and others, briefly
38 Con ___ (tenderly)
39 Something that shouldn't be flat
41 Patrons of the arts
42 Green-skinned god
43 Old Jewish community
44 Pines
45 "Puss in Boots" figure
46 Former carrier name
47 Land heavily
48 Acronymic weapon
50 "Mr. ___" (1983 Styx hit)
55 19th Amendment beneficiaries
56 Cable network with the motto "Not reality. Actuality."
57 Panhellenic Games site
58 Elementary school grads, typically
63 Ascendant
64 Torch bearer
66 Key group
67 Objected to a shearing, possibly
68 Pines
69 "Shucks!"
71 With deviousness
72 Michael of "Juno"
73 Lodge
74 Diner of 1970s–'80s TV
77 Giveaway at the poker table
78 Make
79 Not just big
80 Fictional island in two Alistair MacLean novels
81 Augurs
85 Situated at the thigh
86 Bearer of a dozen roses, maybe
87 A, in Arnstadt
88 Turn down
93 Showing deviousness
94 Person of Perth
96 Nurses old grudges, say
97 Runcible spoon feature

by Patrick Berry

**98** Banks known as Mr. Cub
**99** Wayne's pal in "Wayne's World"
**100** Fish
**101** TV host with "New Rules"
**102** Unable to relax
**104** Serious attention
**105** Lemon Juice, e.g.
**106** Home of Hallvard's ruined cathedral
**107** Life saver?
**108** Vivacity
**111** "Incidentally," in chat rooms
**113** Philosophy suffix

## 33

# T MOBILE

## ACROSS

**1** 1988 Grammy winner for "Crying"
**7** Tweak
**13** Bosses
**20** Cry from a balcony
**21** ___ pork
**22** Many a Nevada resident
**23** Dance seen in a Lincoln Center performance of "Don Giovanni"?
**25** Penn State campus site
**26** Also-___ (losers)
**27** Prefix with caching
**28** Baja's opposite
**30** Author
**31** "Hang on ___!"
**32** Locale for a cattail
**33** "None of the leading sales people came in today"?
**36** Grandparents, typically
**38** With a wink, say
**39** Berkeley campus nickname
**40** Celebration after a 1964 heavyweight championship?
**42** "You don't need to remind me"
**48** Not so big
**49** Tampa paper, briefly, with "the"
**50** Blackmore heroine
**51** Washed (down)
**54** Female co-star in "Love Crazy," 1941
**55** Stirrup?
**57** Tolkien creatures
**58** 41-Down was named after one: Abbr.
**59** Scarlett O'Hara's real first name
**60** Voiced
**61** Summer sign
**62** Little dipper?
**63** Claimed

**64** Chop
**65** The Mavericks, on scoreboards
**66** Up for grabs, as convention delegates
**68** Shriners' headwear: Var.
**69** Gob
**70** Ending with soft or spy
**71** Decide to sleep in the nude?
**73** Drink with one's pinkie up, say
**74** Some cats blow on them
**75** Sodium ___
**76** "Around the Horn" cable channel
**77** Summer treats
**79** 1983 #1 hit with the lyric "Put on your red shoes"
**81** What whitewashers apply?
**84** ___ Friday's
**85** Interlocks
**86** ___ acid
**88** Response to the query "Does Ms. Garbo fist-bump?"?
**94** Summer mo.
**95** "Rock 'n' Roll Is King" band, 1983
**96** Make it
**97** Actress Polo
**98** See 33-Down
**99** Polynesian potable
**100** They're often said to be fair
**102** Love before war?
**106** Looms
**107** Shocking, in a way
**108** Leonard of literature
**109** Sting, e.g.
**110** Team that once played at Enron Field
**111** Bob Evans rival

## DOWN

**1** Former German chancellor Adenauer
**2** Imagine
**3** One hit by a tuba
**4** Singer Grant and others
**5** Prefix with -lithic
**6** Stuffs oneself with
**7** Shot, e.g.
**8** Question that may be answered "And how!"
**9** Garfield's owner
**10** For the most part
**11** Country star ___ Lynne
**12** "Così fan ___"
**13** Agcy. with a list of prohibited items
**14** Tree whose two-word name, when switched around, identifies its product
**15** A Fonda
**16** Plane over Yemen, maybe
**17** College town just off Interstate 95
**18** Thief, in Yiddish
**19** Wolf (down)
**24** When doubled, a number puzzle
**29** Credit
**32** "Totem and Taboo" writer
**33** With 98-Across, showy play
**34** Story teller
**35** Judo-like exercises
**37** French beings
**38** Offspring
**41** Town on the Hudson R.
**42** Filmmaker Allen
**43** Pipe shape
**44** Apollo target
**45** Bygone hand weapon
**46** Catch

**47** Crib items
**49** Lugs
**51** Like a corkscrew
**52** What Cher Bono, e.g., goes by
**53** Ceases
**55** Soap units
**56** River to the North Sea
**58** Artist Francisco
**59** Director of the major film debuts of James Dean and Warren Beatty
**62** Not live
**63** Home to Sun Devil Stadium
**64** Tickled
**67** Old Fords
**68** Like Mussolini
**69** Ranks
**70** Didn't miss
**72** Game whose name is derived from Swahili
**73** Sean Connery and others
**74** Turn brown, maybe
**77** Jazz singer Anderson
**78** Busy
**80** Doesn't miss
**81** Most murky
**82** It's worst when it's high
**83** High and softly resonant
**85** Alex of "Webster"
**87** Sweet-talks
**88** Southwest Africa's ___ Desert
**89** Commercial name suffix
**90** Handles
**91** Lifts
**92** "___ could have told you that!"
**93** Seven: Prefix
**94** Speck

*by David Levinson Wilk*

**98** Assns.
**99** Alphabet string
**101** Retired flier
**103** It landed in the Pacific Ocean on 3/23/01
**104** Yucatán year
**105** Drink with a head

# MY TREAT

Note: When this puzzle is done, the circles will contain five different letters of the alphabet. Connect each set of circles containing the same letter, without crossing your line, to make a simple closed shape. The resulting five closed shapes together will form a picture of a 117-Across. The five letters can be arranged to name a good place to get a 117-Across.

## ACROSS

**1** Essence
**5** Start of a nursery rhyme
**9** "I won't bore you with the rest"
**12** Actress Davis
**17** They're often deep-fried
**19** 1964 title role for Tony Randall
**21** ___-jongg
**22** Indy 500 legend
**23** 1950s NBC icon
**24** Spanish for "rope"
**25** Some versions of a 117-Across
**27** Ingredient in a 117-Across
**30** "How is this possible?"
**31** Repeat
**32** Green lights
**34** "___, danke"
**35** Reversal of sorts
**36** "Top Chef" host Lakshmi
**40** Trouble's partner, in Shakespeare
**41** Kimchi-loving land
**42** "___ honor"
**44** Some cuts
**46** "___ straight!"
**48** DKNY competitor
**49** 1960s campus grp.
**51** "In case you weren't listening . . ."
**53** Amazon's business, e.g.
**55** Whence spiderlings emerge
**59** Ingredient in a 117-Across
**64** Suffix with meth-
**65** Island visited by Captain Cook in 1778
**67** Year Columbus died
**68** French kings' coronation city

**69** Imprudent
**71** David of television
**73** Brawl
**75** Thin Japanese noodle
**76** Salsa seller
**78** Ready, with "up"
**80** Broadway lights
**82** Word with black or stream
**83** Utensil for a 117-Across
**86** Sugary drinks
**88** ___ nothing
**89** Like the buildings at Machu Picchu
**91** Watched
**92** ___ Fields
**95** Filmmaker Riefenstahl
**96** Senator Hatch
**98** ___ nova (1960s dance)
**102** Characters in "The Hobbit"
**104** "Web ___" (ESPN segment showing great fielding plays)
**107** Sniggled
**109** A stake, metaphorically
**110** Holly genus
**111** Attack fervently
**113** Doing some cartoon work
**115** Cruise, say
**117** Something delicious to drink
**121** Version of a 117-Across
**123** What a graph may show
**124** Baltimore and Philadelphia
**126** Come to ___
**127** "Catch-22" bomber pilot
**128** "Later, alligator!"
**129** Versatile utensil
**130** Whizzes at quizzes?
**131** Name connector
**132** Pizazz
**133** Influence

## DOWN

**1** Fellas in "Goodfellas," e.g.
**2** Barely manages
**3** Bad thing to be in
**4** Container for a 117-Across
**5** Cortisol-secreting gland
**6** Family member, in dialect
**7** Construction crane attachment
**8** It's crunched
**9** Baby baby?
**10** Besmirch
**11** Like many a 117-Across
**12** Private eye Peter of old TV
**13** "___ Man" (1992 movie)
**14** Obscure things
**15** Neophytes
**16** Manchester United rival
**18** Bristle
**20** Wild ones may be sown
**26** Lived and breathed
**28** Pizazz
**29** Gobble up
**31** Meas. of screen resolution
**33** Valuable iron ore
**37** Possible response to "You've got spinach between your teeth"
**38** Fails
**39** Excessively orderly, informally
**41** Jewish deli order
**43** State straddling two time zones: Abbr.
**45** Thailand, once
**47** West Coast evergreens
**50** Like mountains and computer images
**52** Burned things

**54** Caustic cleaners
**55** ___ corn
**56** Twisty tree feature
**57** "Beau ___"
**58** ___ sponte (of its own accord)
**60** Pots and pans for baking
**61** Spanish wine
**62** It may be burnt
**63** Hurdles for high-school jrs.
**66** Main lines
**70** Six: Prefix
**72** Mountain sighting, maybe
**74** Mountain
**77** Breathing aids
**79** Movie villain who sought to disrupt a space launch
**81** Union opponent
**84** Utensil for a 117-Across
**85** Field unit
**87** Quantity of a key ingredient in a 117-Across
**90** Scoreless score
**92** Inside look?
**93** The primary instruction
**94** Bit of gymwear
**97** Winnemucca resident, e.g.
**99** Low-rent district
**100** Artist whose name is an anagram of "artisan"
**101** Director Lee
**103** Offer, as a hand
**105** French teacher
**106** It may come after a typo
**108** ___ Pérignon
**111** Need nursing, say
**112** Rents out
**114** Cos. that offer access

*by Pete Muller*

116 Old U.S.P.S. routing
   codes
118 Manitoba tribe
119 Pull (in)
120 "And Winter
   Came . . ." artist
122 Is for two or more?
125 Shade of
   blue

## ACROSS

1 Meaningless
7 Dolt
11 Reached
19 Symphony whose second movement is marked "Marcia funebre. Adagio assai"
20 Ring bearer
21 Dew, e.g.
22 What a poltergeist investigator does?
24 1862 invasion battle site
25 Mount for the god Neptune
26 Monopoly purchases: Abbr.
27 TV show whose name precedes a colon
28 See 49-Across
30 What the tired waiter provided?
33 Worry
34 Totals
36 "Interesting . . ."
37 Noted explorer traveling with a monkey
39 London's locale: Abbr.
40 Fruit for lagomorphs?
46 Shows worry, in a way
49 Old French 28-Across
50 Some people have funny ones
51 Lighten (up)
53 Mauna __
54 Livens (up)
56 Disorderly poultry workers?
62 Opera
65 Practices
66 Sweetheart
67 Wistful remark
70 Result of a bad swing, maybe
71 There may be many in a family
72 Got around
73 __ law (old Germanic legal code)
74 Detectives' aids
75 Attempts to climb a mountain range?
78 "Monk" org.
82 Noshed
83 Snick and __
84 Van Susteren of Fox News
87 Mass of eggs
88 10,000 61-Down
90 Sad sports headline in a Providence paper?
95 Verdi's "__ tu"
96 Actress Gershon
98 Sweetheart
99 Estate total
101 Billy who sang "Rebel Yell"
103 Dusting on the side of a cut gem?
109 Point in the right direction?
110 Friend of Eeyore
111 Bronze, e.g.
112 Like some sabbaticals
114 Point to
116 Churchgoers, sometimes?
120 Didn't just spit
121 Senders of some Christmas gifts
122 Excels
123 Roasters, essentially
124 "Why don't we?!"
125 Get dark?

## DOWN

1 "__ Ramsey" (1970s western)
2 Prize at the Barcelona Olympics
3 Botching
4 Bedding
5 Numerical prefix
6 Basketful, maybe
7 Like some air and dollar bills
8 Snaps
9 A famous one begins "Thou still unravish'd bride of quietness"
10 Buns, e.g.
11 One instrumental in music history?
12 Vodka __
13 Like a lord or lady
14 Undisturbed
15 Follower of Israel?
16 Hinged implements
17 Take off
18 Abdicate
20 Mold
23 "__ will not"
26 Eye layer
28 Peeping Tom, e.g.
29 Little bit
31 Help in making a prediction, maybe
32 Riddle-me-__
33 Monk's title
35 Numerical prefix
38 Unrestricted, as a mutual fund
41 Tom Sawyer's crush
42 Scornful replies
43 "Woe __" (grammar guide)
44 TKO callers
45 Paolantonio of ESPN
47 Like things that go bump in the night
48 MS. enclosures
52 "Love Me Do" vis-à-vis "P.S. I Love You"
55 Actress Lena Olin, e.g., by birth
57 Easter Island is part of it
58 "Born on the Fourth of July" hero Ron
59 Great-grandfather of Noah
60 Web
61 See 88-Across
63 Certain Black Sea dweller
64 It's a gas
67 Taking place in
68 Ellipsoidal
69 Fulfills
70 Morse T
71 "The Balcony" playwright
73 Suffix with hip or tip
74 Stale Italian bread?
76 Neighbor of Colo.
77 Golden __
79 One who's been released?
80 Wires may connect to them
81 Voltaire or Adam Smith
85 Maintaining one's composure, say
86 T or F: Abbr.
89 Rapper __ Wayne
91 Follow
92 With 93-Down, picnic amenity
93 See 92-Down
94 Cheerful
97 Wide, as the nostrils
100 Submit
101 Like Guinness
102 "Pearly Shells" singer

by Ben Pall and David Kahn

104 Change
105 Ole Miss misses,
    e.g.
106 Bad marks?
107 Blocks
108 Drop the ball
111 Taiwan-based
    computer
    maker

113 Home of
    102-Down
115 ___ Jima
116 "Be a ___!"
117 Not settle, say
118 Stephen of
    "Interview With
    the Vampire"
119 Govt. ID

**ACROSS**

1 Punch
4 Birthstones whose name starts with the same letter as their month
9 Senescence
15 Puzzle
20 Advantage
21 "Chasing Pirates" singer Jones
22 "Stop that!"
23 Matt in the morning
24 It means nothing
25 Parting words from the busy type
28 Whom a guy might hang with when he's not with the guys
30 Isn't shy with an opinion
31 Area in a 1969 Elvis Presley hit
32 "The Chosen" author Chaim
34 Cabinet dept. since 1965
35 Pottery base
36 Hans Christian Andersen story
43 Kind of shot
46 Critter with foot-long teeth
47 Dipped sticks?
48 Island known for having "the wettest spot on Earth" (450+" of rain per year)
49 French Revolution figure
51 Adrien of cosmetics
52 Iraq war subj.
53 Hardly breaking a sweat
55 Goldenrod, e.g.
56 Article for Lil Wayne

57 Eastern sect
58 Appears gradually on the screen
59 One of 15, once: Abbr.
60 Major upset, say
62 See 72-Across
65 Monster of Norse myth
66 End of a command at the Battle of Bunker Hill
69 Symbol of strength, to the Maya
72 With 62-Across, Whoopi's "Ghost" role
73 Granter of an honorary degree to George Washington in 1776
74 Farmer's ___
77 Where K-I-S-S-I-N-G happens
79 Hydroxide, e.g.
80 C.I.A. forerunner
81 Palm variety
82 "Godspeed!"
86 Water ___ (dental product company)
87 How some stock is purchased
88 City on the Ruhr
89 Pianist Albéniz
90 TV part
91 Gymnast Comaneci
92 Place with snorts
93 End of a Benjamin Franklin aphorism
96 Bring to a ___
98 9/
99 Pacifist's protest
100 The Jackson 5's first major label
103 Most clueless
108 Papal legate
111 2009 fantasy film based on a best–selling book

114 Goof
115 Former U.N. leader Kofi
116 Key of the "Odense" Symphony
117 "Swan Lake" maiden
118 Arm of a starfish
119 Has over
120 Tree with fan-shaped leaves
121 Grill brand
122 Cause for a TV-MA rating

**DOWN**

1 Contemporary of Freud
2 See 96-Down
3 Vegetable on a vine
4 Cruising the beat
5 Hoi ___
6 Coach Parseghian
7 Varnish resins
8 Jesus, to Christians
9 Quarterfinal groups, e.g.
10 "The way I see it . . ."
11 See 15-Down
12 Jesús, for one
13 Notre Dame football legend
14 Time to enjoy le soleil
15 With 11-Down, leaders
16 Chicago mayor before Emanuel
17 Number with two
18 Riga resident
19 Switch ending
26 Creator of Thidwick the Big-Hearted Moose
27 Watch on the beach, maybe

29 Like bubble gum and questions
33 Skills
35 Main
36 Détentes
37 Classic root beer brand
38 1980s lightweight boxing champ
39 Of the same sort
40 D.C. baseballer
41 "Ya think?!"
42 Stuff in a pit
43 Give a body check
44 "C'est ___"
45 Vols' school
49 Where Julio Iglesias was born
50 Rampaging, after "on"
53 Had been
54 They moved from Minnesota to Los Angeles in 1960
56 1994 Denis Leary/ Kevin Spacey flick
57 Sorority letter
60 Stone in Hollywood
61 Word repeated in "I ___! I ___!"
62 Bellyache
63 Home of the 46-Across: Abbr.
64 "Ta-da!"
66 "Così fan ___"
67 "Buzz off!"
68 Eddie on "Leave It to Beaver"
69 Dovetails
70 Emily Dickinson poem "For Every Bird ___"
71 Bombastic
74 Some clickers
75 Over
76 Military group headquartered in Colo. Spgs.

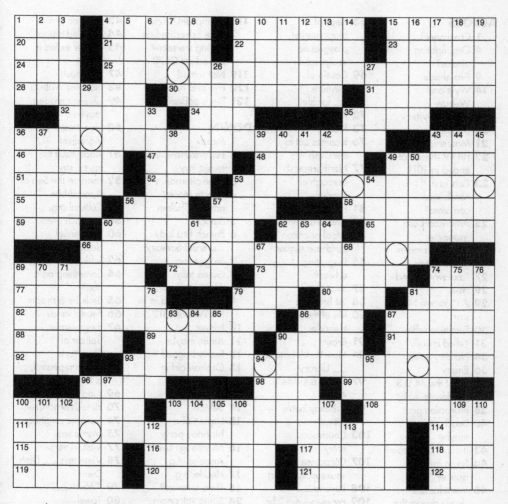

*by Daniel A. Finan*

**78** Architect Saarinen
**79** Hankering
**81** "___ Alive"
**83** Today preceder
**84** "Silent" one
**85** Krazy ___
**86** Something to watch when there's nothing on?

**87** Big name in brewing
**90** Modern update
**93** Clue
**94** San ___, Calif.
**95** Little thrill
**96** 2006 comedy title character from western 2-Down

**97** Buck in the Country Music Hall of Fame
**100** [Kiss]
**101** "Yikes!"
**102** Perfect specimens
**103** Half: Prefix
**104** Cry after hitting a jackpot

**105** "Peter Pan" fairy, for short
**106** Struggle (through)
**107** Surfer's concern
**109** "Dies ___"
**110** Serengeti antelope
**112** Witch
**113** Point of writing?

## ACROSS

1 Crackerjack
4 Org. fighting pirates?
9 Pink shade
14 Wyle and Webster
19 Man of mystery
20 Stylish
21 Mountain ridge
22 Hit TV show that ended in 2011
23 Cuts in a cardboard container?
25 American-born Japanese
26 Prefix with meter or methylene
27 Tax lawyer's find
28 Heel
29 7'1" former N.B.A. star
30 Feminine suffix
31 Yelled initially?
34 Nursery noise
36 Empty
37 26 of the 44 U.S. presidents: Abbr.
38 Instruction part
40 Beach site, maybe
42 It might be skipped
44 So-so formal dance?
46 Went far too slowly during the 10K?
54 State symbols of North Dakota and Massachusetts
55 Leader who said "All reactionaries are paper tigers"
56 Slight
57 "Use the Force, ___"
58 Arizona is the only state to have one
59 Attach to
61 "Rocks"
62 Certain helicopter

63 Piece of black-market playground equipment?
69 Cousin of kerplunk
71 ___ for life
72 Purple shade
73 Press
76 It comes out in the wash
77 Northernmost borough of London
81 Freud's one
82 Antlered animal
83 Wool or cotton purchase request?
85 Disgusting advice?
87 Way out
88 24 hrs. ago
90 Isle of the Inner Hebrides
91 Brown-___
94 New York's historic ___ Library
97 Top of a ladder?: Abbr.
98 Whiskey bottle dregs?
103 Courtroom entry
107 Corporate shakeup, for short
108 Beyond ___
109 People whose jobs include giving tours
111 To have, in Le Havre
112 "I don't give ___!"
113 Nobleman after a banquet?
114 Rita Hayworth's femme fatale title role of 1946
115 Effects of many waterfalls
116 Felt bad
117 Bind

118 Toothpaste brand once advertised as having the secret ingredient GL-70
119 Not settled
120 Hits and runs
121 Rev.'s address

## DOWN

1 Mosey
2 Perform Hawaiian music, say
3 Shell alternative
4 "Uncle Moses" novelist Sholem
5 Smack
6 French first lady ___ Bruni-Sarkozy
7 Staggering
8 Game tally: Abbr.
9 It was invaded in the War of 1812
10 Prayer
11 Airlift, maybe
12 Really bugged
13 Orphan girl in Byron's "Don Juan"
14 Seldom
15 Urging at a birthday party
16 I-5 through Los Angeles, e.g.
17 Heckle, e.g.
18 Thou follower?
24 Some volcanoes
28 Doesn't stop, in a way
32 Pitcher part
33 Animal with a snout
35 Urgent transmission, for short
38 Result of a pitch, perhaps
39 Schedule opening
40 Trolley sound
41 Distant
42 Side in checkers

43 Metered praise
44 Tasseled topper
45 Leader exiled in 1979
47 Not much
48 Nobelist Walesa
49 Queen's request, maybe
50 Skin cream ingredient
51 Adds insult to injury, say
52 Land on the Sea of Azov: Abbr.
53 Cultural org.
59 Stomach area
60 Deferential denial
62 Junk bond rating
64 Something on a hog?
65 Stalk by a stream
66 Feudal lands
67 Ex-governor Spitzer of New York
68 When repeated, a TV sign-off
69 Kind of story
70 Hi-tech organizer
74 Sonoma neighbor
75 Metric wts.
77 Vast, in verse
78 Vietnam's ___ Dinh Diem
79 "What ___?"
80 Towel
82 Reach at a lower level
84 Emoticon, e.g.
86 See 102-Down
89 "___ tu" (Verdi aria)
91 Words following see, hear and speak
92 1972 Best Actor nominee for "The Ruling Class"
93 Winning length in a horse race

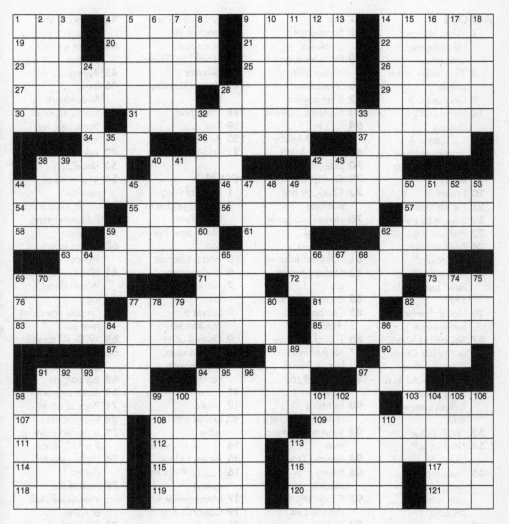

*by Kurt Mueller*

94 Finally
95 Side in a pickup game
96 Minute
97 Swiss quarters?
98 Confederate general who won at Chickamauga

99 Noted 1991 Harvard Law grad
100 Supplied, as data
101 Slot machine symbols, often
102 With 86-Down, what Washington purportedly could not do

104 Boors
105 Banks who was known as Mr. Cub
106 Late bloomer
110 Some notebook screens, for short
113 Fourth notes

## ACROSS

1 When repeated, advantageous to both sides
4 71 answers in this puzzle
9 Get used to it
14 Several CBS dramas
18 "___ Story: A Journey of Hope" (Jenna Bush best seller)
20 Expect
21 French toast piece?
22 It might be pulled
23 Pompeii, e.g.
24 Bride in "The Gondoliers"
25 "What the Butler Saw" playwright, 1969
26 Noted diamond family name
27 See circled letters in 76-/109-Down
30 Restless walker
32 Title character in a 2009 Sandra Bullock crossword film
33 "Well, I'll be!"
34 "Told ya so!" looks
36 "Fear is pain rising from the anticipation of ___": Aristotle
39 Wampum, e.g.
41 Endangered
44 . . . in 119-/120-Across
48 Sweetheart
50 Sweetheart
51 Part of a pack?
52 Panamanians and Peruvians
53 1960 Olympics host
54 Duel tool
55 Radii, e.g.
57 Cut
58 Some drink garnishes
59 Place for some animal baiting
60 Sharpness
62 Bit of physics
63 Hostess's ___ Balls
64 . . . in 116-/117-Across
67 Summer letters
70 Enter, for one
72 Give a hard time
73 Check, as one's numbers
76 Huntee in a game
79 Mounted
80 Authorizes
81 "Of thee" follower
82 Michael Jordan, e.g.
83 Conservative side
85 Comparison's middle
86 T. S. of literature
87 Neither more nor less, in France
88 . . . in 39-/60-Down
90 Item in a restaurant basket
92 Virus named for a river
94 French CD holder
95 Enemy of a Medici
97 Composition of many a cask
98 Techie's hangout
102 It may have sand in it
103 . . . in 17-/43-Down
109 User-edited Web site
110 Words on a sandwich board
112 Emerson's "___ Beauty"
113 "The Neverending Story" writer
114 Upper class?
115 First woman to teach at the Sorbonne
116 "Think" or "Think different"
117 They're stranded, briefly
118 Times past
119 Best ___
120 Rear's rear?
121 Radiator sound

## DOWN

1 Hospital wings
2 Language akin to Kalaallisut
3 Like Gomer Pyle
4 See
5 Had a balance
6 Dry's partner
7 Not yet final, at law
8 Leaves a crooked trail
9 Owned up to
10 ___ Marquez, Nickelodeon cartoon girl
11 ___-at-law: Abbr.
12 Master
13 Game with a setter
14 . . . in 1-/4-Across
15 Pitcher's place
16 "___ out?" (poker query)
17 Merchandise ID
19 Cowardly sound
28 Unfold
29 Miami squad
31 Dada figure
35 Tightfisted sort
37 Silliness
38 Missing, as the start of a party
39 The U.N.'s ___ Ki-moon
40 Definitely not Felix Unger types
42 "___ Pastore" (Mozart opera)
43 Honorary law degs.
44 Inches for pinches
45 Buenos ___
46 Lake ___, Switzerland/France separator
47 Some tails, for short
49 Add to, perhaps
53 Uncle ___
54 Brief word of caution
56 . . . in 12-/35-Down
57 Pulitzer-winning Sheehan
60 France from France
61 "Do You Hear What I Hear?," e.g.
62 "In case you didn't hear me . . ."
65 1970s TV spinoff
66 Wrap for a queen
68 Big bargain
69 Ankle supports
71 Piece of work?
74 Even chances
75 A perfect score on it is 180: Abbr.
76 Daily weather datum
77 Aoki of the World Golf Hall of Fame
78 Off-road specialist
79 2003 Affleck/Lopez flick
80 Century 21 competitor
83 "I'm listening"
84 ___ leash
87 "View of Toledo" artist
88 U.K. carrier, once
89 Word with cherry or cotton
91 Rush igniter

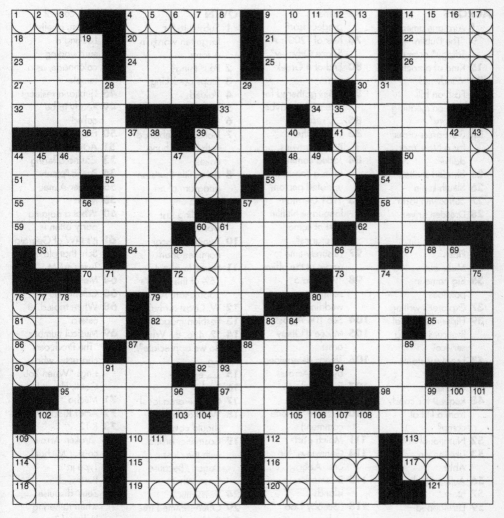

by Pamela Klawitter

**93** Offshore accommodations
**96** Actors' grp.
**99** Sally ___ (teacakes)
**100** Show-biz father and son
**101** Graceful word?
**102** Program coordinator?
**104** Vituperate
**105** Japanese noodle
**106** Part of AARP: Abbr.
**107** Small: Suffix
**108** Outlet
**109** Mode
**111** Strauss's "Ariadne ___ Naxos"

## ACROSS

1 Airplane amenities
9 "The Dublin Trilogy" dramatist
15 Kind of attraction
20 Windward
21 Fashion frill
22 Add-on meaning "galore"
23 Start-press order for a New York daily?
25 Shaded shelter
26 Sleuth Lupin
27 Suffix with form
28 Dresden's river
30 St. Pete-to-Savannah dir.
31 Flaps
32 Make out
35 Big name in potatoes
37 Explorer's writing
39 Flippered animal that runs a maid service?
43 Legal assistants
46 Mart start
47 Sparks
48 Request for candy from a kid at camp?
52 Nutritional abbr.
53 Like the yin side: Abbr.
56 Author Sinclair
57 Start
59 Dewlapped creature
62 When to call, in some ads
64 "Rocky III" co-star
65 Gnarly
67 Ohio university
68 Congratulatory phrase at a "Peanuts" bar mitzvah?
74 "Sounds like ___!"
75 Western Indian
76 High lines
77 Romeo's predecessor?
78 Keir of "2001: A Space Odyssey"
80 End of a Greek run
82 Ones gathered for a reading, maybe
85 ___ result
86 One of the Bobbsey twins
88 Jaded comment from a constantly updated person?
93 1981 German-language hit film
96 Part of some itineraries?
97 Leisurely time to arrive at the office
98 1970s, to a schmaltzy wedding band?
104 See 106-Across
105 Musée d'Orsay artist
106 Things determined by 104-Across
107 Everybody, to Erich
110 "___ me" (phone comment)
111 Match part
114 Geneviève, for one: Abbr.
115 Denmark's ___ Islands
118 "Scooby-Doo" girl
120 Amnesiac's vague recollection of having a hobby?
125 Construct
126 Environment
127 TV character who worked for Steinbrenner
128 Six-pack holder?
129 Certain newspaper advertisement
130 Washed

## DOWN

1 Substitute for forgotten words in a song
2 Pour thing?
3 Stops panicking
4 Valued
5 Prefix with -centric
6 "I can't believe it!"
7 Holiday celebrated with bánh chung cakes
8 Asian title that's an anagram of an English one
9 Unsettling last words
10 Two-time Oscar nominee Joan
11 Home to about 15% of the world's population: Abbr.
12 W. Coast air hub
13 Fashion magazine
14 "2, 4, 6, 8 - Who do we appreciate?," e.g.
15 ___ egg
16 Back
17 College-area local
18 What a chair should cover?
19 Cosmetics brand with the classic slogan "Because I'm worth it"
24 Swiss mix
29 Often-trimmed tree
32 Designed for two
33 Takes in
34 "___ out!"
36 Serpentine shape
37 "Beatles '65" and others
38 Hanauma Bay locale
40 Antipollution mascot Woodsy ___
41 AOL's Web site, e.g.
42 Birth control option, briefly
44 Lacking a surrounding colonnade, as a temple
45 Ljubljana resident
49 Ready to be called
50 French meat
51 Active
53 Casino offering
54 Poetic "plenty"
55 Singer Aimee
58 Muffs
60 What a pajama party often is
61 It's NW of Georgia
63 Sch. that plays Texas A&M
64 Memory: Prefix
66 Calendario unit
68 When tripled, et cetera
69 Musical number
70 "The Producers" character who sings "When You Got It, Flaunt It"
71 Mucho
72 Actor Rickman
73 K-12
79 "Broken Arrow" co-star Michael
81 Type in
83 Portrayal
84 Zeus' disguise when fathering Helen of Troy
87 Blood-typing system
89 Modern party planning aids
90 Sports column
91 Go south, as sales
92 Scot's "wee"
93 In excelsis ___
94 Japanese "thanks"
95 Frequent, in verse

by Tony Orbach and Janie Smulyan

98 Stand on short feet
99 Straight
100 Eve who wrote "The Vagina Monologues"
101 __ egg
102 Beat it
103 Best in crash-test ratings
108 Order to a barista
109 "Zigeunerliebe" composer
112 "La Bohème" soprano
113 Key of Brahms's Symphony No. 4: Abbr.
116 Eleven, to Héloïse
117 Edwardian expletive
119 Ones putting on a show, for short
121 They: Fr.
122 German rejection
123 Cause of some repetitive behavior, in brief
124 A Stooge

## ACROSS

1 Animal with a huge yawn
6 Garden support
10 ___ of roses
15 "Swans Reflecting Elephants" artist
19 Formula One driver Prost
20 Bandleader Puente
21 Religion founded in Iran
22 Dash
23 Reduces significantly
25 "Your Movie Sucks" writer
26 Billion: Prefix
27 "A penny saved is . . ."
30 "___ me anything"
32 Winery wood
33 Needle case
34 Like a black hole
35 "Where there's a will, there's . . ."
42 Mama Cass
43 Partner of 74-Across
44 Spread out
45 E-mail alternative
48 Effrontery
49 Entertainment providers at a sports bar
52 Pop's ___ Tuesday
53 Fill
54 Perfect service
55 Certain commando
56 "Where there's smoke, there's . . ."
60 Founder of United We Stand America
62 Despicable
64 John who searched for the Northwest Passage
65 Buddhist teaching
66 "People who live in glass houses . . ."
71 Rhododendron cousin
74 Partner of 43-Across
75 Chinese "path"
76 Stinks to high heaven
80 "He who laughs last . . ."
84 Russian council
86 Land in a river
87 Some are queens
88 Part of a cul-de-sac address, maybe: Abbr.
89 Neighborhood east of SoHo
91 "This ___ You're Talking To" (Trisha Yearwood song)
92 "Riddle me, riddle me ___"
93 Public respect
96 Managed
97 2, 3, 4 or 6, for 12
99 "If at first you don't succeed . . ."
102 Revenue line
105 It can make a 10 a 9
106 Alley ___
107 Sante Fe-to-Denver dir.
108 "Don't bite the hand . . ."
115 Legend of the Himalayas
116 Oldest von Trapp child in "The Sound of Music"
117 Protein building blocks
120 Reposed
121 Looped handles
122 Bone-dry
123 Sacred city of Lamaism
124 Mrs. Garrett on "The Facts of Life"
125 Places to live in the sticks?
126 Struck out
127 Stupid, in Sonora

## DOWN

1 Is sick with
2 Sick
3 Analgesic
4 Boulevard where Fox Studios and the Los Angeles Convention Center are located
5 "Almost finished!"
6 Wasted
7 Former Yankee Martinez
8 Departing words?
9 Synthesizer designer Robert
10 Helped in a job
11 Middle Eastern salad
12 Area of Venice with a famous bridge
13 It has banks in Switzerland
14 Director Martin
15 Step
16 It's out of this world
17 Port on the Gulf of Guinea
18 Silly
24 Western terminus of I-90
28 ___ Majesty
29 Contraction with two apostrophes
30 Relationship disparity, perhaps
31 Console
36 Naught
37 Rapscallion
38 New newt
39 Part of T.A.E.
40 Comet part
41 "That's good enough"
45 C-worthy
46 Scintilla
47 TV warrior for good
50 It's north of Baja, informally
51 Prime cut
53 A star may represent it
55 ___ blue
57 College cheer
58 Bog buildup
59 "Star Trek" role
61 Cooking pots
63 Baylor's city
67 Applied some powder to
68 Wasted
69 Title girl in a 1964 Chuck Berry hit
70 Toe woe
71 Come from ___
72 Fanboy's reading
73 Stud money
77 Javanese or Malay
78 Ban ___ (Kofi Annan's successor)
79 Laurence who wrote "Tristram Shandy"
81 "Good grief!"
82 Surly manner
83 Material for a suit?
85 Party of the underworld
90 ___-di-dah
91 Suffix with robot
93 Hebrew letter after koph
94 Fights with
95 Permits
98 It might be on the road
99 One behind the lens
100 Farm mate
101 Didn't suffer in silence

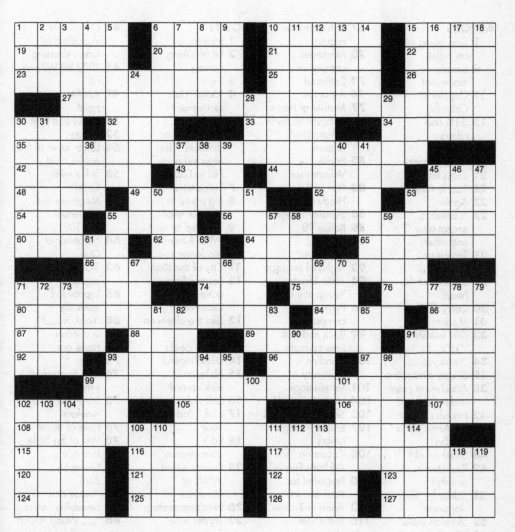

*by Paula Gamache*

102 Flair
103 Forward
104 Exempli gratia, e.g.
109 Economist Greenspan
110 It has a period of 2(pi)
111 No pressure

112 Its highest point is Wheeler Peak: Abbr.
113 Current carrier
114 Nymph spurned by Narcissus
118 August hrs.
119 ___ Tomé

## ACROSS

1 One going into an outlet
6 Sonata movement
11 Org. for Lt. Columbo
15 33⅓ and others
19 Buzz
20 Huge quantity
21 Cross letters
22 "___ la Douce"
23 Again
25 "I before E except after C" and others
27 Tampa-to-Orlando dir.
28 Swelling of the head
30 Carry illicitly
31 Modern: Ger.
33 Old Turkish V.I.P.'s
34 "Now you ___ . . ."
35 Skippy alternative
38 Attachment points under the hood
42 Finnish city near the Arctic Circle
46 Oodles
48 Street on old TV
49 Racketeer's activity?
51 "Ideas for life" sloganeer
53 Skips on water
55 "The Canterbury Tales" pilgrim
56 Sight near a drain
57 Also
61 Dues payer: Abbr.
62 Mark Twain, e.g., religiously speaking
64 Sp. miss
65 Human, e.g., foodwise
67 Salad orderer's request
70 Mercedes competitor
73 Bothered
74 Attractive
77 Mother of Horus, in Egyptian myth
79 "Mona Lisa" feature
82 Prince Valiant's son
83 Part of the Hindu Godhead
88 Summer hangout
89 Italian 10
91 Organic compound
92 Rights of passage
94 1936 Loretta Young title role
96 Pioneering computer
99 Back end of a time estimate
100 Carolina university
101 Terminology
104 ___ Banos, Calif.
105 Skipping syllables
107 Edible Andean tubers
108 Cousin on "The Addams Family"
110 Prepared for YouTube, say
113 Tyson nickname
116 Suffix with planet
119 "Just a sec"
121 Hillary Clinton and Nancy Pelosi
124 "Fargo" director
125 "This ___!"
126 Inner tube-shaped
127 Perplexed
128 Objectives
129 Firm part: Abbr.
130 Bag of chips, maybe
131 Unlocked?

## DOWN

1 Maven
2 Bit of Viking writing
3 Sign
4 Ladies' club restriction
5 Miracle-___
6 Nicolas who directed "The Man Who Fell to Earth"
7 Twice tetra-
8 Big name in upscale retail
9 Cracked or torn
10 What Rihanna or Madonna uses
11 City of the Kings
12 Former Texas governor Richards
13 Like the alarm on many alarm clocks
14 Least hopeful
15 Notes to pick up on?
16 Self-righteous sort
17 Mid 22nd-century year
18 Ed.'s convenience
24 French island WSW of Mauritius
26 Non's opposite
29 Tryster with Tristan
32 Slippery ones
34 Awake suddenly
35 Teased
36 "Have ___ myself clear?"
37 2003 Pixar film
39 "___ further . . ."
40 U.S.A. or U.K.
41 ___ Bator, Mongolia
43 Stoic
44 Occasional ingredient in turkey dressing
45 1972 Bill Withers hit
47 Applies, as paint
50 Banks and Pyle
52 PC key
54 Lower layer of the earth's crust
58 Suffix with Capri
59 Magazine with an annual Hot 100
60 Neighbor of Que.
63 Stood like a pigeon
66 Improvised musically
68 "Lord, is ___?"
69 In concert
71 Hope grp.
72 Spot
74 One concerned with el niño
75 Sans-serif typeface
76 Field of stars?
78 Will of the Bible
80 Pick 6, e.g.
81 Someone ___
84 Zero
85 "Sense and Sensibility" sister
86 "___ Wood sawed wood" (old tongue-twister)
87 Hears again, as a case
90 Treats with scorn
93 It often has dashes
95 Fatigue may be a symptom of it: Var.
97 Approaches boldly

PARDON "E" INTERRUPTION

*by Alan Arbesfeld*

**98** O.K. Corral gunfighter
**102** Senior
**103** Capital of Eritrea
**106** Little hopper?
**109** Crown holder
**110** Viva ___

**111** Home ___
**112** One may be good or dirty
**113** Wee, informally
**114** Suffix with arthr-
**115** Sergeant in "The Thin Red Line"

**117** "___ sorry!"
**118** One of them does?
**120** Annual b-ball event
**122** Has been
**123** Palindromic girl's name

# PARDON "E" INTERRUPTION

## ACROSS

1 Director
6 Stereo syst. component
10 Recipe abbr.
14 Number crunchers, for short
18 State capital whose name comes from the French for "wooded area"
19 Mississippi River's largest tributary
20 The Hermit Kingdom, once
21 Lie a lot
22 Island from which Tiberius ruled
23 Lively dance performed as a six-pack is being laid to rest?
26 Canine king's regime?
28 Small chain component
29 Baker of jazz
30 Dominant theme
31 West African monetary unit
32 Ones crunched during crunch time?
35 Tanned skin
38 Hostile feelings
41 Eco-warriors?
48 Grammatical topic
49 Earth tone
50 Smoke
51 Web address component
54 Beat soundly
56 Encounter with an Alaskan bear?
59 Beneficiary of a 2008 bailout
63 Expected
64 Very unpleasant
65 Red Scare prosecutor Roy

67 Mr. of old cartoons
68 1813–14 vice president
70 Fan club focus
71 Stockpile
73 Hundred Acre Wood young 'un
74 Not permanent
76 Set of shot glasses for Christmas?
80 A man or a mouse
83 ___ equivalent (measure of explosive strength)
84 Eggs served raw
85 W.W. II title
88 Native New Zealander
89 Sharpshooter Oakley when she was a charming young musician?
93 Have an emotional impact
96 "Or ___ what?"
97 Interject
98 Canning seal
99 Paterson's successor as New York governor
104 Newborn on a ranch
107 Sneaky trick
108 Interstellar valet's job?
113 Ship info kept for the Spanish Armada?
115 Foo Fighters frontman Dave
117 Golf rarities
118 Drew on a screen
119 A.L. M.V.P. in 2005 and 2007, informally
120 House that won't catch fire
121 Old Harper's Weekly cartoonist

122 Wheelless vehicle
123 Desires
124 Bygone communication

## DOWN

1 1970 #1 hit for the Jackson 5
2 Waterfall sound
3 Sufficiently aged
4 "Hamlet" courtier
5 Consider carefully
6 Stiffly awkward, as movement
7 One doing course work
8 ___ Minh (1940s independence movement)
9 "Miss Julie" composer Ned
10 Shinto shrine entrance
11 Filled in
12 Cook so as to lock in the flavor, say
13 Comrade
14 Bogeymen's hiding places
15 Hoi ___
16 Compound also called an olefin
17 Puts on the ballot
20 Mathematician Gödel
24 Comrade
25 Continuing to criticize unnecessarily
27 Pop name
32 Border
33 "What nonsense!"
34 Plan for the evening?
36 Start of a Wagner title
37 Biblical priest at Shiloh

39 Stable sounds
40 Hurt badly
42 Opposing
43 Snug retreat
44 "Wall Street" character Gordon ___
45 ___ Chicago Grill
46 Far-away connector
47 Notorious investor
51 Brabantio's fair daughter
52 Not deceived by
53 "Gotta go," in chat rooms
55 "Last Time I Saw ___" (Diana Ross song)
57 Seer's perception
58 Blue uniform wearer
60 All-Star Dick of the 1960s–'70s Knicks
61 Dumbfounded
62 Knuckle-headed action?
65 U.S.N. rank
66 It's due south of Iran
68 "C'mon, sleepyhead!"
69 Starchy staple of Africa
72 Bloodmobile supply
75 Tuscaloosa university, for short
77 Smidgen
78 Workers' rights agcy.
79 W.P.A. initiator
81 Like the climate of 66-Down
82 "So I ___"
86 "Evita" narrator
87 Predatory fish
89 Like the day of the summer solstice

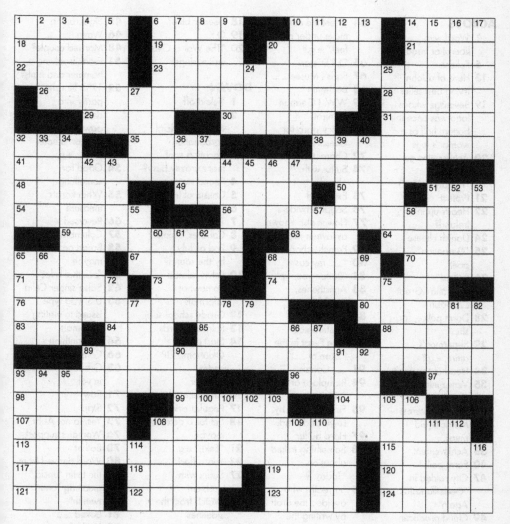

*by Patrick Berry*

90 Smiley's creator
91 Is caught up in the Rapture, e.g.
92 "Cool"
93 Dennis of the court
94 Orchestral work premiered in 1805

95 Moves laterally
100 Tried to convince
101 "That's fine"
102 Thousand thou
103 Certain dental repair
105 Aboveboard
106 Valley ___
108 Ring

109 Richard of "Bee Season"
110 Outhouse door symbol
111 Take turns?
112 One going on foot?
114 HP products
116 Salty fillet

## ACROSS

1 Word with liberal or visual
5 Foliose
13 Hero of a John Irving best seller
19 Beverage whose logo was once the bottom half of a woman's legs
20 Actress who co-starred in "Havana," 1990
21 Protect
22 Heads-up in Ireland?
24 Danish cheese
25 "Gerontion" poet
26 "Yikes!"
27 Australia's Great ___ Basin
28 Dorm police, for short
29 Superman's attire, e.g.?
34 Head of London?
35 Venezuela's Chávez
36 Security interest
37 Metric liquid meas.
38 Achievement
40 Farm pails?
47 City raided in "Godzilla Raids Again"
49 Cloud producer, informally
50 ___ Highway (route from Dawson Creek)
54 Willing to do
56 Fluid
57 Boxer on season four of "Dancing With the Stars"
60 Aggregate
61 Like items at a supermarket checkout
64 "I feel the earth move under my feet," e.g.?
65 Q.E.D. part
67 Paris's Musée ___
68 Benjamin
69 W.W. I German admiral
70 Fancy garb for Caesar?
72 Characterized by
74 Suffix with absorb
75 Exploited
76 Sugar providers
77 Flower also known as love-in-idleness
79 French school
80 "___ my case!"
81 "Button your lip!"
83 Antisthenes, notably?
88 Veronese masterpiece "The Feast in the House of ___"
91 ___ Canals
94 Birthplace of the Rep. Party
95 First tribe met by Lewis and Clark
97 Hard butter
98 Something talked about on "Today"?
105 Surrealist who avoided the draft by writing the day's date in every space on his induction paperwork
106 Victuals
107 Michael of "Juno"
108 "Who ya ___ call?"
110 Unnatural
111 Extremely occult?
115 Happy
116 Set sail
117 Tick off
118 Deeper blue?
119 O.K.
120 "The War Is Over" writer/singer

## DOWN

1 Ticked off
2 Beer served without artificial carbonation
3 Vacation spot that's crazily busy?
4 Round storehouse
5 Cousin of Inc.
6 "Ick!"
7 Tennis's Ivanovic
8 Cabbies' clients
9 End of July by the sound?
10 Pelvis-related
11 Somewhat informal?
12 Grade school subj.
13 Pointer's words
14 Start of all Oklahoma ZIP codes
15 Tumbler
16 Architectural space
17 Regular price
18 Set for a detective, maybe
21 "Eek!," e.g.
23 Yearn (for)
27 Suffix with problem
30 Watch from the sidelines
31 Río makeup
32 Kind of pad
33 Certain triple-decker
39 U.K. decoration: Abbr.
41 Bitter, in a way
42 "Ghosts" playwright
43 What Bryn Mawr College is not
44 N.Y.C. subway inits.
45 Skyscraping
46 Wows
48 Married couple?
51 Prank involving a hammer and nails?
52 1986 film shot partly in a decommissioned power plant
53 Mint on a hotel pillow, e.g.
54 Good for something
55 What karats measure
56 Reversed
57 Columbia athletes
58 Bread on the table, maybe
59 "___ that a lot"
62 Salsa singer Celia
63 U.S. visa type issued to visiting diplomats
64 Labyrinthine
66 Complete: Prefix
68 Gradual increase in vol.
71 Row
72 Strip
73 Yes, to no: Abbr.
76 Woman's support
78 Bother
80 Word derived from the Latin "uncia," meaning "one-twelfth"
81 Baked ___
82 Uncle Sam, for one
84 "Hmmm . . ."
85 Quick
86 Followers: Suffix
87 French vote
89 Nail polish, e.g.
90 Collisions
91 Sticky roll?
92 "C'est si bon!"
93 Put in one's two cents' worth
96 Like custard

*by Dana Delany and Matt Ginsberg*

**99** "This has got me fuming!"
**100** Die out
**101** Creamy shades
**102** Dashes may be part of them
**103** Speak to the masses
**104** Betray

**109** Capital near the 60th parallel
**111** No. typically between 2.0 and 4.0
**112** Omaha Beach craft, for short
**113** One of these days
**114** Kind of jacket

## ACROSS

1 *Nitty-gritty, as of negotiations
6 *Boater
11 Sponge (up)
14 *Title figure in an Aesop fable
19 Royal African capital
20 Something plighted
21 Co. once owned by Howard Hughes
22 "L'shanah ___!" (Rosh Hashana greeting)
23 Amtrak train
24 Emulated the phoenix
26 New Mexico county
27 Roughly plan
29 Effects
31 Losing casino roll
32 Not included
34 James ___, duettist on the 1982 #1 hit "Baby, Come to Me"
36 It might be French, Swiss or Italian
37 Insipid writing
40 Globular
42 Fight (off)
43 "Well, that's odd"
44 Go ___ great length
46 More placid
48 Boss
50 Corporate owner
52 Passé
54 Term of address in Dixie
55 Susan of NPR
58 *Work on at a desk, say
60 Shot up
64 Death, in Dresden
65 Thief
67 Take no action regarding
69 Bale binder
70 Settled down
72 Grunts may come out of them
74 Author Shute of "On the Beach"
76 Throw out
77 *Bracket shape
79 Mini-tantrums
81 Barrio babies
83 Eavesdrop, maybe
84 Exactly like
86 Log holder
88 What Chesapeake dogs are trained to do
90 Golden rule word
92 Leader of Abraham?
94 Time of lament
95 Ayn Rand protagonist
99 "I have been half in love with ___ Death": "Ode to a Nightingale"
102 Locus
103 "Il était ___ fois . . ." (French fairy-tale starter)
104 Ancient kingdom in Asia Minor
106 Incredibly stupid
108 Newsman Baxter on "The Mary Tyler Moore Show"
109 Kitten's cry
110 Fishermen with pots
112 Onetime weight-loss drug
114 Exclamation after a workout
116 Convertible
118 The dot on the "i" in the Culligan logo
122 ___ acid
124 Alabama speedway locale
126 2011 revolution locale
127 Crazy
128 Britney Spears's "___ Slave 4 U"
129 More judicious
130 Stimulant
131 Really feel for?
132 La. neighbor
133 Stellate : star :: xiphoid : ___
134 Artery opener

## DOWN

1 Some intimates
2 Billiards need
3 Have ___ in one's bonnet
4 See 87-Down
5 Library area
6 Poetic stanza
7 Many a vaudevillian
8 Listed
9 Polished off
10 Question from one in another room
11 Bad marks
12 Because of
13 Roast go-with
14 The "it" in the lyric "turn it on, wind it up, blow it out"
15 Campus drillers
16 C
17 Frozen food brand
18 Ad-filled weekly
25 4 on a phone
28 Cool sorts
30 Computer option for a document
33 Singer Washington
35 *Ernest and Julio Gallo product
37 Regulars on VH1
38 Asia Minor
39 Model
41 The Whale constellation
45 Pro ___
47 Enzyme regulating blood fluid and pressure
49 Cabbage dishes
51 Original "Wagon Train" network
53 Classic McDonnell Douglas aircraft
56 Goes bad
57 *Usual amount to pay
59 Act like a protective mother
61 Hit one out of the park, say
62 Sap
63 Innocent
66 Actress Knightley
68 "The ___ Tailors," Dorothy L. Sayers mystery
71 N.Y.C. landmark
73 Trite
75 Ignore, in a way
78 Fishing line fiasco
80 Tick off
82 Monterrey Mrs.
85 One with endurance
87 With 4-Down, $MgSO_4 \cdot 7H_2O$
89 Fingers, for short
91 Source of many English words that come to us via French
93 "Strap yourselves in, kids . . ."
95 *Part of a boxer's training
96 Time it takes to develop a set of photos, maybe
97 Scrupulously followed, as the party line
98 No-win situation?

by Kay Anderson

**100** One living off the land, maybe
**101** One-piece garment
**105** Where kids get creative in school
**107** *It's pitched for a large audience
**111** Fifth of eight

**113** Learn to get along
**115** Bit of smoke
**117** *Common secret
**119** Smelly
**120** Israeli conductor Daniel
**121** After-dinner drink
**123** Iowa college
**125** Margery of rhyme

## ACROSS

1 Group working on a plot
6 Seurat painted in one
10 "Look what ___!"
14 One of Santa's team
19 Old Olds
20 Biblical shepherd
21 Alma mater of football great Roger Staubach
22 Opt for the window instead of the aisle?
23 Don't . . . !
26 Ottoman relative
27 Lover of Bianca in "Othello"
28 See 3-Down
29 Plea to the unwelcome
31 Loo
33 Bug-eyed primates
35 "Dream on"
37 Priestly robe
38 Don't . . . !
40 Us, e.g.
42 Attack like a bear
44 First person in Germany?
45 Stir up
46 "___ is life . . ."
47 Like some wrestlers' bodies
48 "___ for Cookie" ("Sesame Street" song)
50 It's not good when it's flat
51 Word processing command
52 Don't . . . !
56 Skirt chaser
57 Good news for a worker
58 It's passed down through the ages
59 Like some old-fashioned studies
60 Homeric cry?
63 Apothecary weight
64 More, in scores
65 Bass in a barbershop quartet, e.g.
66 Old Tokyo
67 Do-it-yourselfer
69 Filing aid
70 Open
72 Established facts
73 Don't . . . !
78 Person with a code name, maybe
79 Puts words in the mouth of?
80 A trucker may have one: Abbr.
81 Hurricane of 2011
82 Advanced sandcastle feature
83 Target of some pH tests
84 Org. for some guards
86 Famous Georgian born in 1879
87 Camera operator's org.
88 Don't . . . !
92 30, for ⅓ and ⅙, e.g.: Abbr.
93 Start without permission?
95 Possible result of a defensive error in soccer
96 Rogers on a ship
97 Sharpens
98 E-mail from a Nigerian prince, usually
99 Now or never
101 Indulge
103 Don't . . . !
108 Distanced
109 Biblical twin
110 Filmmaker van Gogh
111 One of the Allman Brothers
112 Harry Potter's girlfriend
113 Trick out, as a car
114 In view
115 Palais du Luxembourg body

## DOWN

1 Trade's partner
2 ___-American
3 One may be seen on a 28-Across's nose
4 Indo-European
5 Stats on weather reports
6 Sunbathing sites
7 Can't stand
8 "Automatic for the People" group
9 iPod type
10 Liquid, say
11 "Matilda" author
12 "___ had it!"
13 Poor character analysis?
14 Building material for Solomon's Temple
15 Shade of green
16 Don't . . . !
17 UV index monitor, for short
18 Total hottie
24 Shipwreck spot, maybe
25 Ones with crowns
30 End of a series: Abbr.
31 Biblical twin
32 Basic skateboarding trick
34 "If only!"
35 It has a crystal inside
36 Brand for people with milk sugar intolerance
38 Got started
39 Figure of speech
41 Not the ritziest area of town
43 Small dam
46 "Ditto"
48 France's equivalent to an Oscar
49 Two who smooch, say
50 Mawkish
51 Gilbert Stuart works
53 Hacking tool
54 Spanish newspaper whose name means "The Country"
55 Bring up
56 Done in
59 Packer of old
60 He was named viceroy of Portuguese India in 1524
61 "Heavens!"
62 Don't . . . !
65 Look down
68 A big flap may be made about this
69 Possible change in Russia
71 Banks on a runway
73 Briton's rejoinder
74 Long-armed simian, for short
75 Element in a guessing contest
76 Chilling, say
77 Concern when coming up, with "the"
79 Archetypal abandonment site
83 Corporate type
84 Inexperienced with
85 Witticisms
86 Aníbal Cavaco ___, Portuguese president beginning in 2006
88 Kind of keyboard

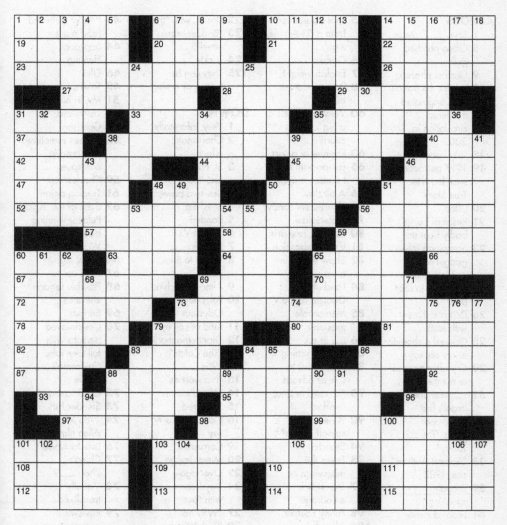

**by Josh Knapp**

## ACROSS

**1** Bryn ___ College
**5** Often-parched gully
**9** Goal of phishing
**13** Where the Baha'i faith originated
**17** It entered circulation in 2002
**18** "My heavens!"
**19** 1997 best seller subtitled "Her True Story"
**20** Lifted
**21** Result of being badly beaned?
**23** Scraping kitchen gadget with nothing in it?
**25** Big name in root beer
**26** Drill attachment with teeth
**28** Offered a shoulder to cry on, say
**29** Cry after a series of numbers
**32** ___ Meir Tower, Israel's first skyscraper
**34** CBS's "The ___ Today"
**35** "Author! Author!" star, 1982
**39** Broadly speaking
**41** Leonine movie star of old
**45** Pale yellow-shelled sea creature?
**47** Differ
**49** Contraction before boy or girl
**50** October haul
**51** Year the Paris Métro opened
**52** Front-wheel alignment
**53** Vlasic pickles mascot

**55** That babies come from a 53-Across, e.g.
**56** Gather
**57** English weight
**58** Return address info
**60** View the effects of a big lunch in court?
**63** Promise of a sort
**65** Person with a headset, maybe
**66** A bit slow
**67** Fluorescent candy?
**75** Materialize
**80** Register, to a Brit
**81** It's an imposition
**82** Show shock, in a way
**84** Land of King George Tupou V
**85** Memorable mission
**86** ___ in ink
**87** Jewelry setting
**89** Alternative to Ole or Edvard
**90** "R" card in Uno, in effect
**92** "Cheers" spinoff mania?
**94** Stanch
**95** Eases the misgivings of
**97** Star-struck entourage
**98** Funny Poehler
**100** Allies have one
**102** Post-solstice celebration
**103** Kind of tape
**107** Arrives
**109** Crew
**113** Hapless Roman ruler?
**115** Taser for children?
**118** Campfire treat
**119** Hit ___ note
**120** Tiny-scissors holder
**121** Cone former

**122** Desire, with "the"
**123** "Buddenbrooks" novelist
**124** Trickle
**125** They can be prying or crying

## DOWN

**1** Very, informally
**2** Charismatic effect
**3** St. Paul's architect
**4** Downed power lines, e.g.
**5** Bonded
**6** Turkish V.I.P.
**7** Häagen-___
**8** Things to think about
**9** Almost matching
**10** Polyphemus, to Odysseus
**11** Kind of colony
**12** Giant who made "The Catch," 1954
**13** "No worries"
**14** Mil. educators
**15** Sheltered
**16** Quiz bowl lover, say
**19** Corrupts
**20** Mirror image
**22** Over again
**24** Daydreams, with "out"
**27** "Why not!"
**30** Black Watch soldier's garb
**31** Vast, old-style
**33** Scavenging Southern food fish
**35** Stockpile
**36** Foamy mugful
**37** Climbing aid
**38** Falls into line
**40** Clear
**42** "The only rule is that there ___ rules"

**43** Pittsburgh-based food giant
**44** Soprano Fleming
**46** Glut
**48** Take a whack at
**51** My, in Bretagne
**54** Garrulous Garrison
**56** Entrees sometimes prepared in crockpots
**59** Charles, e.g.
**61** Tipping point?
**62** Subj. of the 2005 Pulitzer-winning book "Ghost Wars"
**64** Hags, e.g.
**67** Picks up
**68** Possible lagoon entrance
**69** Serious
**70** Unemployed persons with full-time jobs
**71** California's ___ Castle
**72** O.T.B. conveniences
**73** Slender fish
**74** 1983 Woody Allen film
**76** Less fortunate
**77** China's Zhou ___
**78** Visually transfixed
**79** Reviewers' comments on book jackets, typically
**83** Distrustful
**87** God, with "the"
**88** Cut-off pants?
**91** Not consent
**92** Like some chickens
**93** Mea ___
**96** Cheer for
**99** Swamp
**101** "My heavens!"

by Paul Hunsberger

103 Mosquito
    protection
104 Cartridge filler
105 "Great" red
    feature of Jupiter
106 Fat unit
108 The ___ Owl,
    "L.A. Confidential"
    coffee shop

110 Fix
111 Golf great
    Ballesteros
112 Timeline segments
114 When repeated,
    name in old
    Hollywood
116 Outstanding
117 Goose egg

Note: Ten famous people are attending a costume party in this crossword. After the grid is filled, change the two circled letters in each theme answer to "unmask" a celebrity.

## ACROSS

1 Tierra en el agua
5 Horror movie locale, in brief
10 Run ___ of
15 "Whoa! Calm down!"
19 Be featured (in)
20 Words on a Spanish valentine
21 Temerity
22 Choir part
23 Rods on a cowboy's truck
25 Environmentally sound keyboard
27 Prepare the soil for planting, perhaps
28 Multicapable
29 DLXXVI doubled
30 Lily type
32 Foreign visitors?
33 Only nonsentient zodiac symbol
36 In style
37 Voting to pass
38 Empathetic words
40 Password preceder, generally
41 Example, for instance: Abbr.
42 007 strategy
44 High card up one's sleeve
46 Baltimore daily, with "the"
47 ___ voce
48 French river or department
49 Web programs
53 Property claims
55 Some sexy nightwear
60 Clingy wrap
61 Ties up
63 Memo abbr.
65 "To Live and Die ___"
66 Narrow overhang
68 Government resister standing ready
70 It might be in a belt
71 More than attentive
72 Immature egg
73 East Coast rte.
74 Was sincere
76 Strong point
78 It often involves a Snellen chart
80 ___ about
82 All, in old-time stage directions
84 Modern address
85 Shock a fairy-tale monster
89 Nocturnal birds liable to keep people awake
91 Take most of
94 Burglar discouragers
95 Billiards shot
97 Fannie ___
98 "Pastorals" poet
99 Former Portuguese colony in China
100 Certain game-ending cry
101 Industrial hub of Germany
103 1983 domestic comedy
104 Like invalid ballots
107 Fries, e.g.
109 Soup spoon designed for shellfish
111 Last costume at a costume party
113 Requiem hymn word
114 Visibly stunned
115 Michael and Sonny's brother in "The Godfather"
116 Cleaner target
117 Five-spots
118 Transport, as across a river
119 1999 Broadway revue
120 Seasonal worker, say

## DOWN

1 U.N. member since '49
2 Like some newly laundered shirts
3 Ointment base
4 Bitterly cold
5 Californie, e.g.
6 Collection of specialized words
7 Green-headed water birds
8 What wavy lines may indicate in a comic strip
9 Lean-___
10 Celestial being, in France
11 Actor José
12 Trilogy that includes "Agamemnon"
13 Eye layers
14 Carnival follower
15 When the events in flashbacks took place
16 Field with unknowns
17 RR stop
18 "___ knight doth sit too melancholy": "Pericles"
24 Part of "the many," in Greek
26 Canola, for one
28 Clears out of, as a hotel room
29 Hosts, briefly
31 Cheerful and spirited, as a voice
34 Singer Ocasek
35 Fruit drink
37 It might have serifs
39 Before long
40 Straight
42 ___ Vista (Disney video distributor)
43 Boiled cornmeal
45 Cashew, for one
46 Hit hard, as brakes
49 Northeastern Indian state
50 ___ d'Or (film award)
51 Italian "first"
52 Many a "Damn Yankees" role
54 Mutely showed respect
56 Truck fuel
57 Paper collector
58 Kagan of the Supreme Court
59 "The Crucible" locale
62 Pooh-bah
64 Business card abbr.
67 Gets the water out of
68 Many Monopoly spaces
69 They might atone
72 Moved like water into plant roots
75 Very, very funny
77 Short answers?
79 Festive time
81 Note to self
83 "___ in the kitchen with Dinah" (old song lyric)
85 Bad situation
86 Suffix with Cray-
87 Unfilled spaces
88 Mesmerized states
90 Newspaper section that competes with Craigslist
91 Hockey team's advantage
92 Smallish marsupial
93 Prize
96 Elk's weapon

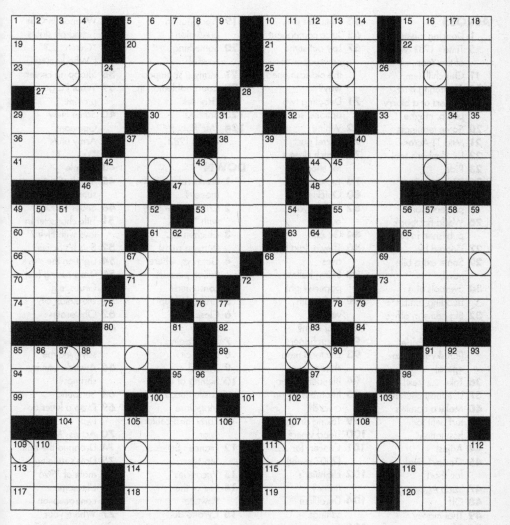

by Eric Berlin

## ACROSS

1 Dancing misstep
5 Time's 1981 Man of the Year
11 Churchill item
16 Chattering bird
19 Subject of a blurry photo, maybe
20 Some terminals
21 Mild 11-Across
22 Ice climber's tool
23 Ride
24 Détente as a means of self-preservation?
26 World Factbook publisher, in brief
27 Floored by
29 Some extra bills, maybe
30 Symbols of a budding romance
32 Big name in office supplies
33 "The ___ Bride" (Rimsky-Korsakov opera)
36 Take ___ (rest)
37 Like most churches
40 Make a homie's turf unfit for habitation?
44 Adjust
45 "Today" rival, for short
47 Veep Agnew
48 Off
49 Thai money
50 Dissertation
53 Where the 34th Infantry Division fought: Abbr.
54 Joint legislative assemblies
55 Israel's Weizman
56 Seven, for one
58 Songs for one
60 Eye part
61 Diminutive of a common Russian man's name

63 Antiulcer pill
65 Juice component
67 Lay out some newspaper copy the old-fashioned way?
71 Debating two options, say
72 Whine
73 Barrel part
75 Match closers, for short
78 Tucson sch.
80 Quickly
82 "While you ___ out . . ."
84 Go off
86 They're laid by aves
88 Shiny, hollow paperweight
89 Prefix with venous
90 Star men?
91 Churchgoers
93 Electoral map shade
94 Blender maker
95 Rhombus on an award?
99 Taking drugs
100 Dead letter?
101 Concert for ___ (2007 event)
102 Highflier's home?
104 Derailleur settings
106 Cartoon character whose last name is Höek
107 Dressing place
111 P
112 What a mysterious restaurant critic has?
116 1968 live folk record
117 Company with Patch Media
118 Sourpusses

119 Precipitation prediction
120 Something special
121 Many a shampoo
122 Court nobleman in "Hamlet"
123 Bottoms
124 "Mr. Roboto" band, 1983

## DOWN

1 Banks raking in the money?
2 Criticize severely, with "out"
3 Chichén ___ (Mayan ruins)
4 Getaway where Italian pies are consumed?
5 Crumpled (up)
6 Close to, in poetry
7 Skyscraping
8 Dutch city
9 Mailed
10 Setting of the castle Rocca Maggiore
11 Early third-century year
12 France's Belle-___-en-Mer
13 Vacancies
14 Foe of the Pawnee
15 Cyrano de Bergerac wooed her
16 Strength required to lift a car?
17 Revolutionary line
18 What a raised hand may mean
25 "Can't beat that contract"
28 Duke ___, Rocky's manager/trainer
31 1986 Indy 500 winner

34 Weapon in Clue
35 Ticked-off states
37 "Quién ___?" ("Who knows?")
38 Shopping center
39 What PC gurus provide
40 Some New Guineans
41 Army units
42 "Yes ___?"
43 Couple
45 Scholastic measure: Abbr.
46 Seder serving
51 Title character in love with Elvira
52 Snitch's activity
54 Light on the stove
56 Drag-racing fuel
57 Grubs, e.g.
59 Ukrainian city
62 Obliterates
64 Last thing a fellow actor says, maybe
66 Awards won by shrimps?
68 Surround
69 Drop a letter or two
70 Actress Mimieux
74 Dropped the ball
75 Dole's running mate of 1996
76 Like some contraception
77 Where your opinion on "One lump or two?" counts?
79 Skirt
81 Nascar Hall-of-Famer Jarrett
83 Spots for hammers and anvils
85 Sharp irritation
87 Berry in some energy boosters
89 Slice of old Turkey?

by Brendan Emmett Quigley

**91** Bird hangouts
**92** Target competitor
**96** Intl. humanities group
**97** Bowler's target
**98** Refrain bit
**99** End of a pricing phrase
**102** Japanese beer
**103** Fire-___ (carnival performer)
**104** Home for a certain old woman
**105** Tattoo removal reminder
**108** Like some sparkling wines
**109** Side (with)
**110** Sauce thickener
**111** Car wash need
**113** A single may get you one, briefly
**114** PC key
**115** Like some flat-screen panels, for short

**ACROSS**

1 Small amount
6 Nab, as a base runner
13 Well-known maze traveler
19 Slings
20 "I kid you not!"
22 "Things Fall Apart" author Chinua ___
23 Full-length
24 See highlighted letters intersected by this answer
26 Game hunters
28 Business card abbr.
29 Friend of Fifi
30 Fleur-de-___
31 Frozen beverage brand
32 One in debt
34 Author ___ Hubbard
35 Guess on a tarmac: Abbr.
36 Geological feature on a Utah license plate
38 Polite
40 Some batteries
41 Speak horsely?
43 ___ hall
44 Tennis's Berdych
45 Type
46 Golfer nicknamed "The King"
47 Year Michelangelo began work on "David"
48 As ___ (usually)
49 Charades participant, e.g.
52 Newsroom workers, for short
53 "Unfortunately, that's the case"
55 "Hurry!"
57 Obedient
58 Umpire's ruling
60 "I ___ the day . . ."
61 Priestly garment
64 Folkie Guthrie

65 Repeated musical phrases
67 Mazda model
69 Facility often closed in the winter
71 Home state for 86-Across: Abbr.
72 Soviet space station
73 Zig or zag
74 Home to the Venus de Milo
76 "Easy as pie"
80 Majority figure?
82 Texans' org.
85 Palindromic vehicle
86 Cheney's successor
87 82-Across stats
88 Launch
90 Jack or jenny
91 Beginning of un año
92 Eggs in a sushi restaurant
93 Freshen, as a stamp pad
94 Isn't wrong?
96 Popular pie flavor
97 Ends
98 PC key
99 1977 thriller set at sea
100 Comedy Central's "___.0"
101 Prefix with -gon
103 Pointed tool
104 ". . . . ___ saw Elba"
105 Co. that owns Moviefone
106 Commonly called
109 See highlighted letters intersected by this answer
114 Child's pet
115 Phenomenon associated with the Southern Oscillation
116 Message seen after 13-Across dies
117 Setting for van Gogh's "Cafe Terrace at Night"
118 Phillies div.

119 Drama has it
120 Shooting sport

**DOWN**

1 So
2 Character in "The Hobbit"
3 See highlighted letters intersected by this answer
4 Critical situation
5 Cosmetician Lauder
6 They have mtgs. in schools
7 Not std.
8 Share
9 Harvey of "Reservoir Dogs"
10 Two-for-one, e.g.
11 Flunk
12 Media watchdog org.
13 "Going Rogue" author
14 Rheumatism symptom
15 1969 film with an exclamation point in its title
16 When the table is set
17 Missing parts
18 Realizes
21 Jewel holder
25 Book after Joel
27 Cousin of an oboe
32 See highlighted letters intersected by this answer
33 Sassy
34 Site of a key battle in the War of 1812
35 Flotsam or Jetsam in "The Little Mermaid"
36 Fleet
37 He played the candidate in "The Candidate," 1972
39 "___ in the Morning"
40 '10 or '11 person, now
41 Buster

42 Shop posting: Abbr.
44 Follow
45 Aviation pioneer Sikorsky
46 Designer of the pyramid at the 74-Across
50 See highlighted letters intersected by this answer
51 It's for the birds
54 Garlicky mayonnaise
55 "___ for Cookie" ("Sesame Street" song)
56 Totaled
59 Ashanti wood carvings, e.g.
62 See highlighted letters intersected by this answer
63 Reason to doodle
66 Apple debut of 1998
67 "I'm less than impressed"
68 Mouse in a classic Daniel Keyes book
70 Contact ___
73 RCA products
75 "I didn't mean to do that!"
77 Quite a schlep
78 "Do the Right Thing" pizzeria owner
79 Thomas who lampooned Boss Tweed
81 "You have no ___"
82 "Tell Me More" network
83 Age-old philosophical topic
84 Fictional reporter
86 Buzzers
89 ___ Park, home for the Pittsburgh Pirates
94 Cézanne's "Boy in ___ Vest"
95 Bonus to something that's already good

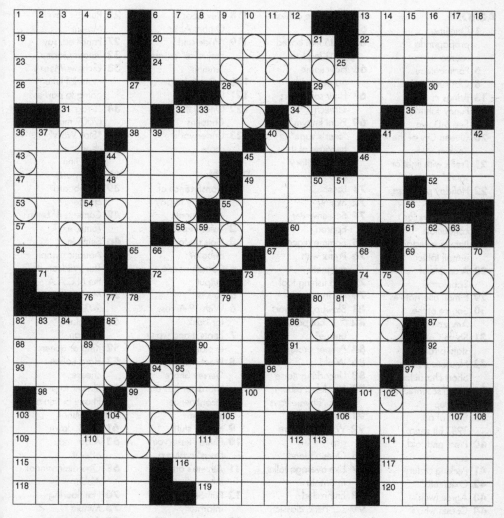

*by Joel Fagliano*

**96** Spanish chickens
**97** Active
**99** Doubting words
**100** Representative
**102** Musical symbols that resemble cross hairs
**103** Gulf of ___
**104** A very long time
**105** Top

**106** "Show Boat" composer
**107** Writer James
**108** The "S" of TBS: Abbr.
**110** Unaccounted for, briefly
**111** Take sides?
**112** Prefix with culture
**113** Boss of bosses

## ACROSS

1 Onetime propaganda source
5 Portmanteau
8 Obstruct
13 Brings in
18 Funny Johnson
19 See 6-Down
20 Queen City of the Rockies
21 Prefix with light or sound
22 Holiday purchase, informally
24 Tone setters for conductors
26 Item in a certain e-mail folder
28 A couple of Spaniards?
29 E-mail alternatives
30 Source of the Amazon
31 South Carolina's state bird
32 Neurotic Martin Short character
35 Not discounted
36 Give up
38 Start of a 1957 hit song
40 Press and fold, say
41 Pecking order?
42 Oxidized
43 Agree (with)
44 Cousin who's "altogether ooky"
45 Vague early afternoon time
47 Like certain investments
49 Soaked
53 To the point, to lawyers
55 Times ___
57 Succeed
59 Bridge expert Culbertson
60 Go back and forth

62 Some are cohesive
64 Territory
65 1985 film based on "King Lear"
66 How some games finish
67 How some cars screech
69 Plant known as "seer's sage" because of its hallucinatory effect
71 Loser
72 Skinny
74 Screenwriter Ephron
75 Somme place
76 Prefix with magnetic
77 Old fishing tool
79 An instant
81 Blowup, of a sort
82 ". . . but possibly untrue"
84 Peeper protector
86 Wield
88 Uncorking noise
90 His debut album was "Rhyme Pays"
91 Grating
92 W. Hemisphere grp.
95 Queen's land
97 Like average folks, in Britain
98 Enthralled
99 ___ Park, classic Coney Island amusement locale
100 V formation?
102 Shop chopper
104 Bounce (off)
105 Mil. officers
106 Avg. level
107 Change quickly
110 Incredibly nice
115 Matter in statistical mechanics
116 Bulldog
117 Dispatch boats

118 Neighbor of Oman: Abbr.
119 "Pride and Prejudice" actress Jennifer
120 9-Down holder
121 Pickup line?
122 One of the Chaplins
123 Underworld route

## DOWN

1 Transference of property to pay assessments
2 Asian republic
3 Gets up for the debate?
4 Certain poetic output
5 Reveal
6 With 19-Across, far back
7 Beats it and won't explain why?
8 Proof that a "Jersey Shore" character has an incontinence problem?
9 Heady stuff
10 Entire "Reservoir Dogs" cast, e.g.
11 Athlete's attire, informally
12 Pampers maker informally
13 Arrests an entire crime syndicate?
14 Inits. in '70s and '80s rock
15 Slayer of his brother Bleda
16 Like some majors
17 Impudent
20 Longtime ESPN football analyst Merril ___
23 Protected images, for short

25 Russian novelist Maxim
27 Fancified, say
32 Singer Gorme
33 Eschews Mensa material when going to parties?
34 "Drag ___ Hell" (2009 movie)
36 "Star Wars" character ___-Gon Jinn
37 SALT party
39 Dashboard choice
42 Contents of Lenin's Tomb, e.g.?
46 Settle in
47 Aquatic nymph
48 The Wildcats of the N.C.A.A.
50 Merits at least a 20% tip?
51 "Airplane!" woman
52 King or queen
53 Hard Italian cheese
54 Slower to pick up
56 Phone button trio
58 ___ Minor
61 Break down
63 A bar may offer it
68 One-dimensional: Abbr.
70 Flat flooring
73 Minute
78 Scout's mission
80 Assertive comeback
83 118-Across is in it
85 Super Bowl IV M.V.P. Dawson
87 Scoring stat for N.B.A.'ers
89 Wallop
91 Motorola phone line
93 Departure from the norm

by Joe DiPietro

**94** Untraditional, as some marriages
**95** Charges
**96** Give a hard time
**99** Soup kitchen implements
**100** They're shown by X's, O's and arrows

**101** Luggage attachment
**103** Some annual bills
**104** Major org. representing entertainers and athletes
**108** Anita of jazz

**109** Desideratum
**111** ___ Fit
**112** Brooklyn's Flatbush, e.g.: Abbr.
**113** Go unused
**114** Symbol for electric flux

## ACROSS

1 "Right back at cha!"
9 Unclear
15 Sandcastle engineering equipment
20 Took one step too many, maybe
21 She was beheaded by Perseus
22 "Dallas" Miss
23 One of St. Peter's heavenly duties?
25 "The Untouchables" villain
26 "How's it ___?"
27 Ship part
28 Roast slightly
29 Mujeres con esposos
31 Place for un béret
33 Conquer
36 Kitty, in Segovia
37 Singer Cassidy
40 One side of a quad, maybe
42 "Snakes on a Plane," e.g.?
46 Brand of tea
48 Term on a tide table
50 Subject of a Magritte painting
51 Doc workers' org.?
52 What a lazy mover prefers to carry?
56 Projections on some globes: Abbr.
57 Your, in Tours
58 Blues instrument
59 Harsh cry
60 Cheap and flimsy, as metal
62 Big bump
63 Poet Mark

64 "___ Fan Tutte"
65 Bob, for one
67 Workout class on a pleasure cruise?
74 William Morris workers
75 Cousin of an ampule
76 Things rings lack
77 Egg foo ___
78 Makeshift Frisbee
81 Film special effects, briefly
82 Rangers' venue, for short
85 Ax
86 Number of X's in this puzzle's answer
88 Unbelievable court infraction?
91 Game with 108 cards
92 Mouselike animal
94 Fictional Jane
95 Biblical dancer
96 Cabby's nonstop patter?
100 Key with four sharps: Abbr.
102 Curt
103 "Family Guy" wife
104 Melodic passages
106 Provide a gun for, maybe
108 "Shakespeare in Love" star
111 Anthem contraction
112 Crystal on the dinner table?
114 Bloke
118 Dickens's Drood
119 Guests at a Hatfield/McCoy marriage ceremony?
123 Appropriate
124 Playground retort
125 Classic Freudian diagnosis

126 Stinger
127 Stonewallers?
128 Looks down on

## DOWN

1 Single partygoer
2 Classical Italian typeface
3 Christmas party
4 Occurring someday
5 Daughter of Loki
6 Horror film locale: Abbr.
7 Garnered
8 "The Simpsons" teacher Krabappel
9 Letters of surprise, in text messages
10 Classmates, e.g.
11 Lets in
12 City that was the site of three battles in the Seven Years' War
13 Org. with a sub division
14 Has a beef?
15 Mark Twain and George Sand, e.g.
16 1960s–'70s San Francisco mayor
17 Opera whose second act is called "The Gypsy"
18 Singer Ford
19 Cinco follower
24 Limb perch
30 "Raiders of the Lost Ark" locale
32 College in Beverly, Mass.
34 Fine fiddle
35 Rat-a-tat
37 Orly birds, once
38 "You're so funny," sarcastically
39 "Family Ties" son
41 It's west of 12-Down: Abbr.

43 "You put the ___ in the coconut . . ."
44 Marcos of the Philippines
45 "Morning Train" singer, 1981
47 Ancient May birthstones
49 Thing that may break people up
53 Rtes.
54 Polar hazard
55 Money-related: Abbr.
61 Automaker since 1974
62 Triangular sails
63 "Shoot!"
65 1997 winner of Wimbledon and the U.S. Open
66 Step down, in a way
67 Union concession
68 Creature whose tail makes up half its body's length
69 World heavyweight champion who was once an Olympic boxing gold medalist
70 Egg: Prefix
71 Feudal estate
72 "Et violà!"
73 Geom. figure
78 ___ sci
79 Peeper problems
80 Doing injury to
82 Othello, for one
83 Basic arithmetic
84 Lottery winner's feeling
86 Easy eats
87 Poorer
89 Word with level or devil
90 Arrow maker
93 Mendes of "Hitch"
97 Charge, in a way
98 Chips away at

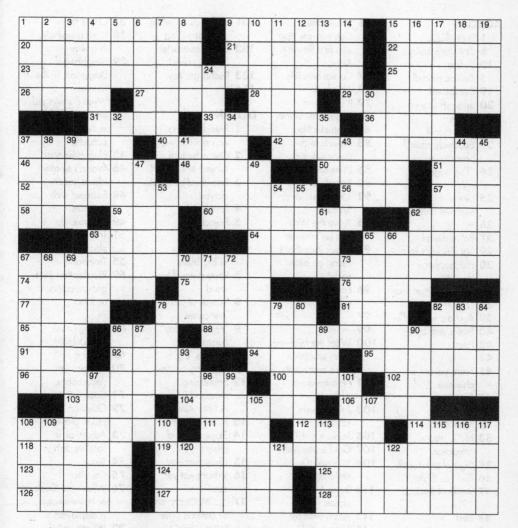

by Andrea Carla Michaels & Patrick Blindauer

## ACROSS

**1** Hall-of-___
**6** Cry like a baby
**10** Evolve
**15** Zodiac animal
**19** Combined
**20** Spanish skating figure
**21** Long rides?
**23** Suddenly smiled broadly
**24** "This might get ugly"
**25** Like a mischief-maker
**26** ---
**27** Polite denial
**29** Sgt. Friday's force
**30** Philosopher Hannah
**32** It may purr or roar
**35** "Zip it!"
**39** Archaic verb suffix
**40** Prefix with byte
**42** Pass
**44** ---
**45** Front part of a chimera
**47** Prankster
**50** ---
**52** Spell caster
**53** N.Y.C. tourist attraction
**54** Sign of pressure?
**56** Get ___ (fight)
**57** Battle of the ___, 1914
**58** Best
**60** ---
**61** Sun spot?
**63** An extremity
**64** ___ judicata (decided case)
**66** Tick off
**68** Grab, with "onto"
**69** Extremity
**70** Infomercial line . . . with a hint to 10 answers in this puzzle
**75** Where the Confederate flag was first flown: Abbr.
**77** Cereal box title
**78** It's a lock
**79** It's uplifting
**80** Sequel title starter
**81** Synthetic fiber
**83** Provide with cornrows, e.g.
**86** Lines on a staff
**90** Belted out
**92** 15-Across, in Spanish
**93** "Love the Way You Lie" rapper
**95** Snack item that's round on both ends?
**96** Former Chevy subcompact
**97** ---
**99** ---
**100** What the hyphen in an emoticon often represents
**101** Nonstandard: Abbr.
**103** John Belushi catchphrase
**105** Miner's aid
**107** Gold units: Abbr.
**108** Minimalist's philosophy
**110** Dean Martin classic
**113** Asian wild ass
**115** Miner's aid
**117** Baby ___
**119** Pitching awards
**121** Spirited?
**126** Mythical con man
**127** Neighbor of Somalia
**128** Will-o'-the-wisp feature
**129** God wounded by Diomedes in the "Iliad"
**130** Glove material
**131** It's not good when it's outstanding
**132** Exiled character in "King Lear"
**133** Recharge, say
**134** ---

## DOWN

**1** President who was not elected
**2** Oscar feature subject since 2001
**3** Snowbird's vehicle, maybe
**4** Toughen
**5** Preacher's exhortation
**6** It's known for its big busts
**7** Repeat word for word
**8** Words of faux innocence
**9** "Freaky Friday" co-star
**10** Bauxite, e.g.
**11** Highway caution
**12** Something punched into an A.T.M.: Abbr.
**13** Hotel amenity
**14** Skipjacks and others
**15** Chowderhead
**16** What's not yet due?
**17** ___ McGarry, chief of staff on "The West Wing"
**18** The U.S. banned it in 1968
**22** Second or tenth, in a way
**28** Gray
**31** Numerical prefix
**33** Oldest desert in the world
**34** Environmental extremists' acts
**36** The "you" of "Here's to you!"
**37** Cheer for
**38** Used a keyhole, in a way
**39** Neighbor of Dagwood, in the funnies
**41** What the winged woman is holding in the Emmy statuette
**43** Blog nuisances
**46** World's smallest island nation
**48** Fastener with two nuts
**49** Equivalence
**51** Treat like a pharaoh?
**55** Transform
**59** Retailer that sells grasshoppers as food
**62** ---
**65** College near Philadelphia
**67** "Go on . . ."
**70** Gymnasium decorations
**71** Cool
**72** Question to a poker player
**73** Adjust, as a satellite dish
**74** Tease
**75** Go after
**76** Where the Code of Hammurabi is displayed
**82** What's up?
**84** How some N.F.L. games are resolved
**85** Many an action movie villain
**87** Entered violently
**88** U.S.S. Ward, e.g.
**89** They're not on your side
**91** Headlines, as a band

*by Joel Fagliano*

**94** Cussed
**98** One who doesn't give tough love, say
**102** Legend
**104** Siouan speaker
**106** White rapper with two #1 hits
**109** ---

**111** Sunny?
**112** ---
**114** Twinkle
**116** Stick on the range?
**118** Barely manages, with "out"
**120** Old German duchy name

**121** Digs
**122** Parrot
**123** Take the wrong way?
**124** Important no. for car buyers
**125** What this puzzle may make you say

### ACROSS

1 City south of West Palm
5 Old man
9 Give for free, slangily
13 Heckle or Jeckle of cartoons
19 Stoker who created Dracula
20 Womb, jocularly
21 Painful boo-boo
22 Winter stash, of a sort
23 Investing in a growth company
25 High-risk investments
27 Hardly parade-worthy, say
28 Antics
29 Ltd., in Lille
30 Hanging piece
31 Like one trying to hit a piñata, often
33 Pronged, as an electrical plug
34 Former Norwegian P.M. Stoltenberg
35 Vardalos of "My Big Fat Greek Wedding"
36 Buttonhole, e.g.
37 Big picture: Abbr.
38 Con target
39 Shocked
42 Bolognese bride
45 Sprint, e.g.
48 It should have no effect
50 "No bid"
52 Not so smooth
54 Without
55 Somewhat
57 One-third of Neapolitan ice cream: Abbr.
59 Like the right third of Ireland's flag
60 Announcer Hall
61 Mrs. Capp and others
62 Add-on features
64 "Cómo ___?"
65 Money . . . or a hint to how six crossings in this puzzle are to be represented, superimposing one letter over another
68 Ora pro ___
71 Bully's coercive comeback
72 Places for picks, informally
73 Admonishment to a puppy
76 Ticks off
78 Gospel singer Winans
79 "That's nuthin'!"
80 Bead maker?
81 Request from a guest over an apartment intercom
83 Holiday attraction at a mall
85 Inaugurated
87 Fame
89 Astronomical distances: Abbr.
91 Eventually
92 Yiddish laments
93 Faunus's Greek counterpart
95 Beef
97 Ukr., e.g., once
98 Certain lap dogs, informally
100 ___ moons
101 French film award
102 The shortest one has only two verses
105 It appears at the top of a page
106 Instruments played with mallets
108 Bit of corporate attire
110 Quotation sources, once
112 Unrecoverable investment expenses
113 More swanky
114 Confab
115 Robert of "The Sopranos"
116 Draft status
117 Trying to pull a fast one
118 Certain
119 Beef
120 Corp. V.I.P.'s

### DOWN

1 Pellet propeller
2 University town named after a Penobscot chief
3 Some liquid assets
4 Ones unlikely to write memoirs?
5 Lacoste offering
6 Gets around
7 #2s, e.g.
8 Director Lee
9 Patient's liability
10 Wilson of "The Internship"
11 Small role in "Austin Powers" movies
12 Ticket to the World Series
13 En ___
14 Source of the line "Thy money perish with thee"
15 Melted Popsicle, e.g.
16 Spot on a demand curve
17 Fully blacken
18 Half-kiss?
24 Musical with the song "Summer Nights"
26 "Old ___"
28 Rock and Roll Hall of Fame inductees from Texas
32 "Not a peep!"
34 Fool
38 What best friends keep
39 Church section
40 Song classic "___ to Be Unhappy"
41 Kids' outdoor game
43 Baptism, e.g.
44 Glowing
46 Head across the Atlantic
47 Big, in ads
49 Ancient Greek coins
51 Convinced
53 It's a legal thing
56 Designer Mizrahi
58 See 62-Down
61 Australian beer brand
62 With 58-Down, financial topic of 2012–13
63 Feudal figures
65 Horrifies
66 Bar selections
67 ___ alike
68 Texans are part of it, in brief
69 Certain bank deposits
70 Key business figure
73 AA or AAA, maybe
74 Opera part
75 Disavow
77 South of 79-Down?
79 See 77-Down
80 Briefing spot
82 Warhol's specialty
84 Squirts
86 Without a contract
88 Crazies
90 Shoulder bone

*by Daniel A. Finan*

**94** Lead-in to 88-Down

**96** Danish bread

**98** Plays miniature golf

**99** Constellation next to Taurus

**100** Unionize?

**101** Social level

**103** Bottle unit

**104** Arizona sights

**106** Lamblike

**107** Ship's keel, e.g.

**109** Radio station on TV

**111** Automaker since 1974

**112** [as written]

## ACROSS

1 Whammy
5 Where les enfants might play
9 Rendered speechless
15 Female lobsters
19 Every which way
20 Subject for a mariachi band
21 Insubstantial
22 Like Voldemort
23 Artist's favorite spiritual?
26 Ablution, e.g.
27 Firefighter's need, maybe
28 Summer Olympics host after London
29 ___ vu
30 Food item a cook might flip
32 Prescription pain medication
35 Nos. in a directory
37 Look for
38 Several, in Seville
40 Cool with what others are doing
42 Go (for)
43 Christmas song line from an artist?
47 Batman villain
51 What Mississippi cheerleaders ask for a lot
52 How you might do something gross
53 Cagney or Lacey: Abbr.
54 Daughter of James II
55 Where there's Wi-Fi availability
57 Get ready to drive
60 Former six-term senator from Indiana
61 More yang than yin: Abbr.

62 Monetary bribes, in slang
64 What a star probably has
65 N.R.A. piece?: Abbr.
68 Artist's favorite Broadway musical?
70 Revival meeting miracles
71 ___ Zulu (warrior dubbed Africa's Napoleon)
72 Atlantean superhero of DC Comics
73 ___ Field
75 Defrocked villain on "Buffy the Vampire Slayer"
76 Vista opener?
77 Roman of film
81 Michigan college
82 ___ generis
83 Part of an umpire's count
86 Put in writing
87 Parts of an orrery
89 Artist's expression for "Such is life"?
92 Easter purchase
93 Worth all the hype, as a film
94 Snorkeling aids
95 "Tsk!"
98 Finger
99 Cuts some slack
103 "Zero Dark Thirty" locale
105 Castaway's construction
107 Rough position?
108 Sedona maker
111 The Roman way
112 How the expert artist passed her exam?
116 "The Cosby Show" boy

117 Last word in the Torah
118 Rain man?
119 Inclination
120 ___ Club
121 River that "sweats oil and tar" in T. S. Eliot's "The Waste Land"
122 Predoctoral tests, for short
123 Approximately

## DOWN

1 Tatooine race in the "Star Wars" saga
2 What's big at the movies?
3 Like old unrecyclable bottles
4 Certain Jaguar
5 Pre-exam feeling, maybe
6 Playground retort
7 South Korea's ___ Tae Woo
8 Buffet cabinet
9 Key of Schubert's "Trout" Quintet: Abbr.
10 Bronze
11 Topper
12 Ancient
13 Patchwork quilts have lots of them
14 "Good point"
15 Artist's line of weary resignation?
16 "On This Night of a Thousand Stars" musical
17 Capone's top henchman
18 Wintry mix
24 Flawed, as mdse.
25 Party host's convenience
31 Reposed

33 "Laborare ___ orare" (Freemasons' motto)
34 What Morehouse College lacks
36 Before, poetically
38 Home of Kings Peak
39 Little muchacho
41 What the tipsy artist had at the bar?
42 Liz of "Garfield," e.g.
44 Pay to cross town, maybe
45 First chimp to orbit Earth
46 Pay to cross town, maybe
47 Pop icon?
48 "The Odd Couple" role
49 Daft
50 "Phooey!"
53 Gauntlet thrower's challenge
56 What the artist confused people with?
58 Norse source for Loki lore
59 Dash
60 Dairy consumer's enzyme
62 Erotic
63 Good wife in "The Good Earth"
65 Org. protecting music copyrights
66 "Congress ___ make no law . . ."
67 Actress Hayek
69 Prefix with poise
74 Pain and suffering
77 "Gay" capital
78 Summer lawn sight
79 New Jersey's ___ University
80 QB mistakes: Abbr.
82 Holy mlle.

*by Tracy Bennett*

**84** Turn to bone
**85** Apiarist's woe
**88** Watchful ones?
**89** Holy city of Iran
**90** Access charge, of a sort
**91** Debatable sighting
**93** Words to live by
**95** Blurts (out)

**96** ___ yoga
**97** Arabic name meaning "wise"
**98** J. Carrol ___, Oscar nominee for "Sahara"
**100** Phycologist's study
**101** Some templegoers
**102** Pro vote

**104** Birdbrain
**106** "___ fair . . ."
**109** Discoveries of Michael Faraday
**110** Regarding
**113** Easter purchase
**114** ___'easter
**115** "Boardwalk Empire" network

## ACROSS

1 Holiday cheer
7 Early round
13 "30 Rock" or "3rd Rock From the Sun"
19 P.G.A. event played on Father's Day
20 Company in a 2001 merger with Chevron
21 Old TV component
22 See 36-Across
23 Tickles
24 Corrects
25 Bobble
27 Wordsworth's "___ to Duty"
28 Short race?
29 ___ Peninsula
31 Opposite of eternally
35 Suffix with green or bean
36 With 22-Across, shortly
37 Accident marker
39 Subject of many a war
42 Cobra's foe
44 Melee
45 Whole ___
48 Stamp, perhaps
49 Express
50 GMC truck
51 GPS lines: Abbr.
52 Texas athletic site
54 Dive, maybe
55 Molding material
58 Robed ruler
59 Seminary subj.
60 New newt
61 Cons
62 Like the 116-Across

67 Common pg. size
68 "___ magic"
69 Auto safety feature, for short
70 Dead-end jobs, perhaps
71 Eye affliction
72 Pizza order
73 A computer may be in it
77 Seventh letter
79 Con
81 Narrow valleys
82 Strong-smelling cheese
86 Lord or lady
87 "Nifty!"
88 How many Playboy bunnies dress
89 Generosity
91 Rise
92 "No ___!"
93 Furtive
95 N.F.L. owner who moved the Cleveland Browns to Baltimore in 1996
97 She outwitted Sherlock
99 ___ greens
102 Versailles resident
103 Is a poor night watchman, say
105 Polo ground?
106 Gargoyle features, often
109 Showy shrub
112 Showy
113 Greets the day
114 "Feeling Good" chanteuse
115 Hide-and-seek cheater
116 5-Down unit
117 Consumer Reports employee

## DOWN

1 Run smoothly
2 Bear, in Baja
3 2012 Emmy winner for Outstanding Drama Series
4 "L'Africaine," e.g.
5 Business titan born July 30, 1863
6 Not conned by
7 Grp. that rarely meets during the summer
8 Take off
9 Give off
10 Light show light
11 Put away
12 Hip-hop's ___ Def
13 Blasted
14 "Garfield" waitress
15 Balcony, e.g.
16 Feature of a 57-Down
17 More curious
18 Unkempt
26 Genetic enzyme
28 Fictional character with steel pincers for hands
29 Give the silent treatment?
30 Before long, poetically
32 Before, poetically
33 Words to live by
34 Exposed
38 Failed investment
40 Off course
41 Tobiko, in Japanese cuisine
43 Bloody
44 A Beatle
46 Poorly insulated, say
47 He wrote "I exist, that is all, and I find it nauseating"
49 Bobble
50 Hook's hand
52 Wake-up times, for short

53 Tolkien creatures
55 Impressive golf shot
56 Many a Dream Act beneficiary
57 5-Down innovation
58 Latin 101 verb
62 Get down pat
63 Up to the task
64 Northeast university town
65 Getup
66 Pac-12 player
71 Winter sprinkle
74 Discharge
75 Ending with cyto-
76 Space rock, maybe
77 List ender
78 116-Across, colloquially
80 Like
82 Shrew
83 Bit of TV real estate
84 Pearl Buck heroine
85 Where 5-Down's company gets an "F"?
87 Bookworm, maybe
88 Casting source for some H'wood comedies
90 Hose holder
91 Harvey of "Taxi Driver"
93 Cone filler
94 "The Big Bang Theory" co-creator Chuck
96 Extinguish
98 Lots
100 Tip for a reporter, maybe
101 Status quo ___
104 Brewery fixture
106 Cooke of soul
107 For
108 Bygone flier
110 Phoenix-to-Albuquerque dir.
111 ___ Lingus

by Andrew Reynolds

## ACROSS

1 Shows worry, in a way
6 Times before eves
10 Ice cream truck music, e.g.
14 Military hat
18 Curved connector
19 Conquest of Caesar
20 Where woolly mammoths once roamed
21 Does some kitchen prep work
22 Harder to come by
23 Tree experts
25 Part of IV
26 Span
27 The jigsaw . . .
29 Antiglare wear
31 Ruling classes
32 The F.D.I.C. was created during his presidency
34 Genteel affairs
35 Sports venue
36 Folklore figures
40 The elevator . . .
45 Pottery decorators
47 Get
48 Tilted
51 Don José in "Carmen," e.g.
52 Column on a Clue notepad
53 The mosquito zapper . . .
57 Conversation inhibiter
58 He said "Every great film should seem new every time you see it"
60 Not the inside track?
61 Wrap (up)
63 Fire
64 Take in
65 T, by telegraph
68 Glands on top of the kidneys
73 Of Nineveh's home: Abbr.
75 Muslim headdress
77 The quiz-grading machine . . .
81 Express, as a deep sigh
83 Coin with a two-headed eagle
84 London weights
85 Agent on "The X-Files"
86 Having a knack for
89 The crosswalk signal . . .
92 Naldi of film
93 Like the samba and salsa
96 Sinuous dance
97 "Charlotte's Web" setting
98 1972 musical or its 2013 revival
100 Quirky
104 The film-processing machine at the movie studio . . .
108 Curling implement
111 Arkansas's ___ National Forest
112 Impossible to tell apart
113 Comes down hard
114 Essays
115 Vladimir's veto
116 Capitol Hill sight
117 Kind of beauty
118 Smooth, in a way
119 Certifications on some college apps
120 "Calm down now"
121 Bar, at the bar

## DOWN

1 Result of some heavy petting?
2 Quatrain rhyme scheme
3 Place to find a date
4 Words of farewell
5 Savvy, in a way
6 High Muslim honorific
7 China setting
8 Rode down a river, in a way
9 Soapbox derby necessity
10 Nonclerical
11 Provider of passports, e.g.
12 Minute
13 With 37-Down, restaurant offering with many small dishes
14 Part of a honeymoon suite, perhaps
15 Prefix with -plasm
16 Paddington Bear's country of origin
17 Attends
21 Wine's partner
24 Online news aggregation inits.
28 Right-leaning: Abbr.
30 Caught
32 Coastal feature
33 "The Souls of Black Folk" author, 1903
35 Item dropped on Wile E. Coyote in Road Runner cartoons
37 See 13-Down
38 ___ rock
39 Parts of Eastern Eur., once
41 Highland headwear
42 Tidy up, in a way
43 Carry-___
44 Licks, e.g.
46 Mailing label abbr.
49 "Can't Get It Out of My Head" band, briefly
50 S.F.'s division
53 Spells badly?
54 Childish retort
55 Much-hyped Google product
56 Like some hot cereals
59 Teller of tales
62 Hung some strips
66 On sale
67 Lack
69 It makes a flea flee
70 "Te ___" (Rihanna song)
71 Biography subtitled "A Revolutionary Life"
72 Platform locales: Abbr.
73 A.M.A. part: Abbr.
74 Tart dessert
76 Stop-and-start, start-and-stop
77 Funny Drescher
78 Car make whose name sounds like a Cockney greeting
79 "Uh-huh, sure"
80 Job listing letters
82 Kay's follower
85 Go soft
87 Dinner in a can, maybe
88 Haunted house sound
90 Pride of St. Louis
91 Onetime NBC news anchor
94 Hippie T-shirt technique

by Steven Ginzburg

**95** "I agree!"
**99** Classes
**100** "Laborare ___ orare" (Freemason motto)
**101** Chasten
**102** Hot ___
**103** Caddie selections
**104** Braille, essentially
**105** Biblical prophet
**106** Useless
**107** Echidna food
**109** It may get dipped in milk
**110** Fig. near an m.p.g. rating

## ACROSS

1 Phonies
6 Cat nipper?
10 1977 double-platinum Steely Dan album
13 Capacitance measure
18 Newfoundland explorer
19 16 23-Acrosses
20 Input for a mill
21 Tolerate
22 Vaquero's rope
23 See 19-Across
24 Eat heartily
26 Where most things rank in importance to a Muslim?
28 Foe of Frodo
29 Certify (to)
30 Fannie ___
31 Mid sixth-century year
32 Casts doubt on
35 Low notes?
38 Haunted house sound
39 Bathroom installation
42 Webster's directive to the overly formal?
45 Raises
46 ___ raise
47 Folder's declaration
48 Plaintive
49 Upper ___
50 Single
51 Madam
52 Exciting matches?
55 Series of measures
57 Burns books?
59 Fancy
61 Exchange news?
62 Equipment list for a hashish-smoking fisherman?
67 Baby no longer

68 "Do I ___!"
69 News of disasters, e.g.
70 One might be mean or cross
71 Total
74 Hide
78 Way, in Pompeii
79 Berlin Olympics hero
82 Word on either side of "à"
83 One getting special instruction
84 ___ Plaines
85 1986 rock autobiography
86 Departed from Manama, maybe?
89 Sounds often edited out for radio
90 Hand for a mariachi band?
91 "Everything must go" events
92 Cover, in a way
94 One may be kept running in a bar
95 The South, once: Abbr.
98 Número of countries bordering Guatemala
101 Subsidy
102 Niece's polite interruption?
106 Close to losing it
108 Antiknock additive
109 Caustic
110 Current carriers
111 Throwaway publication
112 Get the old gang together
113 Part of a barrel
114 Commotions
115 Common symbol in hieroglyphics

116 Depleted of color
117 Strength of a solution

## DOWN

1 "Skedaddle!"
2 Eastern Mediterranean port
3 Lessen
4 Speck
5 Space specks
6 Fair alternative
7 Moon goddess
8 "Whole" thing
9 Cooler
10 Actress Woodard
11 Old ad figure with a big nose
12 Turkish big shot
13 Prepares to eat, perhaps
14 Is against
15 Ready (for)
16 Commotions
17 Bumper bummer
19 Organized society
25 Welcome look from a Bedouin?
27 Jessica of "Valentine's Day"
28 Special ___
33 Not so hot
34 Slather
35 Game for those who don't like to draw
36 Hip
37 Contemptible one
39 Mooch
40 German W.W. II tank
41 Annually
42 Foresail
43 Thurman of "Kill Bill"
44 Miss piggy?

45 1953 A.L. M.V.P. Al
49 Ancient Hindu scripture
50 Often-blue garden blooms
52 What many Bay Area skiers do on winter weekends?
53 ___Kosh B'Gosh
54 Levels
56 Festival setup
58 1930s migrant
60 Tinkers with
62 Pitch recipient
63 Mate for Shrek
64 Trump, for one
65 Birds' beaks
66 One who's all wet?
67 Queen's "We Will Rock You," to "We Are the Champions"
72 Extends too much credit?
73 Quaker cereal
75 Determinant of when to do an airport run, for short
76 Hawaii's ___ Day
77 Big or top follower
80 One type of 66-Down
81 Historic exhibit at Washington Dulles airport
83 Beauty's counterpart
85 Blow away
86 "A ___ cannot live": Martin Luther King Jr.
87 Clash
88 Jai ___
91 Blossoming business?
92 King Arthur's father
93 Military blockade

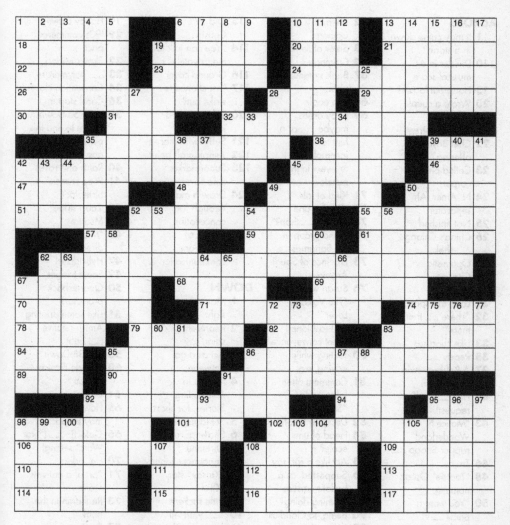

*by Dan Schoenholz*

**95** Bamboozle
**96** Dish (up)
**97** Insect trapper
**98** Intimidates
**99** Battalion, e.g.
**100** Italian bell town
**103** "No way!"
**104** "30 Rock" setting, briefly

**105** When Stanley cries "Hey, Stella!" in "A Streetcar Named Desire"
**107** Beats by ___ (headphones brand)
**108** Historical period

## ACROSS

1 It may come down in a storm
10 Divider in a musical score
13 Hang-out locale?
20 Wrote a couple of letters?
21 Montréal street
22 Chef Boyardee offering
23 Called on the carpet
24 N. Amer./Afr. separator
25 Not finished
26 China's Chiang ___-shek
27 Optimistic
28 Change
30 Visit anew
31 Loop transports
32 "There ___ there there"
33 Like choruses
35 Ready-___
37 A Bobbsey twin
39 Less certain
40 Half-___ (coffee request)
43 "Malice N Wonderland" rapper Snoop ___
46 Trains
48 "Tootsie" Oscar nominee
50 "You want a piece ___?"
53 Main hood in "Little Caesar," 1931
55 Without face value, as stock
57 Brink
58 Two-Face and the Riddler, to Batman
59 French children's song
61 "You Gotta Be" singer, 1994
62 Allen of "Candid Camera"
63 Sister of literature
64 Originates
67 Bank statement abbr.
68 Sea eagle
69 Gray areas, maybe . . . or a hint to 12 incomplete answers in this puzzle
71 Kind of lab
72 Cpl., for one
73 "What ___ thou?"
74 Island group in the Bahamas
75 Province of Saudi Arabia
76 Susan who wrote "The Volcano Lover"
78 Old-fashioned street conveyance
80 Texting while driving, e.g.
81 Comment often followed by "So sue me"
82 Designer Geoffrey
84 Head of une école?
85 Act like a rat, say
86 Supported, as a ballot measure
88 Nothing doing?
90 Being, to Claudius
92 Before, in sonnets
93 Primitive drive
95 Airport info: Abbr.
97 Monotonous routine
101 Hide
103 Virginie, e.g.
106 Ski-___
107 Type units
111 Honor at graduation?
112 Checkbook record
113 Old TV's Cousin ___
114 "You can talk to me privately"
116 Ground cover
117 Last chance to strike out?
120 Whitewashed, with "over"
121 Suffix with morph-
122 Jumping-off point
123 Supermarket time-saver
124 Draw a mark through for cancellation
125 Means of one-to-one communication

## DOWN

1 Movie theater sight
2 Represent as a saint, say
3 Act as a go-between
4 Figures in Astounding Stories, for short
5 Set (against)
6 Shavings, maybe
7 Old-time announcer Johnny
8 "Kinsey" star, 2004
9 Little sucker?
10 "___ yourself"
11 Just going through the motions, after "on"
12 Air-conditioning on a hot day, maybe
13 More curmudgeonly
14 Office PC hookup
15 Certain car gears
16 Prong
17 Masonry containers
18 Gen. Robert ___
19 Hobby activity
29 '90s commerce pact
32 Skater Midori
33 ___ polymerase
34 Convention closer?
36 Carol starter
38 With 56-Down, where to find this puzzle's 12 theme answers
40 Rants and raves
41 Pope Francis' birthplace
42 Court stripe
44 Mixture
45 "Michael Clayton" director Tony
47 Hybridized
49 Some fridges
50 Quarterback protectors
51 Like some printing
52 Amish relative
54 ___ Light
56 See 38-Down
60 Tour de France season
61 Urges
65 How picnic drinks may be packed
66 Galactic ___ ("Star Wars" setting)
70 Fleur-de-___
71 Part of a nativity scene
73 Real pain in the butt?
77 Driving aid
79 Feature of St. Basil's Cathedral
82 Olympic racers
83 "Fanny" author Jong
87 A swimmer might rightly be scared to see one
89 New Guinea port from which Amelia Earhart left on her last flight

*by Elizabeth C. Gorski*

**91** Army fig. who knows the drill?
**94** Fire extinguisher
**96** Go to sleep
**98** Cry of victory
**99** Posting, say
**100** Bottom of a contract

**102** Gave up
**104** Listening, with "in"
**105** Counters
**107** Locale for finished works that haven't yet appeared
**108** Big-screen format
**109** Dogpatch creator

**110** A, e.g.
**112** Org. in "Monk"
**115** Super ___ (old video game console)
**118** Driver's ID: Abbr.
**119** Superfund org.

## ACROSS

1 Item whose name is derived from the Latin "aquarius"
5 Auto parts giant
9 Pot user, maybe
14 Peyote and saguaro
19 Rossini's William Tell and others
21 Lump in one's throat
22 First acrylic fiber
23 Superlative for Sirius
24 Rush job?
26 Home security system component
27 Big kahunas
28 Stationery item: Abbr.
29 Had
30 Log
32 Abbr. on a lawyer's stationery
34 Censure
35 Berry used to make gin
37 They have pluses and minuses
39 In ___
41 ___-pedi
42 Medicine label info
44 Putting out on an anniversary, maybe
48 Bosch's "The Garden of Earthly Delights," for one
50 Lustrous fabric
52 Provide with a quality
53 Daisylike bloom
54 Massive ref.
56 Maze explorer
58 Turn over
59 Disencumber
61 Not beat
63 Collapses
65 Drain
68 White-suited "Dukes of Hazzard" villain
69 Spartan
70 ___ Party
71 Some bio majors
73 Fails to
75 Court judgment
77 Barrett of gossip
78 "Phooey!"
80 ___ Moines
82 Mentions
86 Apple line
88 Experience you might want to forget
90 Guaranteed
92 Darwin stopping point, with "the"
94 Founder of the Missionaries of Charity
96 Epitome of cool, with "the"
97 Lead singer on "Octopus's Garden"
98 Singer Peniston
99 Einstein and Camus
100 Hint-giving columnist
102 Three, for a short hole
104 Postwar prime minister
106 Simpson case judge
107 11th-centruy hero, with "El"
109 Religious art figures
110 Country crooner Randy
115 Emergency Broadcast System opening
118 Kind of treatment
120 Still goopy, as concrete
121 Poet/dramatist Federico García ___
122 Pixar movie between "Toy Story" and "Toy Story 2"
123 Verse-writing
124 Jerks
125 Some screens, for short
126 Glacial

## DOWN

1 Goes down
2 Suffix with hard or soft
3 Girl's name that's also a place name
4 Semis
5 Unprepared
6 Hydrocarbon suffix
7 Basil sauce
8 One end of New York's Triborough Bridge
9 Cry of epiphany
10 Suggests
11 Director George
12 Bull or cow
13 Tear
14 Nike rival
15 Parenthesis shape
16 Butcher's tool
17 Layered dessert
18 Head of state?
20 He wrote "It is life near the bone where it is sweetest"
25 French waves
28 -
32 Kaley of "The Big Bang Theory"
34 Eccentric
36 -
37 Pantry lineup
38 Squad, e.g.
39 -
41 Author Zora ___ Hurston
43 Athlete's foot treatment
44 Where Charlie may ride forever, in song
46 Connecticut city
47 Carom
48 Words of explanation
49 Blue flick
50 Hollywood's Davis
52 Crow, e.g.
54 Byes
58 Thingamabobs
60 Cow's fly swatter
63 Dummy
65 Bad thing for a roommate to do
67 Sweater option
68 Rosemary piece
69 Rosemary feature
70 Like some codes
72 -
74 -
77 1990s craze
79 Related on the mother's side
81 Renowned jeweler
84 Sag
86 Rug fiber
88 Jeff Bridges sci-fi classic
89 Start of a count-off
90 "___ who?"
92 TV show on which Charlie Sheen replaced Michael J. Fox
94 Best-selling author who once worked for Britain's MI6
96 Markdown markers
98 Author Nin

by Victor Barocas

**100** New DNA evidence may lead to one
**103** It's been shortening for over 100 years
**105** -
**106** Ask for money
**107** Prefix with musicology
**108** -
**110** Imitation
**112** Year the emperor Claudius was born
**115** 1991 P.G.A. champion John
**117** -
**119** Is unwell
**120** Obscure
**121** Skinny
**122** Fuss
**124** French possessive
**125** "___ cool!"
**127** British dessert, for short

## ACROSS

1 Star of four Spike Lee films
8 Exercised on a track
14 Longtime Ed Asner role
18 Birds at a ballpark
19 1954 film septet
20 White: Fr.
21 Away, in a way
22 Gustav Holst septet
23 Barista's offering
24 Cable alternative
25 [typo not fixed]
26 Star of a 1981 Broadway revue subtitled "The Lady and Her Music"
27 Add one's views
29 Style
31 Second-in-command: Abbr.
32 41-Across athlete
34 How his-and-hers towels are sold
35 "Gossip well told," per Elbert Hubbard
37 Comebacks
39 Bud
40 Hydrocarbon ending
41 See 32-Across
42 Electrical unit, old-style
45 Webster's second?
47 Quick punch
50 Author Janowitz
52 Bud's place
53 Strike turf before the ball, in golf
54 Bye line?
56 Olympic venues
58 It may extend for many minutes
59 Thoughtful exercise
60 Overseas market
62 Tease
63 Unspecified degrees
65 Comic strip cries
67 Waltzed through
69 ___ de carne asada
70 Burj Khalifa locale
72 Joint
76 Fashion label ___-Picone
78 Prickly sticker
79 Letter with a limited amount of space
81 Savvy
82 Radar reading
84 Steel giant, formerly
85 Chug
87 End of an argument
88 Singer at Obama's 2009 inauguration
89 Baseball All-Star who was also a football Pro Bowler
90 Edamame source
92 Cross-state rival of CIN
93 Arizona's ___ Cienegas National Conservation Area
94 Hot prospects, say
97 Home base for many a mission
99 Like Victorian streets
102 Honorarium
103 Nirvana's "Come as You ___"
104 Paid to play
107 It has 135° angles
109 Proust title character
111 See 115-Across
112 Campers' letters
114 ___ by chocolate (popular dessert)
115 Certain 111-Across specification
117 Ghostly sound
119 First film Tarzan
120 White Russian, e.g.
121 1918's Battle of the ___ Forest
122 Formula One units
123 "The Terminator" co-star
124 Neighbor of Archie Bunker

## DOWN

1 "I ___ it!" (Skelton catchphrase)
2 Bond villain ___ Stavro Blofeld
3 Popular snack brand
4 Actress/screenwriter Kazan
5 Stretchiness
6 Assesses
7 "Be right there!"
8 Heap
9 Poet Khayyám
10 Artillery crewman
11 Founder of the New York Tribune
12 Have something
13 Tiddlywink, e.g.
14 Peruvian pack
15 Warren of "Bring Me the Head of Alfredo Garcia"
16 Free
17 Rapper who feuded with Ja Rule and Nas
19 Round figure
20 Second-tier, among celebs
28 Women's rooms?
30 Actress Belafonte
31 & 33 Skeptic's advice . . . or a "noteworthy" hint to seven Across answers in this puzzle
36 Colorful songbird
38 Brazilian greeting
39 Pop/rock group with a 2002 hit co-written with Mick Jagger
42 Story coloring?
43 1980s British band
44 Big deliveries?
45 Paganini or Rachmaninoff
46 "He makes no friend who never made ___": Tennyson
47 Schooner sail
48 Health org. since 1847
49 Dickens pen name
51 Raiding grp.
53 Polish the old-fashioned way
55 Air safety org.
57 ___-rock
61 Apotheosizes
64 Uncle ___
66 Wrap (up)
68 Hollow
71 Homemade bomb, for short
73 Website heading
74 Before, in verse
75 Sanguine
77 Recently
80 Met, as a challenge
83 "U.S.A." is part of one
86 Ended up?
91 Acronym for the hearing-impaired
92 Louis Armstrong instrument
94 "___ Republic"
95 Celebratory gesture
96 Alaska town that is mile 0 of the Iditarod Trail

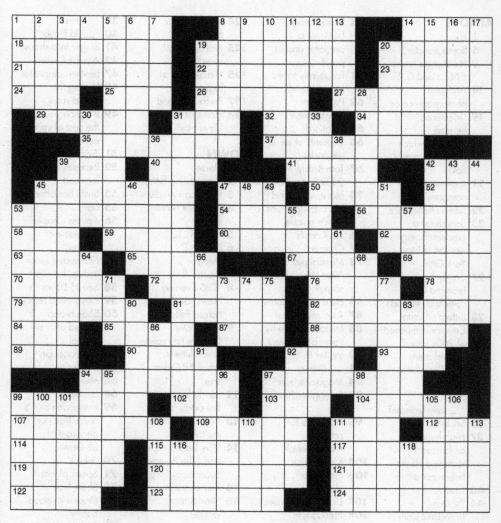

### by John Farmer

**97** Does a surfboard stunt

**98** 1913 Literature Nobelist from India

**99** Douglas Hofstadter's "___, Escher, Bach"

**100** Amtrak bullet train

**101** Sign of approval

**105** Scratching (out)

**106** "Meditation XVII" writer

**108** N.R.A. piece?: Abbr.

**110** Vegas casino with a musical name

**111** Newsweek, from Jan. '13 to Mar. '14

**113** "Terrible" toddler time

**116** Auden's "___ Walked Out One Evening"

**118** Often-partnered conjunction

## ACROSS

1 Fix
5 Some powder
9 Hurdles for future E.N.T.'s and G.P.'s
14 Antiqued photograph color
19 "Idomeneo" heroine
20 River into which the Great Miami flows
21 Japanese copier company
22 Some title holders
23 Search for a cradle-robbing woman in New York City?
27 Candy bar featured in a "Seinfeld" episode
28 Bittern's habitat
29 Country composed of 200+ islands
30 Start of many Brazilian place names
31 Salts
33 "___ any wonder?"
35 Sticky handle?
37 High-handed ambassador stationed off the Italian coast?
43 Cast
44 TV show broadcast from Times Square, for short
45 French/Belgian river
46 Turbaned type
47 Musician with the gold-selling album "Sugar Lips"
50 Billet-doux recipient
54 Four-time Best New Age Album Grammy winner
55 Peace treaty between a predator and its prey?
61 Frequently faked luxury brand
62 Palindromic constellation
63 Relation?
64 Contents of some six-packs
67 Tom Brady, in the 2002 Super Bowl?
74 More, in Madrid
75 ___ cube (popular 1960s puzzle)
76 ___ Canals
77 Charred
78 Musical piece for a "Star Wars" battle scene?
84 Here, in Honduras
87 As a result
88 Mistakes made by some bad drivers
89 Writer H. H. ___
91 ___-Honey
94 Magazine user?
95 Smuggler-chasing org.
98 Advocate for pro-am tournaments?
105 Kind of kick
106 Pixar title character
107 Like some excuses
108 Pseudonym preceder
110 Change
112 Short-winded
115 Turning point
116 Diminutive Aborigine?
121 Engage in excessive self-reflection?
122 Marathoner's woe
123 Sections of a natural history museum, maybe
124 Super Soaker brand
125 Not approach directly
126 Himalayans of legend
127 Prefix with god
128 Home of Wind Cave Natl. Park

## DOWN

1 Nurse
2 Stop getting better
3 Broadcast medium
4 City near Mount Rainier
5 "Mazel ___!"
6 [Pardon]
7 Director Wertmüller
8 "CBS Evening News" anchor before Pelley
9 1969 Peter O'Toole title role
10 Union letters
11 Small 58-Down size
12 Ready for a frat party, say
13 "Would you like me to?"
14 "The Dark Knight" and "The Bourne Supremacy," e.g.
15 Mer contents
16 Newspaper worker
17 "Casablanca" heroine
18 Concerning
24 Skater's jump
25 Time piece
26 X Games fixture
31 Acad., e.g.
32 Brief remark upon retiring
34 Milk-Bone, e.g.
36 Stroked, in a way
38 Arabic for "commander"
39 ___ avis
40 "___ la Douce"
41 Singer Winehouse
42 Actress Carrere
47 Lenovo competitor
48 Having the fewest rules
49 It'll grab you by the seat of your pants
51 Twice tetra-
52 Berkeley campus, for short
53 Sushi bar offering
55 Lip
56 Actress Chaplin of "Game of Thrones"
57 Nonkosher lunch orders, for short
58 See 11-Down
59 Playground retort
60 Shoe brand named after an animal
64 Taj Mahal city
65 Inclination
66 Mex. miss
68 ___ Bear
69 Hungarian man's name that's an anagram of 38-Down
70 "Nuts!"
71 Speak pigeon?
72 Short trips
73 Ones with good habits?
78 Seductive singer
79 Frozen dessert brand owned by Mrs. Fields
80 Rule
81 Book of Judges judge
82 Bring down the house?
83 Disdainful response
84 "Mad Men" channel

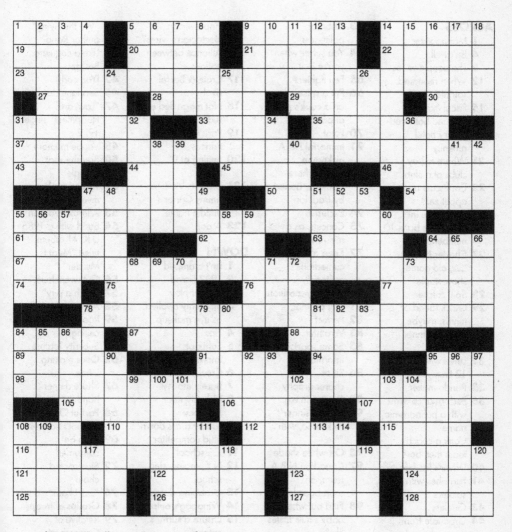

*by Pete Muller and Sue Keefer*

**85** Neighbor of Vt.
**86** Dumped (on)
**90** Very blue
**92** Accessories for hoofers
**93** Ancient Mexican
**95** Like role models
**96** Small mosaic tile
**97** Small ___
**99** Pussy ___ (Russian girl group)
**100** Opposite of brilliance
**101** Job security, for some
**102** Split
**103** Carrier to Ben Gurion
**104** Onetime White House family
**108** Some concert gear
**109** Diva ___ Te Kanawa
**111** H.R.'s, e.g.
**113** Withered
**114** Checkup, e.g.
**117** Shampoo, maybe
**118** Ascap rival
**119** Inflation indicator: Abbr.
**120** D.C.'s ___ Stadium

## ACROSS

1 Monopolizer
4 Isn't well
8 The people vs. us
12 When repeated, spirited
15 Fiscal exec
18 Hot and bothered
20 Luxury hotel amenity
21 Where to buy clubs at a club
23 Confiscate a chef's appetizer?
25 "Count me in!"
26 10, for the base 10 number system
27 Charles Nelson ___, old game show staple
28 Spill catcher
29 Quick round of tennis, maybe
31 Pulitzer winner James
32 Lewis with 12 Emmys
35 Rondo maker
36 Performance artist with a palindromic name
37 Conk a coach's team member?
40 Driver's lic. info
41 Furnishes with soldiers
43 Clueless
44 Graduate from Barnard, say
45 Old Roman well?
46 Disney dog
48 HVAC measures, for short
49 Certain radio user
51 Like most fish
53 View from Long Is.
55 Close a VW Beetle owner's car door?
60 Like much rush-hour traffic
61 Bud
63 Abbr. of politeness
64 You suffer when you're in it
65 Feu fighter?
66 Put a spice mix on a cook's piece of poultry?
70 Point
71 Immortal P.G.A. nickname
73 Island where Homer is buried, by tradition
74 Exclusive
75 Cancels, as a mission
77 Keep a bad comedian onstage?
80 Poetic preposition
81 Not prompt
82 Perfect
83 Wrathful
85 Some sports cars, informally
86 Bit of choreography
88 The "g" in e.g.
91 "Baby" singer's nickname, with "the"
93 Off-white shade
97 Canadian N.B.A. team, on scoreboards
98 Find out what a baby's milk tastes like?
101 "True Blood" network
102 ___ store
103 Apples introduced in 1998
104 Asian holidays
105 Full
107 Magician David
109 Latin dance
111 Valleys
112 Observation of cardinals, say
114 Hop over an electrician's wires?
116 Alliance between nations
117 Crate & Barrel rival
118 Not magnified or reduced
119 Paris's Parc ___ Princes
120 Setting at 0° long.
121 U.S.A.F. V.I.P.
122 Jimmy Carter's middle name
123 A pop

## DOWN

1 Isn't cramped
2 1992 David Mamet play
3 Smoothly applied, as eye makeup
4 Tips
5 Suffix of imprecision
6 Creepy look
7 Barely moves?
8 Irish city near Killarney
9 Loudly dress down
10 uBid competitor
11 ___ school
12 N.Y. engineering school
13 Grabbing distance
14 Windbag's output
15 Ensure a surfer's safety?
16 Like many accents
17 Run
19 Commando movie accessories
22 ___ mai (dim sum dish)
24 Rifle attachment
30 "See?!"
32 Group of unsolicited manuscripts
33 ___ radio
34 "We the Living" author Rand
38 Like a coquette
39 Besides
42 [You cad!]
45 Sea lane danger
47 "Love and Happiness" singer, 1972
48 Vague memory
50 Squishy seat
51 Goggle
52 Take a mechanic's inventory?
53 Allergic reaction
54 Band with a 1985 U.K. #1 album titled "Meat Is Murder"
56 Gut wrencher?
57 "Such a pity"
58 Agreement
59 Rooms with high ceilings
60 Security feature
62 Ones making intros
67 Shore dinner handout
68 Part of Obi-Wan Kenobi's costume
69 Fit to be consumed
72 Blue-roofed chain
76 "___ I hear"
78 Groups of troops
79 Relative of Camembert
84 One side in "The War of the Worlds"
85 Shade of black
86 Like Julius Caesar
87 Where to write your name on an I.R.S. form
89 Zenith competitor
90 Org. that registers pointers

by Joe DiPietro

**91** Muff
**92** "Just arrived!"
**94** N.B.A. Hall-of-Famer nicknamed Handy Andy
**95** Something easy as pie
**96** "Luck Be a Lady" composer/lyricist

**98** Jacket part
**99** "C'mon, help me out"
**100** Ultimate purpose
**106** They make indents
**108** Suffix with fluor- or chlor-

**109** Pickled veggie
**110** Discipline
**113** High-profile interviewee
**114** Fiddler's tune, maybe
**115** Sleeper, for one

Note: In this crossword, the completed solution conceals a familiar three-word phrase related to the puzzle's theme. 70-Across provides a hint on how to find it.

## ACROSS

1 Crew's colleagues
5 Dojo needs
9 Classic sci-fi film billed as "a horror horde of crawl-and-crush giants"
13 "La-La" lead-in in a 1974 Al Green hit
16 Iberian wine city
18 "Vincent & __" (film about the van Gogh brothers)
19 Rings of angels
21 What X-O-X lacks?
22 "Macbeth" king
23 Words on a fragile package
26 Irascible
27 "Mona Lisa," e.g.
28 Thumbs-up
29 Harridan
30 Orchestra section
31 Mouthpiece for the head?
34 Jiffy
35 Not post-
37 Old piece
38 Little dog, for short
39 __ Aviv
40 Strawberry blond sister of Barbie
43 Hindu "Mr."
44 "Swans Reflecting Elephants" and others
46 1960s–'70s series starring Efrem Zimbalist Jr.
49 Oscar winner Hathaway
51 Material beyond the terrestrial plane, in medieval science
55 Hello or goodbye, maybe
57 PC key
59 First word in 104-Across
61 Cum __

62 __ engr.
63 Like hit shows, often
67 Pitchfork-wielding groups
69 Boo-boo
70 How to get a message out of the boxes
74 Van Morrison song "__ the Mystic"
75 Numerical prefix
76 "Only the Lonely" singer
77 Part of a wriggly field?
78 Foreordained
80 Understands
82 Maker of the Sorento
83 Gallivants, with "about"
85 Boo-boos
87 Pale
89 Like citrus fruits
92 Like video games, nowadays
94 __ Lingus
96 Round Table assignments
99 Old PC monitor feature
102 Ernie's instrument on "Sesame Street," informally
103 Italy's main broadcasting co.
104 TV channel with lots of bells and whistles
105 Take up, as a skirt
107 Rotary alternative
112 Covent Garden performance
114 Newspaper columnist, humorously
115 Grampa Simpson
116 Snockered
117 Anders Celsius and Greta Garbo, for two
118 DDT and others

121 "Is Anybody Goin' to San __" (#1 Charley Pride song)
122 Bullet, in poker
123 Cartoonist Wilson
124 Help illicitly
125 Alley flanker
126 Hide/hair link
127 Looking up
128 Chant at a bullfight
129 Satirical 1974 espionage film

## DOWN

1 With 97-Down, classic puzzle type
2 Like eyebrows
3 Ones getting the red-carpet treatment, say
4 "The Spiderwick Chronicles" co-author DiTerlizzi
5 Antarctic summit between peaks named for faith and charity
6 Words after "win by" or "hang by"
7 What lobsters and crabs have
8 Nursery purchase
9 Baltimore club, for short
10 Ethan of "Before Sunrise"
11 Giant Manning
12 Company that pioneered walkie-talkies
13 "__ Mater" (hymn)
14 African capital
15 Organic chemistry group
16 Lilac and lavender
17 Turns into mush
20 Oaf
24 Not ephemeral
25 All ChiSox home games are played on it

32 __ Lee
33 Pro with books, for short
35 Slapstick prop
36 Play watcher
41 Motocross entry, for short
42 Pirate's cargo
44 Frenzied as if possessed
45 East German secret police
47 Where a mattress goes
48 Shapes like squares
50 Country that has two oryxes on its coat of arms
52 Like much processed wheat
53 Roman magistrates
54 Push off
55 Food item named after an Austrian city
56 Film set on Pandora
58 Snarly dog
60 Recedes
62 Blackmail, e.g.
64 "Well, now!"
65 Beat
66 Uncle Pedro, e.g.
68 Sign of a successful show
71 One with a name on a plaque, maybe
72 Nickname for baseball's Dwight Gooden
73 Rolling Stones #1 hit with the lyric "You're beautiful, but ain't it time we said goodbye?"
79 Hefty thing
81 Wrinkly dog
84 Ones providing cold comfort, briefly
86 Big wheel's wheels
88 "You betcha"
90 Dim bulbs have low ones

by Mike Selinker

**91** Horse hue
**93** Prefix with skeleton
**95** 1970 John Wayne western
**97** See 1-Down
**98** Placid
**99** Self-image?
**100** Like the Palace of Versailles
**101** English landscapist famous for "The Burning of the Houses of Lords and Commons"
**104** Irritates
**106** Electromagnetic device
**108** Op. ___ (footnote phrase)
**109** Some West Coast wines
**110** Magazine to which Obama gave his first postelection interview in 2008
**111** N.F.C. West player
**112** Admit
**113** Trifling
**117** Wilts
**119** "___ my destiny be Fustian" (Dickinson poem)
**120** Was idle

## ACROSS

1 Boxes up
8 Hidden
14 Astronomer Halley
20 Sheer, informally
21 Individually
22 Not get gratis
23 Clan garb
24 A "Star Trek" officer and a physician are going to board a plane?
26 Attack, as ramparts
27 Cracker topper
29 German Dadaist Hannah
30 Makes stronger?
31 Kind of court
34 Without ___ in the world
36 Atlantic fishery auditors?
39 "Galatea of the Spheres" and others
41 Comcast media holding
44 Ones giving their addresses
45 Hedge shrub
47 Dog command
48 Non-Eur. U.S. ally
49 Baseball features
53 French article
54 To boot
56 Minute
59 Work agreeably in a greenhouse?
62 It's opposite julio on a calendario
63 "No challenge at all"
64 "Dat ___" (classic jazz song)
65 Called the shots
67 Dead-doornail connection
68 Delicate first-date topic
72 Moon feature
73 Aristocratic practice
75 Bacteriologist Julius
76 "Happy Birthday" on a cake, e.g.?
80 Naysayer
81 Reproductive parts of flowers
82 Folk rocker DiFranco
83 Ball game
85 Québec place name starter
86 Buster Brown's dog, in old comics
87 Verizon competitor
90 Positions oneself to hear better, say
93 Wood-shaping tool
94 Reagan attorney general
95 Sexy operators?
99 Cell part
101 Femmes fatales
102 Bank heist, e.g.
104 Lion portrayer
107 Word with sea or seasoned
108 Bar, legally
112 Where frogs shop?
115 Religious recluse
117 Consternation
118 O.K. to serve
119 Medication for a narcoleptic
120 Cabernet Sauvignon alternative
121 Ran out
122 Immediately

## DOWN

1 They're probably close: Abbr.
2 Undiluted
3 Large sport fish
4 Draw
5 Hotel amenity
6 Directional suffix
7 Hitchcock genre
8 Common aquarium feature
9 Show up
10 Grp. in a 1955 merger
11 "Wag the Dog" actress
12 Fashion designer Marc
13 Family tree listing: Abbr.
14 Prefix with dermis
15 Longtime home of the Cotton Bowl
16 Reflective material
17 Unbalanced
18 Florida State player, casually
19 Prohibitionists
25 Oil source
28 Model Carol
32 Clutch, e.g.
33 Recipe amt.
35 Stronghold
36 Tortile
37 Italian princely family name
38 Sand ___ (perchlike fish)
39 Drab-looking
40 Bygone Chevrolet
42 Salve
43 Engine specification: Abbr.
46 Drinks now, pays later
47 Make more enticing
50 Footless creature
51 Barnyard sound
52 Enters furtively
55 Chevron
57 Exhibit fear, in a way
58 Quarter
60 Green spot
61 1960–'70s pitcher Blue Moon
63 Ticked (off)
66 Locked?
68 One 60-trillionth of a min.
69 "True"
70 Dimwit
71 Charmers
73 Start of a choosing rhyme
74 "Can ___ now?"
76 "___ light?"
77 "Metamorphoses" poet
78 Sight at many a barbecue
79 Setting of the 2012 film "John Carter"
80 Combine name
84 Hoarders' problems
88 Rinds
89 Fourth Arabic letter
91 Go along with
92 "WKRP in Cincinnati" news director Les ___
94 To a greater extent
96 Reduced
97 Got emotional, with "up"
98 Baseball's Bando
100 Mountainous land
101 Postal symbol, once
102 Bud
103 Super-duper
105 Uncle of Enoch
106 "I ___ thought"
109 Part of a space shuttle's exterior
110 ___ & Carla (1960s duo)
111 Cooped (up)
113 No longer playing: Abbr.
114 They may improve in crunch time
116 Birthplace of the bossa nova

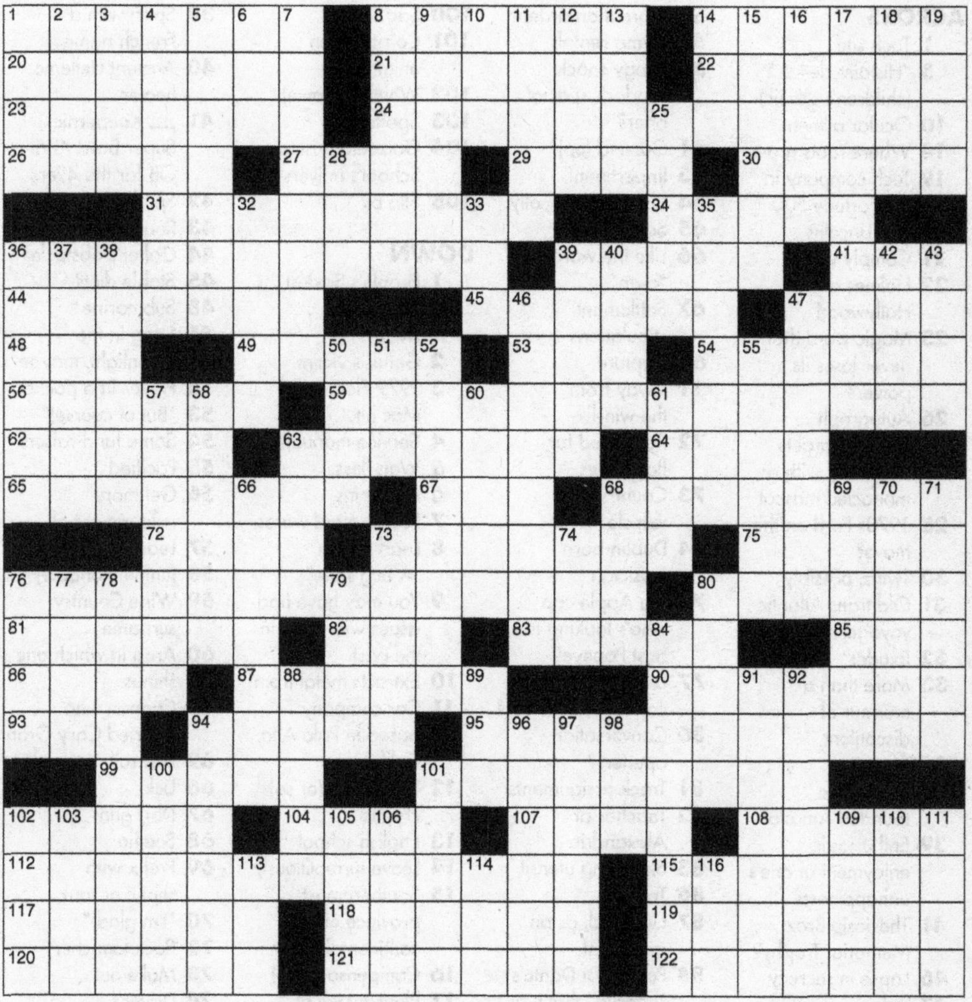

*by Norm Guggenbiller*

## ACROSS

**1** Tach site
**5** "Histoire de ___" (children's classic)
**10** Ocular ailment
**14** Where roots grow
**19** Tech company in the Fortune 500
**20** Like Lincolns
**21** Comply with
**22** Holmes of Hollywood
**23** Magic word that never loses its power?
**26** Autograph seekers' targets
**27** Company with a monocled mascot
**28** 1970s Ford on the move?
**30** Twins, possibly
**31** Old trans-Atlantic voyager
**32** Exudes
**33** More than a murmur of discontent
**36** Ruptures
**37** Bezos who founded Amazon
**39** Enthusiastic enjoyment of one's unhappiness?
**41** The Josip Broz Memorial Trophy?
**46** Lapse in secrecy
**47** Balance sheet nos.
**48** Stumper
**49** Hindustan capital of old
**50** Common ingredient in Nigerian cuisine
**51** Bag End resident
**53** "North Dallas Forty" star
**54** Tenderloin cut
**55** Hands-free microphone's place

**56** More than ardent
**57** Camp rentals
**58** Stingy snack vendor's special offer?
**61** Gussied (up)
**63** Impertinent
**64** Rises dramatically
**65** Say uncle
**66** Like the word "cwm"
**67** Settlement stipulations
**68** Capture
**71** Away from the wind
**72** Rock used for flagstones
**73** Country club vehicle
**74** Dublin-born musician
**75** Big Apple cop who's looking to bust Popeye?
**77** Learn all about the capital of Ecuador?
**80** Conversation openers?
**81** Track assignments
**82** Teacher at Alexandria
**83** Skimming utensil
**86** Tootle
**87** Unsound, as an argument
**88** Portion of Dante's "Inferno" that was wisely excised?
**91** Photo processing centers
**95** To date
**96** Christmas decoration that automatically steers toward lovers?
**98** "Here lies One ___ Name was writ in Water" (words on Keats's tombstone)
**99** Tiny pasta

**100** Sad sack
**101** Constellation animal
**102** Whittled (down)
**103** Spotted
**104** Goizueta Business School's university
**105** Slip by

## DOWN

**1** People's Sexiest Man Alive . . . twice
**2** Genesis victim
**3** 1979 Fleetwood Mac hit
**4** Service manual?
**5** Waterless
**6** Maintains
**7** Rubbermaid wares
**8** Lead bug in "A Bug's Life"
**9** You may have had issues with them in the past
**10** Extracts metal from
**11** Car company based in Palo Alto, Calif.
**12** Seven-foot (or so) cryptid
**13** English school
**14** Leave surreptitiously
**15** Southernmost province of continental Spain
**16** Compensate (for)
**17** Pleasant vocal qualities
**18** Spanish "weight"
**24** Elite squad
**25** Sonata segment
**29** Take a stab at
**31** Genoese delicacy
**33** Frightful
**34** Defendant's declaration
**35** Incur cellphone charges, maybe
**36** Model A features
**37** Fitting punishment

**38** Sport with a French name
**40** Ancient Hellenic healer
**41** ___ Kaepernick, Super Bowl XLVII QB for the 49ers
**42** Spoils
**43** Round house
**44** Golfer's obstacle
**45** Stable diet?
**48** Submarine
**51** Sang in the moonlight, maybe
**52** Player in a pocket
**53** "But of course!"
**54** Some fund-raisers
**55** Pacified
**56** Get more mileage out of
**57** Learn fast, say
**58** [unmentionable]
**59** Wine Country surname
**60** Area in which one shines
**61** Cannon who married Cary Grant
**62** Like sulfuric acid
**66** Lick
**67** Dart gun
**68** Seethe
**69** Prefix with septic or tank
**70** "I'm glad!"
**72** Rock launcher
**73** Make out
**74** Driver's recommendation
**76** Overlarge
**77** Paint option
**78** Orbital decay result
**79** Small game
**81** Three-time Olympics host
**83** One of the Obamas
**84** Seinfeld called him "the Picasso of our profession"

*by Patrick Berry*

**85** Overlarge
**86** Mesoamerican crop
**87** Tempered by experience
**88** Stare stupidly
**89** Impediments to teamwork

**90** Medical breakthrough
**91** ___ soup
**92** Sensor forerunner
**93** Give orders to
**94** Poseidon ruled them
**97** Pop lover

## ACROSS

1 Treats, as a bow
7 Org. for lab safety?
12 Inits. for cinephiles
15 QB datum
18 G. P. ___ (early book publisher)
19 Layered
20 Refined resource
21 Name-dropper's word?
22 Movie franchise since 1996
25 Crosswords, e.g., in the 1920s
26 Like bourbon barrels
27 Grp. with a staff of Aesculapius
28 Metaphor for obsolescence
30 Setting for "Mork & Mindy"
35 Kind of raid
36 Playing
37 Rideshare rides
38 Whistle-blowers?
40 One of three stars in the Summer Triangle
42 One of a race in Middle-earth
43 Painter's deg.
45 Caroline du Sud, e.g.
46 Publisher's entreaty
48 Some wraps
50 Sonata starters
53 Plant whose seed is sold as a health food product
55 Twin of Jacob
56 Actress Sorvino
57 Cat's resting place, maybe
58 "Gilligan's Island" castaway
61 When doubled, a sad sound effect
62 No longer exists
63 "Be My Yoko ___" (Barenaked Ladies single)
64 When doubled, a hit song of 1965 and 1989
65 Porter
67 '50s duds
69 Carry or iron follower
70 Bupkis
71 Overcast
72 AARP concern
73 Pub offering
75 NATO member?: Abbr.
76 Pub offerings
77 Not even close
78 Eponym of a Southern "-ville"
79 Sport using xisteras
81 Word with solar or sound
83 Bide one's time
86 Beverages in bowls
87 Apple variety
88 Jaw
90 Doozy
92 Went off?
95 Isle where Macbeth is buried
96 Film bit
97 Score abbr.
98 Violation of the first and second laws of thermodynamics
103 Achieve
105 Just what the doc ordered?
106 Go cold turkey
107 That, in Tabasco
108 Underdog's saying
114 Personal digits: Abbr.
115 ___ the Eagle (a Muppet)
116 Date for New Year's Day
117 Barely get
118 Kicker's prop
119 Draft org.
120 Paintball mementos
121 Animal with a star on the Hollywood Walk of Fame

## DOWN

1 Tach readout
2 "Bien sûr!"
3 Some map lines: Abbr.
4 Feared red state
5 Nymph of Greek myth
6 Fire sign
7 Intention
8 Floral components
9 Teaser
10 ___ Millan a k a the Dog Whisperer
11 Some teasers
12 Additionally
13 In the 70s, say
14 Shakespeare heroine
15 Computer programming problem
16 In the vicinity of
17 Singer Pendergrass and others
19 Jalopies
23 Daredevil's asset
24 ". . . and ___ it again!"
29 Sharon's predecessor
30 Beachgoer's pride, informally
31 Doozy
32 ___ Independent Press Awards
33 In transit
34 [sigh]
39 Cold-blooded
41 Joy of TV
43 [air kiss]
44 Something you might get shot for?
47 Red or white vessel
49 "It can't wait!"
50 Place where many screens may be set
51 "___ Voices" (best-selling New Age album)
52 Imagine, informally
54 Peace Nobelist Sakharov
56 Much mail to mags
58 Rapper Nicki
59 Helen Keller brought the first one to the U.S.
60 First publisher of Hunter S. Thompson's "Fear and Loathing in Las Vegas"
62 It's a challenge
66 ___ in cat
67 Proof-ending word
68 Hindu title of respect
72 Hypothetical words
74 Little confabs
76 Red Scare target
77 Philosopher Rand
80 Main line
81 ___ City (Baghdad area)
82 Hand holder
84 "Eat, Pray, Love" locale
85 "Worst car of the millennium," per "Car Talk"
87 "___ hand?"
89 Onetime Krypton resident
91 Lick
92 Brief
93 Actually
94 Fits
95 Sweater's line?
99 Trim
100 Discharge
101 Normand of the silents

*by Jeff Chen*

**102** Stomping grounds for Godzilla
**104** H H H H
**109** "It can't wait!"
**110** Prevailing party
**111** Talking-___
**112** French pronoun
**113** Tours summer

## ACROSS

**1** In tandem
**8** Decorative shoe features
**15** Like some feet and envelopes
**22** Bill
**23** It's often swiped by a shopaholic
**24** Go from A to B?
**25** Nickname for the 122-/124-Across
**28** Stops: Abbr.
**29** Jazz/blues singer Cassidy
**30** Shoelace tip
**31** Barely make, with "out"
**32** "___ two minds"
**33** ___ Bell (Anne Brontë pseudonym)
**35** Like eggs in eggnog
**37** Class for some immigrants, for short
**39** Jump back, maybe
**40** With 105-Across, historical significance of the 122-/124-Across
**48** It's ENE of Fiji
**49** "Wheel of Fortune" buy
**50** Declined
**51** It fits all, sometimes
**55** Up on things
**58** Part of a page of Google results
**63** 1796 Napoleon battle site
**64** Freight carrier: Abbr.
**66** Young and Sedaka
**67** Italian possessive
**68** Von Furstenberg of fashion
**69** "___ luck!"
**71** European capital once behind the Iron Curtain
**73** Comic finisher

**75** Ocean
**76** Item dropped by Wile E. Coyote
**77** Times Square flasher?
**78** "So nice!"
**79** Masked warrior
**80** Beer belly
**83** Chemistry suffix
**84** Ultimate
**85** Day ___
**87** They really click
**92** It may be corrected with magnification
**98** Piece at the Met
**99** El Al destination: Abbr.
**100** German cry
**103** Inherit
**104** Italian writer Vittorini
**105** 122-Across
**112** Like most houses
**113** Expensive patio material
**114** Comment before "Bitte schön"
**115** Components of fatty tissues
**118** Bit of jive
**119** French wine classification
**120** It may leave you weak in the knees
**122 & 124** Dedicated in October 1913, project represented by the 13 pairs of circled letters
**126** Captain
**130** ___-turn
**131** "Alley ___"
**132** Sports org. headquartered in Indianapolis
**136** Wearing clothes fit for a queen?
**138** Concerned

**146** Kindle downloads
**148** Follows the east-west route of the 122-/124-Across?
**151** Doll
**152** Tropicana grove
**153** Knight's trait
**154** Follows
**155** Sauce brand
**156** ___ of time
**157** Kind of question

## DOWN

**1** Targets
**2** Weightlifting move
**3** Hedgehop, e.g.
**4** Many, many
**5** Sue Grafton's "___ for Evidence"
**6** "Tartuffe" segment
**7** TV's Griffin
**8** ___ kwon do
**9** Tulip festival city
**10** Web periodical
**11** Cicero's 350
**12** Rhine tributary
**13** For now, for short
**14** Campus political grp.
**15** Mt. Rushmore's home: Abbr.
**16** Heavy volume
**17** Bowl over
**18** Sony co-founder Akio
**19** Elementary
**20** Kind of service
**21** Intentionally disregarding
**26** Keep one's ___ the ground
**27** Historic march site
**34** Vivaldi's "___ Dominus"
**36** Latin 101 verb
**38** In stitches
**39** Caesar and others
**41** Motorola phone
**42** Eurasian ducks
**43** Funny Garofalo

**44** "You're the ___ Love"
**45** Figure on the Scottish coat of arms
**46** Radio booth sign
**47** Make over
**51** Pueblo pot
**52** Whistle time?
**53** 1999 Ron Howard film
**54** "Of course, Jorge!"
**56** Group in a striking photo?
**57** "This ___ a test"
**59** Prefix with -scope
**60** Not fer
**61** Or or nor: Abbr.
**62** "May It Be" singer, 2001
**65** Over there
**67** "So-so"
**70** Sea grass, e.g.
**72** Charges
**74** 1980s–'90s German leader Helmut
**75** ___ B'rith
**81** Bell Labs system
**82** Try
**85** Popeye's ___' Pea
**86** Sarge's charges: Abbr.
**87** Phoebe of "Gremlins"
**88** Buddhist who has attained nirvana
**89** What's a strain to cook with?
**90** Stun with a gun
**91** Very, in Vichy
**93** Gruesome sort
**94** Body type
**95** Actress Graff
**96** Sounds from pens
**97** Jottings
**100** When some local news comes on
**101** Revolutionary figure
**102** China cupboard
**106** Sacred cow
**107** London greeting

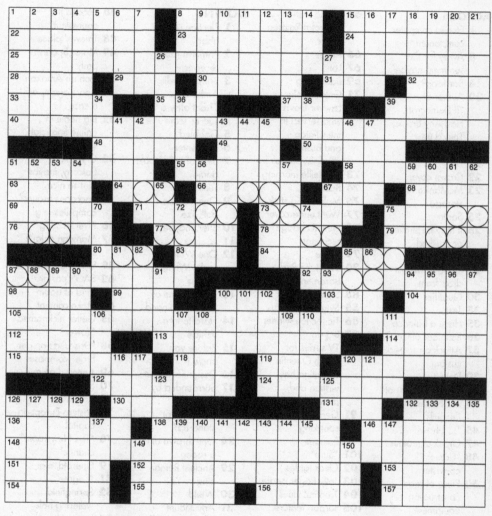

by Elizabeth C. Gorski

## ACROSS

1 Etched computer component
8 Away for the summer, maybe
14 Bar food?
20 Author of "If Democrats Had Any Brains, They'd Be Republicans"
21 Fix
22 Crown cover
23 McMansion's storage
25 Santa ___
26 It may be stroked or crushed
27 Difficulties
28 Remove the last drop from
30 Qualifier
33 Test ___
35 Have a balance
36 Religious office
37 Attack on sacred custom
39 Dotty?
43 Brief letter sign-off
44 ___ Nashville Records
45 "___-haw!"
47 Greek characters
48 "Camelot" co-writer
50 Piece of road construction equipment
56 Grassy expanse
58 Exams with analytical reasoning parts: Abbr.
60 Grp. with the platinum album "Out of the Blue"
61 Graf ___
62 Look for
63 Marshmallowy treat

64 Vodka with a Chocolat Razberi flavor
66 Keeps
67 Lot
69 Badgering
71 Great leveler
72 Lawyer Davis who served in the Clinton and Bush administrations
73 Marseille morning
74 Buenos ___
75 Make a big stink
77 Went undercover
78 New ID badge recipient
79 Gaffe
80 What the Red Baron engaged in
83 Sly one
85 Symbol of Horus
86 Tic-tac-toe winner
87 Big do
88 TV series for which Quentin Tarantino has written and directed
91 Generally speaking
96 Famous
101 "Sure"
102 Clear tables
103 Jolly Roger pirate
104 Tropical vines
105 Jordan feature
109 Barn seat
111 ___ Tour
112 "Hot" dish
113 They may keep you on your toes
120 Pass
121 "You betcha!"
122 Four-star figure
123 Dishwasher, at times
124 February forecasts
125 Comes in behind

## DOWN

1 Election results abbr.
2 Primitive radio receiver
3 British novelist Anthony
4 Chant after a soccer score
5 Gobbled
6 ___ center
7 Start of a Scrabble game
8 Tees off
9 One may be doll-size
10 Biter, maybe
11 ___ loss
12 One White of rock's White Stripes
13 Like the time of Franz Ferdinand
14 Hard-to-turn vehicle
15 Before you know it
16 Designer Helmut
17 Surrounded by
18 Order
19 Stood out at stand-up?
24 One thrown at a rodeo
29 Ancient Roman king
30 Wield
31 Any Mount Olympus dweller
32 Like some rioters
34 Provider of a trip across a desert?
35 Well-financed grp.?
38 Boxer's target
40 Rhapsodizes over
41 Be flat
42 Sources of some lethal injections

46 Second lt.'s equivalent
48 Thieves' place
49 Major Spanish daily
50 Icon on Amazon
51 Hears again, as a case
52 Big name in online financial services
53 Cry from a balcony, maybe
54 Not so nice
55 Raccoons around campsites, e.g.
56 River of song
57 Many an actor's second job
59 Vaio manufacturer
62 SAG's partner
63 Kind of boom
64 Make content
65 Golfer nicknamed "Tower"
68 "Das Lied von der Erde" composer
69 Antlered animal
70 Stole material
73 Cat calls
76 Eastern European capital
78 "The Newsroom" channel
79 Emerald, e.g.
81 "I agree"
82 Springfield watering hole
84 Lamar Hunt Trophy org.
88 Some 99-Down
89 Curse
90 Connections
91 Bar food?
92 Indian neighbor
93 One way to dress in drag
94 Court inits.
95 Cajun dishes
97 "Whew, that wore me out!"

by Brendan Emmett Quigley

98 Video game losses
99 88-Down, e.g.
100 Brit's diaper
106 Pen parts
107 Different
108 Raspberry
110 Carrier that owns the airline Sun d'Or

114 Rink org.
115 Cleaning solution
116 Daniels who directed "The Butler"
117 Words said before a kiss
118 Afts and eves
119 ___-mo

# STOLEN PRODUCE

## ACROSS

1 Winner of the 2005 and 2007 Grammys for Best Spoken Word Album
6 Relief for the snowbound
10 Seal words
15 Put one's hands together
19 Setting for Henry James's "The American"
20 Actress Chaplin of "Game of Thrones"
21 Company whose logo was, appropriately, crooked
22 Burrow, perhaps
23 Many service dogs, after 29-Across?
25 Roi's wife
26 ___ Stanley Gardner
27 French colony until 1953
28 The Warrior Princess
29 They get stuffed at Greek restaurants
31 Rapper with the 2013 #1 album "Born Sinner"
33 Sees red
34 Eighty-sixes
35 Foil user's words
38 Foreshadows
39 A/C measures
40 Serious break, after 48-Across?
42 Author John Dickson ___
43 Mao ___-tung
46 Harvests
47 "I don't know why ___ this way"
48 Schedule planners

50 Years, for Cicero
51 On the q.t.
53 Sail extender
54 She, overseas
56 Greek goddess of witchcraft
59 Salinger title girl
60 Legendary Scottish swimmer, after 66-Across?
66 Tart treats
68 Potter's base
69 Painted crudely
71 Gulf of ___
72 Marx without much to say
74 Cruiser repair site
77 List component
81 Circus founders, after 89-Across?
84 "The Lion King" lioness
85 Overflowed
87 Swelled head?
88 Ice cream brand
89 Ice cream treats
91 Shield border
92 Mastodon features
93 Clobber
94 Jet Ski competitor
97 Forces from office
98 Begins to wake
99 Where Margaret Thatcher studied chemistry, after 108-Across?
101 Winglike
102 "The King and I" role
106 Ulrich of Metallica
107 Obliterate
108 Short-lived pests . . . or an alternative title for this puzzle
110 Prefix with -genarian
111 Money holders
112 Guam, e.g.: Abbr.
113 Only inanimate zodiac sign

114 Lee of Marvel Comics
115 Beginning
116 Northeast vacation locale, with "the"
117 "The Lion's Share" author

## DOWN

1 Car with a lightning bolt in its logo
2 The Tide
3 River of Pisa
4 Tokyo beauty, maybe
5 Smokestack emission
6 Poe poem
7 Tony winner Lena
8 All that ___ bag of chips
9 Second word of "A Tale of Two Cities"
10 "The more the ___"
11 N.B.A.'s Shaquille and Jermaine
12 Psychedelic experiences
13 Shape (up)
14 Glenfiddich bottle size
15 Wipes off, say
16 Caterpillar, for one
17 Dancer Alvin
18 Iron
24 Book in which Moses is born
29 Split the check
30 They're way out
32 Buds
33 Ball game
35 Med. test
36 Saints' home, for short
37 Feds
38 Frederick's of Hollywood purchases
39 Flutter, as one's eyes

41 Adjusts carefully
42 Twin-hulled vessel
43 Many a broken statue
44 Tighten one's belt
45 Politico Kefauver
48 Hockey fake
49 Phone button
51 "Here's looking at you, kid" addressee
52 Mother, e.g.: Abbr.
55 Psychedelic drug
57 Mary Lincoln, née ___
58 Jackson-to-Birmingham dir.
60 Earthy pigment
61 Santa ___
62 Damages
63 "Law & Order: SVU" force
64 Many a collector's resource
65 Preacher, for short
67 Fourth-longest river of Europe
70 Powerful line
73 Puck's master
75 "Over There" soldiers
76 Word of woe
78 Does what George Washington couldn't?
79 Oscar winner Jannings
80 Lead-in for physics . . . and pieman?
82 Enthusiastic reply
83 Grease dissolver
85 Casual top
86 Medal awarded to MacArthur in W.W. I and W.W. II
89 Superlative for Atlanta International Airport

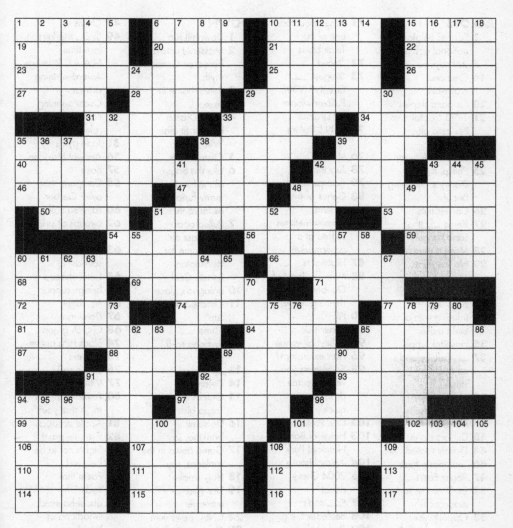

by Andy Kravis and Victor Barocas

**90** "Holiday Inn" co-star
**91** Favored against the field
**92** Scrap
**94** Performs unaccompanied
**95** Perfect
**96** Vessel with an arch
**97** Some exams
**98** Drink loudly
**100** Andrews of Fox Sports
**101** Vicinity
**103** Penpoints
**104** Great-grandson of Mark Antony
**105** Quickly, quickly
**108** Org. "protecting America's consumers"
**109** Marco Rubio's home: Abbr.

## ACROSS

1 Former Belgian national airline
7 Just says no
14 Cremona craftwork
20 Origami staples
21 1993 5× platinum Nirvana album
22 Wise guy
23 *The Lone Ranger*
25 Phillip, e.g., in Disney's "Sleeping Beauty"
26 Carrier inits.
27 Kemo ___ (the Lone Ranger)
28 Move a muscle?
29 No longer in enemy hands
30 Kind of appeal
32 Base, e.g.
34 Infusing with a soda maker
35 Hospital supply
37 ___ Fáil, Ireland's coronation stone
38 Strike callers
39 Massachusetts motto starter
40 Dietary claim
44 Deeply rooted
46 Toothpaste type
47 *Roger Ebert*
52 84-Down writer's monogram
53 Opportunities, metaphorically
54 Hands (out)
55 Trig ratio
59 Old camera settings, for short
61 Add (up)
62 François Truffaut's field
63 Sweet-talk
64 *Porky Pig*
69 Fixes up, as a run-down house
70 Cato's man
71 When doubled, one of the Teletubbies
72 "Now!"
73 "August: ___ County" (2008 Pulitzer winner for Drama)
74 "S.N.L." alum Cheri
76 Mimicry
78 July third?
79 *George Burns*
83 Genus of small rodents
86 Items sometimes sniffed at a supermarket
87 Highlights
88 Mille ___ (part of Québec with a rhyming name)
90 Fill
91 Other side
92 Volleyball venue
96 Hair extensions?
98 Something you want to come down from quickly
102 Dry: Prefix
103 Home of Banff National Park
104 Animal house
105 2004 Chevy debut
107 "___ can't"
108 Beefeaters, e.g.
109 *Red Skelton*
112 Record of the Year Grammy nominee for "Lose Yourself"
113 Primary pigment for printers
114 Rays' div.
115 Luna's counterpart
116 Auto steering system components
117 Potential sweethearts

## DOWN

1 Downhill run
2 Massenet opera based on Greek myth
3 Bears' home in Texas
4 2005 Drama Pulitzer finalist Will
5 Costner role
6 Like the origin of the food in many fusion restaurants
7 Pulled apart
8 Compass dir.
9 Nickname for Huntington Beach, Calif.
10 Bologna's place
11 Clinched, with "up"
12 "Time ___" (bygone sci-fi series)
13 ___-based
14 Defames
15 One of the von Trapp girls
16 Do some banking, say
17 Going down in the rankings, say
18 Holy smoke
19 First Mets manager
24 CNBC news item
29 Mag proofs
31 Shallot, e.g.
33 Keyes and King
34 Mosey along
36 "Beowulf" quaff
38 Jesse and Leo of TV sitcoms
41 Poky sorts
42 Order to go?
43 Onward
44 Sees through
45 Latte option
47 Ópera venue
48 Chops up
49 S. ___ Merkerson, four-time N.A.A.C.P. Image Award-winning actress
50 Oscar-winning Forest Whitaker role
51 Judo gyms
56 Ancient Mexican
57 Base
58 Company that owns Gerber
60 Layered coifs
62 Groups of strings, maybe
63 Sword fight sounds
65 Letter-shaped bridge support
66 Mr. Right
67 Dominant
68 Church group
74 Black Hills native
75 Sweetie
76 Lace's end
77 Vittles
80 Possible answer to "Is that you?"
81 Apple product
82 Extreme point
83 Sights not to be believed
84 Poem that ends "This ghoul-haunted woodland of Weir"
85 What a judge might do during a hearing
89 "A Sentimental Journey" author
91 Thomas Jefferson or Jimmy Carter, once
93 Virgil hero
94 Bit of field sport equipment
95 Lifts

by Alan Olschwang

**97** Where to find "books in the running brooks," per Shakespeare
**98** Star, maybe
**99** Indian melodies
**100** Nobelist writer Andric
**101** Go by bike

**104** Beginning of some temple names
**106** Preceder of "di" or "da" in a Beatles song
**109** Invoice fig.
**110** Since 1/1
**111** "___ Sylphides" (ballet)

## ACROSS

1 Shade of brown
6 Javert's portrayer in 2012's "Les Misérables"
11 Rice, e.g., informally
15 Come (from)
19 All-time leader in R.B.I.'s
20 Vegetables also known as lady's-fingers
21 Common quatrain form
22 Indian tourist destination
23 Paintings of French estates?
25 Spin, of a sort
27 Tanning aid
28 Carrier for Casanovas?
30 Time of one's life?
31 Thanksgiving, e.g.: Abbr.
33 Having failed to ante up, say
34 Italian tourist destination in the Mediterranean
37 "Anything you can do I can do better" and others
39 Supreme Court justice known for his trenchant dissents
43 Spurs
45 Relative of mono-
46 Medium for body art
50 Roman roads
51 "So pret-t-ty!"
52 Aid for a submarine séance?
56 Google : Android :: Apple : ___
57 Quarreled
59 When scores are settled?

60 Cake with a kick
61 "That's clear"
62 Venus de ___
63 Post production locale?
65 Kings and queens: Abbr.
66 Achieve nirvana
69 Having little give
70 Skiing maneuver at a bend in the course
72 Like cutting in line
73 Savoir-faire
74 Glorify
75 Navigation hazards
78 Dish Network competitor
81 4×4, e.g.
82 Hawaiian wine lover?
84 Get behind
85 Vice ___
87 Big name in batteries
88 Substantial shoe spec
89 Figure with horns
91 Untrustworthy sorts
93 Odin's home
95 Time off
96 "That'll never happen!"
100 Scrape (out)
101 Moo ___ pork
103 Last words from a coxswain?
107 American alternative
111 "Stay cool!"
112 Garlicky sauce in central Europe?
115 English princess
116 Food item often seasoned with cilantro
117 Like some patches
118 Sporty car roofs
119 High land

120 6'9" or 72% free throw avg.
121 Swift composition
122 "Narcissus and Goldmund" author

## DOWN

1 One side in a computer rivalry
2 Home of the Waianae Range
3 Start of some blended juice names
4 Gunfire, in slang
5 Not far from, in poetry
6 Putsch
7 Studio behind "Suspicion" and "Notorious"
8 ". . . ___ quit!"
9 Whiskered creature
10 International gas brand
11 Stan Lee's role in many a Marvel film
12 Skip ___
13 They come from the center
14 Wee ones
15 Living room?
16 Not supportin'
17 "Dies ___"
18 Girl in tartan
24 Docs united
26 Keys with tunes
29 Turn out
31 Muscle ___
32 Extremely sharp
34 Self centers
35 Lariat part
36 All the writings of a Persian faith?
37 Fictional Billy
38 Hit show with many hits
40 "Happily ever after" with Han Solo?

41 2004 movie set in 2035
42 Indian state known for its tea
44 Most reliable
47 Seasonal beverage
48 Small difference
49 Girl's name meaning "loved"
53 Word between last names
54 Convinced
55 Wailing Wall pilgrim
58 Got back to, in a way
60 Support
62 Toon with a polka-dot hair bow
64 Goggled
65 New York's ___ Island
66 Charlatan
67 100 cents
68 "Operators are standing by" and "Call now!," e.g.
70 Many Eastern Europeans
71 "WWE Raw" airer
73 Up to, informally
76 "Almighty" item: Abbr.
77 Quiet
78 Was mortified, hyperbolically
79 What chopsticks come in
80 Hole in the wall
82 Kind of exam or kit
83 "Is this the spot?"
86 Hot herbal beverage
90 Learned
92 Brown weasels
94 History and biography
97 Pressed charges against?

by Julian Lim

**98** Actress Durance who played Lois Lane on "Smallville"
**99** Fancy neckwear
**101** "And ___ Was" (1985 Talking Heads single)

**102** ___ bar
**103** Singer Lambert
**104** Cry made while wiping the hands
**105** Some stopovers
**106** Recess
**107** Big Apple sch.

**108** Ski-___ (snowmobiles)
**109** Challenge for Hannibal
**110** Quit lying
**113** Sounds by a crib, perhaps
**114** Indian tourist destination

## ACROSS

1 Parade organizer
6 Fake
11 One-named singer with the hit "Locked Up"
15 Pat gently
18 Recipe amount
19 ___ mama (tropical drink)
20 Belittling
22 "Greetings, Ms. Retton!"
24 Orwellian state
25 Right angle
26 Turkey isn't one
27 One who's done the "I do's"
28 "___ further review . . ."
29 Handle again?
31 "Very nice, Ms. Kennedy!"
34 Eight, for starters?
35 March org.?
36 Admiral's inits.
37 "Hurry up, Ms. Brennan!"
44 Little birdie
46 3.0 or 4.0
49 Like some queens
50 Sports-league-backed cable network
51 Market makeup: Abbr.
52 Summer month in France
53 Kind of cat
54 Feature of Oz's Wicked Witch of the West
55 "Cheer up, Ms. Teasdale!"
57 Advanced deg.
58 Bearded one
59 Title character in an A. A. Milne play
61 Person who holds property in trust
62 "Am I the one, Ms. Andrews?"
66 "Si!" at sea
69 Shorties
70 "Hurrah!"
71 Scuba tank meas.
74 "You look hot in a thong, Ms. Hawkins!"
76 Firenze's home
79 Bad mark
80 "___ off!"
81 German name part
82 Rock genre
83 Barbecue needs
84 Go off
85 Nothing special: Abbr.
86 "I need a hand, Ms. Fleming!"
88 N.R.C. forerunner
90 Classical "You too?"
93 Big ___ Conference
94 "Leave it alone, Ms. Zellweger!"
100 "Absolutely Fabulous" or "Father Ted"
103 Jai ___
104 First razor with a pivoting head
105 Yvonne with the 1978 #1 hit "If I Can't Have You"
107 Portuguese "she"
108 Pitcher Valenzuela
110 "Time to show your cards, Ms. Field!"
112 Pulled
113 TV's Ashley and Mary-Kate
114 Kate's TV partner
115 Maxime or Marie: Abbr.
116 Fury
117 Agemates
118 More Solomonic

## DOWN

1 HBO host Bill
2 Singer with the hit albums "19" and "21"
3 Remember
4 Designer inits.
5 2,000 pounds
6 Food source
7 "Oh, now I see"
8 1980s–'90s Corbin Bernsen TV drama
9 Cuffed
10 ___ de Nil (pale yellowish green)
11 Hound
12 Main cause
13 Figure skating champion Brian
14 Cavil
15 Bread flavorer
16 Par ___
17 "Moneyball" subject Billy
19 Urged
21 All ___ Day
23 Breakfast order
27 Global commerce grp. since 1995
30 Alpine climber's tool
32 Seaside eagle
33 No longer closeted
37 Not serious, in a way
38 Sushi fish
39 Cause of yawning
40 "Can ___ next?"
41 Port city from which Amelia Earhart last flew
42 Older form of a word
43 Always
45 La ___, Dominican Republic (first Spanish settlement in the Americas)
47 Whine
48 Suit to ___

51 Military wear, for short
52 Date for Denis
54 Away for a while
55 The "S" of R.S.V.P.
56 Matching
58 Blokes
60 Aqua, e.g.
62 Noisy birds
63 Fairies' land
64 Having a projected date of
65 Drapery material
66 Athlete who wrote "A Hard Road to Glory"
67 Junior, e.g.
68 Egg choice
71 Botanists' microscopic study
72 Persuaded
73 "___ jungle out there"
75 Cutthroat
77 Sports org. supported by 66-Down
78 Beat it
79 Hype
83 Logging aid
85 Home theater brand
86 Aqua, e.g.
87 Broadcast as an encore
89 Barely managing, with "out"
91 Power in old Hollywood
92 Singsong syllable
94 Drifts
95 Northern native
96 Film fish
97 Football Hall-of-Fame coach Greasy
98 "Family Ties" mom
99 Black-berried tree
100 Gran Turismos and others

*by Gary Cee*

**101** Dragon puppet
**102** One-third of an old Hollywood trio
**106** They carry charges
**109** ___ Lingus
**110** Cut
**111** Rope-a-dope boxer

## ACROSS

1 Shot from a gun
4 Hummus, e.g.
7 One-named rapper with a hyphen in his name
12 $C_2H_5OH$
19 "Yuck!"
20 Disney deer
21 Company named for a volcano
22 Ones with bouquets, maybe
23 Actress ___ Dawn Chong
24 Aught
25 Subject for the philosopher Heidegger
26 Dressed with elaborate care
27 Passage from life to death
30 Scorecard column
31 Unwritten reminder
32 Wedges, e.g.
34 Sources of feta and ricotta cheese
38 Biological ring
39 Round trip . . . or the subtitle of "The Hobbit"
41 -
42 "This I Promise You" band
43 Neptune's home
44 Brewer's oven
45 "Really?"
46 Fins
48 Aquatic singer
49 -
50 Camp treats
53 Astronomical datum
54 20-Across, e.g.
55 Nutritional std.
58 Eponym of Warsaw's airport
59 Numismatic classification

60 Private gatherings
63 Having macadamias or pecans, say
64 Part of E.S.L.: Abbr.
65 Word with holy or sacred
66 Sweats
67 Met one's potential
69 Old capital of Europe
70 Cat also known as the dwarf leopard
71 51-Down unit
72 YouTube posting, for short
73 Firm (up)
74 Basketball play
75 Inexpensive reprint, maybe
78 -
79 Ocean menace
80 Less prudish
82 Deuteronomy contents
83 German Expressionist Otto
84 Sin city
89 2005 nominee for Best Picture
90 -
92 Name on some European stamps
93 "Do the Right Thing" pizzeria
94 Where the wild things are?
95 Steeply discounted product, maybe
97 Distort
98 1980 hard rock album that went 22× platinum . . . or a hint to how to cross this puzzle's 27-Across
99 University in Lewiston, N.Y.
103 Speculate, say

105 Cadenza or Forte maker
106 Terre in the mer
107 Some badges
108 ® accompaniers
109 Not a reduction: Abbr.
110 South of Spain?
111 Anne Bradstreet, for one
112 Lane in Hollywood
113 Fa-la connector
114 Conan's network

## DOWN

1 Director with three Best Foreign Film Oscars
2 Messengers, e.g.
3 Todd of Broadway
4 Tooth decay, to professionals
5 Not going anywhere?
6 Michael or Sarah
7 Daughter on "Bewitched"
8 The Carolinas' ___ River
9 End in ___
10 Comfort or country follower
11 Badger
12 Seen
13 Revisits an earlier time
14 Speeds
15 Tucked away
16 Prefix with smoker
17 What a picker may pick
18 "Purple haze"
28 Lots
29 Plebiscites
30 Stands one's ground
32 Clothing lines
33 Metal fastener
34 Yves's "even"
35 Amphibious rodent

36 Autobahn hazard
37 With 60-Down, carnival treat
40 Stir
41 It might be heard when a light bulb goes on
43 Parisian possessive
45 -
47 Try very hard
48 Remain undecided
49 Korean money
50 Coach with two Super Bowl championships
51 Collection of vehicles available to personnel
52 Makes a choice
53 Look after
54 -
56 Three-time N.B.A. All-Star Williams
57 Part of P.D.A.: Abbr.
58 Jim Cramer's network
59 Cause of an audio squeal
60 See 37-Down
61 It's caught by a stick on a field
62 Busy as ___
65 Go pfft, with "out"
68 Yuri's "peace"
69 Publicize
73 Atlas index listings
74 One was blown in Ellington's band
76 Quizzes
77 Presentation opening?
78 Dial-up unit
79 European capital on the Svisloch River
80 Scale abbr.
81 ___ pro nobis
82 -

by Alan DerKazarian

**83** Bishop's place
**85** Libran stone
**86** Arp or Duchamp
**87** Lowest bid in bridge
**88** Buoys, e.g.
**90** Mire
**91** Support group since 1951

**92** Cause of weather weirdness
**94** ___
**96** Dickens villain
**97** Goods
**98** Nickname for Georgia's capital
**99** Small amount of drink

**100** Oath-taking phrase
**101** ___-high
**102** "Little Caesar" weapon
**103** Superseded
**104** Dish made from a root

## ACROSS

1 Palindromic band name
5 Tosca's feeling for Cavaradossi
10 Spring for a vacation
13 Hawaiian tourist purchases
17 "__ yourself"
19 Cow catcher
20 Red wine drinker's paradise?
22 Employee at the Ron Paul Archive?
24 Pitch that fixes everything?
25 "Strange Magic" band, briefly
26 Dollar bill featuring a portrait of Duran Duran's lead singer?
28 IRS Form 5498 subject
29 Street caution
31 Ball with a yellow stripe
32 Shiner?
33 Willowy
37 Like a robot's voice
39 Still
41 Architect Saarinen
42 Blue expanse
43 Follow closely
44 Hair-raising shout
46 "__ te absolvo" (priest's phrase)
47 The one puppy that can read?
53 Creator of perfect whirlpools?
56 Baath Party member
57 Uncommunicative
59 Political title of the 1930s–'40s
60 Counter formations
62 Mix in a tank
64 Overextend oneself?

68 Classical guitarist Segovia
70 Adds to the batter, say
72 In a kooky manner
73 Buttonholed
75 Given a home
77 Triumphant song
78 "This isn't making sense"
80 Whom John Bull symbolizes
82 Have an objection
83 Minor-league championship flag?
86 Alienate a New Jersey city?
88 Biblical priest of Shiloh
89 Blue expanse
90 "Man of Steel" actress Adams
92 Sully
93 Go on strike
95 Film crowd
97 CBS spinoff that ran for 10 seasons
102 How sports cars are contoured
105 "Cover __ Face" (P. D. James's first novel)
106 Distress
107 Actor Jack of oaters
108 Cousin of a crumble
109 Begat a soft place to sleep?
112 Burlesque garment
113 "Charge!," to Duracells?
117 Satisfying finale coming to pass?
119 Labeled idiotic?
120 First name in photography
121 Nickname for Palmer

122 "Don't be a spoilsport!"
123 Savory condiment
124 Variety show fodder
125 Trader __

## DOWN

1 Most qualified
2 Relative of S.O.S
3 Galoot
4 One-hit wonder?
5 Friend of d'Artagnan
6 Thick bunch?
7 Venture a thought
8 Unfeigned
9 Miranda of the Miranda warning
10 Avoid
11 Course listing
12 Percussion instrument in "Maxwell's Silver Hammer"
13 Sophisticated
14 Automaker that started as a bicycle company
15 Bent pipe
16 "She's a good old worker and a good old pal," in song
18 Med. workplaces
20 Tea go-with
21 "Days of Heaven" co-star
23 Would-be singers' liabilities
27 Little town
30 Site of a 1963 J.F.K. speech
33 Chargers and coursers
34 Forest game
35 "By that logic . . ."
36 Boarder's domain
38 Director Daniels of "The Butler"
39 Of the lymph glands

40 Signet ring feature
45 Dropper?
47 Steven Bochco series
48 Youngest of Chekhov's "Three Sisters"
49 Eldest Best Actress winner
50 Acronymic aircraft name
51 Wistful remark
52 With a will
53 It's "well regulated" in the Constitution
54 Quarrel
55 "Lovergirl" singer
58 Pulsation
61 Morally degraded
63 Fish hawks
65 Cross-promotion
66 Streetcar sound
67 Chrissie in the Rock and Roll Hall of Fame
69 Start of a George Eliot title
71 N.B.A. team originally called the Americans
74 Elephant's opposite, symbolically
76 URL component
79 Zeus swore oaths upon it
81 Excited Oscars attendee
83 Nave furniture
84 Airline that doesn't fly on religious holidays
85 Khartoum's river
87 Run headlong into
90 Datum in a house listing
91 __ Vineyard
94 Confined
96 "I thought __ never leave!"

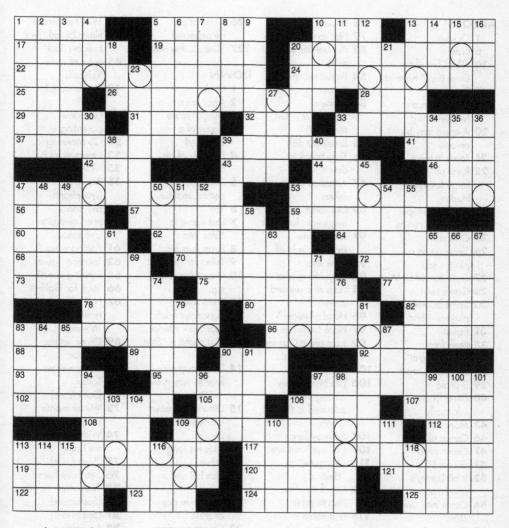

by Patrick Berry

97 Pile on the floor
98 Soothsayers of old
99 Person prone to sunburn
100 Last Hitchcock film with Tippi Hedren
101 Some Google search results
103 Hot pot locale

104 English film festival city
106 It "hits the spot," per old radio ads
109 Begin to show wear
110 Yarn quantity
111 Hair strands?

113 "EastEnders" network
114 Shot spot
115 Metaphysical concept
116 Fortune cover subj.
118 Longtime Sixers nickname

## ACROSS

1 Oceans
6 Bats
10 "The Clan of the Cave Bear" novelist
14 Razz
19 Tennis's Goran Ivanisevic, e.g.
20 A band may be on one
21 Torch-lit event
22 River of forgetfulness in Hades
23 Iron Age people
24 It has nine rooms
25 Ottoman
26 Serve up on a platter, say
27 Collectors of DNA
28 Game twist
30 Some basketball players: Abbr.
31 Espies
33 Profit from
34 "I'm innocent!"
35 Lab safety org.?
39 3-D pic
40 Diner fixtures, informally
43 More rakish
46 Canon offering
47 Clown prop
51 Sitcom ET
52 Walt Disney's middle name
54 Cable inits. since 1996
56 "Be a ___"
57 "Six Million Dollar Man" feature
60 Cabbed it
63 Most likely to be called up
64 From the top
68 Move, informally
69 2400, on the SAT
73 Dolt
74 Like most checks and political candidates
78 Green
79 Not so nice
82 Annual literary prize
83 Picked up, in Britain
84 Home of Velázquez's "Las Meninas"
85 Breakfast dish
86 They break at dawn
87 Angelica and others
89 Like some resolution, for short
91 Showed no restraint, in brief
92 Cask filler
93 Linguistic quintet
94 Parts of sows and cows
96 Head of steam?
97 Place to lounge
99 Jazz great Carmen
103 Cricket's sound
105 Triply
106 Like New Jersey among states admitted to the Union
107 Subway fare
109 Chinese hard-liner
110 "Antigone" or "Elektra"
112 One famed for heartlessness
114 Last name in cookies
115 Some notepad jottings
117 It may be left hanging
119 Take out
120 Farmworker in "The Wizard of Oz"
121 Scale unit
122 Tony winner Tharp
123 Spheres
124 Ice cream brand
125 Recess
126 It's what's to be expected
127 "The ___ the limit"

## DOWN

1 Grab
2 Abbr. on a musical score
3 Cause of a crybaby?
4 Provider of an inside look?
5 Nos. after a period, maybe
6 Yen
7 Last name in "Star Wars"
8 Farm females
9 Takes for granted
10 Charitable giving, e.g.
11 Trees with poisonous seeds
12 Marquis's inferior
13 First name in "Star Wars"
14 Girl group with four #1 hits in the 1990s
15 Often-decorative kitchen item, in Britain
16 Aids for long drives
17 Gas bill unit
18 Crisp
29 Lead-in to pop or pass
32 Chicago setting: Abbr.
34 Japanese computer giant
36 [See above]
37 Last place, with "the"
38 Indy 500 winner Luyendyk
40 2007 title role for Ellen Page
41 In utero
42 [See above]
43 Sharp putdown
44 1974 Fassbinder film subtitled "Fear Eats the Soul"
45 Subj. of some 911 calls
48 Figurehead, for short?
49 Like some parenting
50 QB Manning
53 Ottoman V.I.P.
55 RR stop
58 Brown-___ (sycophants)
59 Like one pre-Columbian civilization
61 Parting word
62 Taunting figure
65 Running pants?
66 Subj. for Galileo
67 N.B.A. Hall-of-Famer Thomas
69 Oscar winner Swinton
70 Oscar winner Tatum
71 [See above]
72 Winter month in Spain
74 Withdraw from the bank?
75 [See above]
76 Seashore fliers
77 Twosomes
80 [See above]
81 [See above]
88 "___ kleine Nachtmusik"
90 Per
93 National rival
95 Her name is Norwegian for "beautiful woman who leads you to victory"
98 Van Gogh painting that once sold for a record $53.9 million

by Jeff Chen

100 Highlight of many a western
101 Fix
102 Ain't right?
104 Concerto movements
105 Broke
108 Didn't get involved

109 Pac-Man screen, e.g.
110 ___'clock scholar
111 Numbskull
113 Loch ___
116 Twosome
118 Canon offering, briefly

# ANSWERS

## 1

```
HER   CABIN    EDNA  QUADS
ORA   ALEROS   BEERHUNTER
LIV   SILENCEOFTHEIAMBS
ACELA    CORNY   AIT
   REBA  POOL    TRIPPY
THEVASTEMPEROR   STARER
REVISION    ABUT   LIMO
UNI   DUNCESWITHWOLVES
SCEPTER  HAP    RIP  ENE
SEWER   EASY  COOKIETIN
   GONGWITHTHEWIND
FLAGPOLES   OREO   EARLS
IAM  ISA   LAS  GASMAIN
FRENCHCONFECTION   NEE
TINE   EVIE    MONGOLIA
HARASS  ABEAUTIFULMINK
 TATTER    CRIT  LINK
    ANI  EERIE   SIEVE
GERMSOFENDEARMENT  MIX
MYHAIRLADY  HEINIE  ANA
AEONS   EROS   DCTEN  DOM
```

## 2

```
AWNUTS  BASICS  JUSTNOW
RHINOS  ORIOLE  ASTRIDE
FOLLOWINGSUIT  WHOOPEE
 SEED  TAOISM   BELL
   ALSO    BEFORELONG
CLOSETOHOME  BUN    CIO
YOOHOO  ADORABLE  MECCA
ROMEO  PROVEN   VALUED
UMPS  CHERI  DNA  EXALTS
SSA  HUE   EASYA  NITTY
   BETWEENYOUANDME
 SPACE  GRIEF   EOS  MAE
STALKS  GAG  OWNER  TILL
WEEKLY   HARHAR  DHABI
ERASE  FOOTSTEP  SEAMUS
EEN   IRR  AHEADOFTIME
POSTOFFICE    EXES
 ABET   MASALA  ATMS
RELIEVE  NEXTTONOTHING
ICANSEE  TREATS  BEARUP
POSTERN  HYDRAS  IDTAGS
```

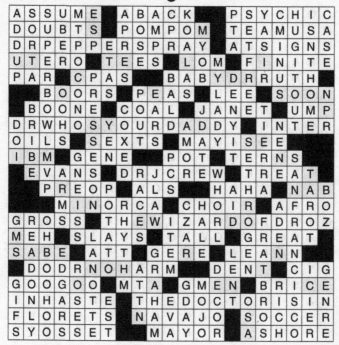

**3**

```
A S S U M E   A B A C K     P S Y C H I C
D O U B T S   P O M P O M   T E A M U S A
D R P E P P E R S P R A Y   A T S I G N S
U T E R O   T E E S   L O M   F I N I T E
P A R   C P A S     B A B Y D R R U T H
  B O O R S   P E A S   L E E   S O O N
  B O O N E   C O A L   J A N E T   U M P
D R W H O S Y O U R D A D D Y   I N T E R
O I L S   S E X T S   M A Y I S E E
I B M   G E N E   P O T   T E R N S
  E V A N S   D R J C R E W   T R E A T
  P R E O P   A L S   H A H A   N A B
  M I N O R C A   C H O I R   A F R O
G R O S S   T H E W I Z A R D O F D R O Z
M E H   S L A Y S   T A L L   G R E A T
S A B E   A T T   G E R E   L E A N N
  D O D R N O H A R M   D E N T   C I G
G O O G O O   M T A   G M E N   B R I C E
I N H A S T E   T H E D O C T O R I S I N
F L O R E T S   N A V A J O   S O C C E R
S Y O S S E T   M A Y O R   A S H O R E
```

**4**

```
  B A N D B   A C K S     S H E A F E D
S E R I A L   S N O O P   S T A L L O N E
C A M A R O   I T C H Y   T E N Y A R D S
A K A   T O M G I R L   S I N K   G U S
R E N T   D E N S E   B E E T   S C A R E
F R I E D   T O M A T O E S   B E A V E R
  N O R   R O T O R S   T E N S E S T
  M A D L I B   G O D S   E A R T H
H O V   O V I D   R A T E D P G   B E S T
E T E   R E G I S   Y A Y A S   G A R T H
W I N T E R   G U M   L E T   J E R S E Y
T O G A S   H I R A M   S E W O N   A R M
O N E L   E A T F R O M   S A L T   T E E
  L E V I S   G U Y S   S L E A Z O
A S H I V E R   A I R M A N   Y E S
N O O N E R   R U N N I N G A   L I G H T
T U R N S   H O T S   S T U N G   S O A R
O R S   T O G O   S T A Y S I N   S N O
I S I T T R U E   A P A C E   A C C O S T
N O N E V E N T   Y U K O N   N A P L E S
E N G A G E D   E D E N   T A L O N
```

## 5

**Puzzle 5**

```
C O A T R A C K ■ C H U T E S ■ A D O B E
O H B O O H O O ■ P O P A R T ■ C R U E T
M A R I N E R S B A T T L E P I R A T E S
A R A L ■ M E S A ■ P O I ■ ■ N E M O ■
S A M S A ■ ■ L E A ■ S P I T ■ A F A R
■ ■ V O T E S O N ■ M A T E R ■ T M I
■ T I G E R S C A N T H A N D L E C U B S
H O V E R C A R ■ S I N G ■ A R N I E
A T O M ■ A U T O ■ T S A R ■ D E E T S
N O R ■ S A G ■ I D E S ■ E E N I E
■ Y A N K E E S D E F E A T R E D S ■
■ L E A N N ■ M O O R ■ R A D ■ N A B
A B O D E ■ T A L E ■ R A T E ■ S A N E
M I L E R ■ M A N S ■ ■ H A V E P I T Y
P A D R E S B O W T O C A R D I N A L S
E L M ■ D I A R Y ■ F O C U S E D ■
D Y A D ■ T A S E ■ T N T ■ ■ S H E B A
■ S E T I ■ R E B ■ U C L A ■ E X E S
N A T I O N A L S T O P P L E R O Y A L S
A L E C K ■ C O U R I C ■ U N I C Y C L E
P A R E E ■ E X P E L S ■ B A D D A T E S
```

## 6

**Puzzle 6**

```
A D E S T E ■ A W O L ■ A N D S O D O I
O I L P A N ■ T B O N E ■ N O R A D U N N
R O L A N D ■ A S N E R ■ S T A Y S M A D
T R I C K Y D I C T I O N ■ U N E ■ P R E
A S S E T ■ A L I ■ D I R T P O R T I O N
■ J O E Y ■ S H A ■ C A T ■ S W E P T
P O P U P S ■ T S A ■ T O N ■ O R E S
A V O N ■ S T R A W M A N S I O N ■
M E L C ■ A G E ■ K O B E ■ T R E C O O L
P R E T T Y I N G ■ B E A V ■ P O R N O
E E N I E ■ F D I C ■ T R I O ■ A L B E N
R A T O N ■ Y A L L ■ S C H I L L I N G
S T A N T O N ■ N A I L ■ T I X ■ A T O B
■ S W E E T N L O T I O N ■ R A T E
R A R E ■ L T R ■ K I M ■ A I S L E D
E W O K S ■ I A N ■ A I M ■ G Y N T ■
B A S E T E N S I O N ■ E P A ■ S A L M A
E S S ■ A L C ■ B O N U S T R A C T I O N
C H A T R O O M ■ Z U N I S ■ R A I N O N
C I N E R A M A ■ E L A N D ■ B L O U S E
A N O D Y N E S ■ D I S K ■ S E N S E S
```

## 7

```
S A A B   G A Y E   O P A L S   R E A R M
P R E Y S U P O N   N A M E D   E N N I O
I N T R O V E R T   U N I F I C A T I O N
C I N D Y   I I N S I S T   A D E S T E
Y E A   R O C C O   C H O I R   R E S T
    C H U K K E R S     P R O F S
D E C R E E S     T A K E I L L   S A D
A A R O N   P E L I C A N S   A S C I I
B R E W   T H E N A N N Y   A T T A R S
S N O   T O M R I D G E   G A S C A P S
    S A W W O O D     P O S T A G E
    S O L O I S T   N A R R A T O R   G O P
A T T E S T   P E R C O D A N   D O N E
G U E S T   A S H H E A P S   N A A C P
E D D   A R C A D I A   S H I I T E S
    G R A M M   S E T S H O T S
A L T O   D E E M S   L I E O N   S I S
M A R S H A   H I A A S E N   D O N N A
B Y Y O U R L E A V E   D I M M E D O U T
E N S U E   A R T O O   Y O G I B E R R A
R E T R Y   Y E A R N   E R M A   S E E N
```

## 8

```
A T O M I C   M E A T C A S E   A F A R
M A R I N O   P I P E O R G A N   N I N E
F R O Z E N W A T E R W O R L D   K R I S
A S Y E   C A R R E   A E S T H E T E
R I P   S E R T A   L G S   R I O   S A T
    L A H R   A L I E N C O N T A C T
P E A N U T S   C A M A R O   S H A F T
T I T A N I C S K Y F A L L   U T E R U S
A N A L   I L E   P E E T   X T R A
    O R D E R E D I N   S A P   E R R
    B I G C O N S P I R A C Y T H E O R Y
T O M   A R C   D E S I A R N A Z
A R I D   M E I S   T R E   A S T O
T I M E R S   S A W T H E D E P A R T E D
A S P C A   E M B R Y O   T A N K A R D
    R O C K Y S L E E P E R   R O S Y
A W E   E E E   E N S   X E D I N   E P A
M I S T R E S S   B E E R S   I D O S
I T S Y   N O T O R I O U S K I N G P I N
S T E P   E R I C A K A N E   A R O U S E
H Y D E   N E R D I E S T   N A T T E R
```

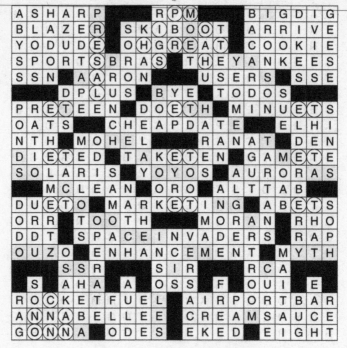

**9**

| A | S | H | A | R | P | ■ | ■ | R | P | M | ■ | ■ | B | I | G | D | I | G |
| B | L | A | Z | E | R | ■ | S | K | I | B | O | O | T | ■ | A | R | R | I | V | E |
| Y | O | D | U | D | E | ■ | O | H | G | R | E | A | T | ■ | C | O | O | K | I | E |
| S | P | O | R | T | S | B | R | A | S | ■ | T | H | E | Y | A | N | K | E | E | S |
| S | S | N | ■ | A | A | R | O | N | ■ | U | S | E | R | S | ■ | S | S | E |
| ■ | ■ | D | P | L | U | S | ■ | B | Y | E | ■ | T | O | D | O | S |
| P | R | E | T | E | E | N | ■ | D | O | E | T | H | ■ | M | I | N | U | E | T | S |
| O | A | T | S | ■ | C | H | E | A | P | D | A | T | E | ■ | E | L | H | I |
| N | T | H | ■ | M | O | H | E | L | ■ | R | A | N | A | T | ■ | D | E | N |
| D | I | E | T | E | D | ■ | T | A | K | E | T | E | N | ■ | G | A | M | E | T | E |
| S | O | L | A | R | I | S | ■ | Y | O | Y | O | S | ■ | A | U | R | O | R | A | S |
| ■ | M | C | L | E | A | N | ■ | O | R | O | ■ | A | L | T | T | A | B |
| D | U | E | T | O | ■ | M | A | R | K | E | T | I | N | G | ■ | A | B | E | T | S |
| O | R | R | ■ | T | O | O | T | H | ■ | M | O | R | A | N | ■ | R | H | O |
| D | D | T | ■ | S | P | A | C | E | I | N | V | A | D | E | R | S | ■ | R | A | P |
| O | U | Z | O | ■ | E | N | H | A | N | C | E | M | E | N | T | ■ | M | Y | T | H |
| ■ | S | S | R | ■ | S | I | R | ■ | R | C | A |
| S | ■ | A | H | A | ■ | A | ■ | O | S | S | ■ | F | ■ | O | U | I | ■ | E |
| R | O | C | K | E | T | F | U | E | L | ■ | A | I | R | P | O | R | T | B | A | R |
| A | N | N | A | B | E | L | L | E | E | ■ | C | R | E | A | M | S | A | U | C | E |
| G | O | N | N | A | ■ | O | D | E | S | ■ | E | K | E | D | ■ | E | I | G | H | T |

**10**

| O | P | A | L | ■ | S | H | A | U | N | ■ | C | A | L | V | E | ■ | A | P | B | S |
| N | O | S | E | ■ | P | A | B | S | T | ■ | A | T | E | A | M | ■ | L | I | R | A |
| T | O | P | S | T | O | R | I | E | S | ■ | G | L | A | R | E | ■ | A | N | O | S |
| A | C | C | ■ | R | U | D | D | ■ | B | R | E | A | K | I | N | G | N | E | W | S |
| P | H | A | R | I | S | E | E | S | ■ | O | R | R | ■ | A | D | R | I | A | N | I |
| ■ | E | V | A | N | ■ | A | G | O | ■ | G | U | N | ■ | A | S | P | E | N |
| D | E | T | A | I | L | S | A | R | E | S | K | E | T | C | H | Y | ■ | P | Y | E |
| A | R | O | M | A | ■ | C | A | N | T | O | ■ | Z | E | E | ■ | I | L | E | S |
| B | I | O | S | ■ | U | F | C | ■ | R | E | F | I | ■ | S | A | D | N | E | S | S |
| A | C | L | ■ | S | P | O | O | N | E | R | I | S | M | ■ | R | O | T |
| T | H | E | L | A | T | E | S | T | ■ | B | A | C | K | T | O | Y | O | U |
| ■ | I | D | O | ■ | T | H | E | J | O | N | E | S | E | S | ■ | E | N | S |
| G | A | L | L | O | P | S | ■ | S | L | A | G | ■ | N | I | N | ■ | L | E | I | A |
| I | S | A | Y | ■ | A | T | E | ■ | O | C | H | O | A | ■ | P | E | S | C | I |
| M | I | S | ■ | T | R | A | F | F | I | C | A | N | D | W | E | A | T | H | E | R |
| M | A | T | R | I | ■ | B | F | A | ■ | U | M | A | ■ | A | S | N | O |
| E | M | P | A | N | E | L | ■ | B | U | S | ■ | T | A | S | T | I | N | E | S | S |
| F | I | L | M | A | T | E | L | E | V | E | N | ■ | L | O | A | N | ■ | A | A | H |
| I | N | A | S | ■ | A | B | A | R | E | ■ | S | T | A | N | D | I | N | G | B | Y |
| V | O | C | E | ■ | T | O | N | G | A | ■ | F | R | I | T | O | ■ | A | E | R | O |
| E | R | E | S | ■ | S | Y | K | E | S | ■ | W | I | N | O | S | ■ | G | R | A | F |

## 11

```
H O P I   R A F T     A C H E   D O D O S
U S E S   A L I S T   L O O S   R H I N O
T H E O L D G R A Y M E R Y L   P A N E L
S A L T I N E S   R U R A L   S E R E N E
      O V E R   B A R T L E T T P E R I L
S N I P E R   R A N K S     H I P   S L Y
P A C E R   H A S T Y   J E E R E D
A M Y S   R A P T   S C A M   R E T R O
R E S   K O D I A K B A R R E L   W H U P
E S T E E M E D   N I X E S   A W A I T S
    E X E C S   W I D O W   S T E R N
M E R I N O   C O V E N   T O O L S E T S
A W O L   M A R K E T S H E R Y L   R H O
P E L E G   S E E S   E T T A   C R A W
    D A R K E N   P L I E S   B O O N E
A M A   G E O   P R I G S   L O L L E D
B I L L O F F E R R E L L   B A R D
A N D E R S   V A U L T   M U S I C A L S
T I R E D   H A N D L E W I T H C A R O L
E M I L E   E D G E   D A N T E   L E G O
D I N A R   F E E S   D E E D   L A S T
```

## 12

```
  S A A B S   R I V A L     A V A S T
A N N U L E T   E R I T U   G R I L L E S
B E A S T I E   S K I F F   L I P L O C K
D E C       L A P     H O E       C H I
U Z I S   Y E L L O W S T O N E   R U N E
L E N A   E X P E D I T I O N S   A M O S
    F D A   N I L L A   C D C
P A L E O   C E D E   O F F S   R E B U S
A A A   M O O R E   D R A M A   I R E
P H D   E D M O N D   S L A V I C   O N E
  Y O S E M I T E   H O M E L O A N
  A P U   D O C   S P A   E M O   N I H
  N A T I O N A L P A R K S E R V I C E
S O L E M N   I O N I A   D E M E A N
U S M A P   M E T G A L A   G A Y L E
B E S T R O N G     N E P A L E S E
    E V E R S O   W B O S O N
H O L Y C O W   A R M E Y   P E D A N T S
T R E V I   M I N D C A N D Y   I N A W E
M E T E S   E N D E A V O R S   E N D I T
L O O S E   N P R N E W S   T E A T S
```

## 13

Grid 13:

| S | C | R | A | P |   | M | E | S | H |   | H | A | R | K | S |   |   | T | S | O |
| T | R | A | V | E | L | O | G | U | E |   | A | R | E | N | A |   | S | H | I | P |
| R | A | D | A | R | A | N | G | E | R |   | D | A | M | E | C | H | E | E | S | E |
| U | Z | O |   | M | O | T | H |   | B | Y | E | B | Y | E |   | I | N | F | E | R |
| T | E | N | S |   | T | H | E | A | T | E | R |   |   | D | A | Y | T | O | N | A |
|   |   | H | A | S |   | A | R | E | A |   | S | C | E | N | A |   | R | O | M |   |
| S | E | N | A | T | E | I | D | E | A |   | K | E | Y | E | D |   | A | U | R | A |
| E | L | U | D | E |   | N | E | S |   | H | E | A | R | P | E | R | L | M | A | N |
| R | A | R | E |   | S | T | D |   | S | E | R | R | A |   | S | O | U |   |   |   |
| M | I | S | D | A | T | E |   | S | H | A | N | A | N | A |   | A | M | P | A | S |
| O | N | E |   | S | P | R | I | T | E | D | E | C | O | R | P | S |   | R | E | A |
| N | E | S | T | S |   | S | T | E | E | P | L | E |   | M | E | T | E | O | R | S |
|   |   | H | A | R |   | S | A | R | I | S |   | P | A | C |   | U | T | A | H |   |
| A | S | S | U | M | E | D | A | M | E | N |   | S | A | N |   | E | L | I | T | E |
| B | A | A | S |   | R | O | G | E | R |   | I | N | S | I | D | E | O | P | E | D |
| S | N | L |   | V | A | P | O | R |   | B | R | O | S |   | O | R | G |   |   |   |
| I | T | E | M | O | N | E |   |   | E | Y | E | B | O | L | T |   | Y | A | Y | S |
| N | A | D | A | L |   | S | A | V | E | U | S |   | V | A | I | N |   | L | E | A |
| T | H | A | N | E | A | L | L | E | N |   | I | M | E | D | N | O | V | E | L | S |
| H | A | Y | S |   | P | A | T | T | I |   | G | I | R | L | G | R | O | U | P | S |
| E | T | S |   | S | P | O | S | E |   | N | O | S | E |   | A | N | T | S | Y |   |

## 14

Grid 14:

| E | L | A | N |   | S | L | A | P |   | I | N | F | I | R | M |   | S | W | A | G |
| L | I | V | E | A | L | O | N | E |   | M | O | O | M | O | O |   | M | A | T | E |
| B&O | R | A | I | L | R | O | A | D |   | S | T | O | P | I | T |   | A | S | S | T |
| W | A | S | N | T |   | S | T | I | L | E | T | T | O |   | O | B | L | A | T | E |
| S | S | T |   | E | Y | E |   | A | T | O | M | S |   | R&B | A | L | B | U | M |   |
|   |   | P | R | O | S | H | O | P |   | W | E | E |   | I | S | A | I | D |   |   |
|   | K | E | A | N | U |   | O | P | E | N | O | N |   | I | K | E |   |   |   |   |
| G | E | T | S | A | L | I | T | T | L | E | R&R |   | Q&A | S | E | S | S | I | O | N |
| R | E | C |   | T | O | N | S |   | P | E | Y | O | T | E | S |   | E | N | D | O |
| O | L | E | M | I | S | S |   | M | I | D |   | N | A | E |   | H | I | V | E | S |
|   |   | T | O | V | E |   | M | A | N | A | G | E | R |   | T | U | N | A |   |   |
| T | H | E | R | E |   | L | A | W |   | L | O | S |   | A | I | M | E | D | A | T |
| A | E | R | O |   | S | E | T | S | A | I | L |   | B | A | J | A |   | E | T | A |
| P | E | A | N | U | T | M&M | S |   | S&P | F | I | V | E | H | U | N | D | R | E | D |
|   |   | N | R | A |   | D | E | T | A | I | L |   | A | R | O | S | E |   |   |   |
|   | S | E | G | U | E |   | A | I | R |   | T | I | T | A | N | I | C |   |   |   |
| T | E | X | A | S | A&M |   | S | L | U | S | H |   | S | A | G |   | E | S | T |   |
| R | A | P | P | E | L |   | H | A | S | A | S | H | O | T |   | H | A | L | L | E |
| E | R | I | E |   | I | N | A | T | U | B |   | A&W | R | O | O | T | B | E | E | R |
| S | A | R | A |   | N | O | D | E | A | L |   | K | E | R | O | S | E | N | E | S |
| S | T | E | T |   | E | D | E | R | L | E |   | S | O | S | O |   | L | A | K | E |

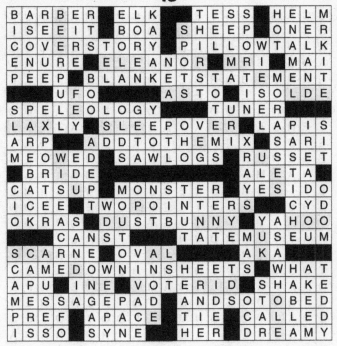

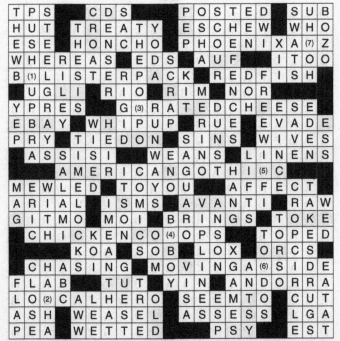

(1) DASH (2) DASH (3) DASH (4) DASH (5) DASH (6) DASH (7) DASH

## 17

Puzzle 17 (completed grid, across entries):

- COAGULATE · PNCPARK · MUY
- OBSESSION · ROSALIE · INE
- WANTEDDEADORALIVE · CBS
- AMESS · DUM · PSHAW
- NARC · BURNEDATTHESTAKE
- LIENEE · ARIA · REED
- HOOKEDONPHONICS · ALDO
- TERSE · ATAN · EAT
- SIDESTEP · ALEKEG · TIDAL
- EGER · BLESSEDEVENT · ELI
- THA · MALTA · NOTON · BAN
- STL · CRACKEDJOKES · ARME
- ESSAI · SOISEE · EMERSION
- TIO · PETA · OPEDS
- FAIT · GROUNDEDFORLIFE
- ALGA · REBS · AIMFOR
- TOUCHEDINTHEHEAD · ASST
- CHAKA · HAM · ETAPE
- EAN · DRESSEDTOTHENINES
- LOA · ITSONME · FOOTNOTES
- LES · NESTLES · AIRCANADA

## 18

Puzzle 18 (completed grid, across entries):

- MCS · DENIM · TAPS · SAABS
- RHO · ALONE · ISLAM · ADMIT
- MARRYINGTHEKALE · FLITE
- OREOS · HORSY · SPEEDUP
- MOSTPASTORS · STAIRRAMP
- AWARDS · BOAST · LEE
- SGT · ATE · IOUS · ARYANS
- CRACKYOURPATE · PIE
- CHOPPER · NIA · BACARDI
- HOMERS · CANDLEWITHHAIR
- ELY · MARS · INEZ · IVE
- RAKINGMYMOUNDS · BOWMEN
- IRONORE · HEE · NOWHERE
- RDA · GROUNDHOWLING
- AFRESH · MOTH · AIL · GTE
- RIO · ABACO · NAUSEA
- TRAILMUCK · BETTERLOCKS
- DENSEST · PIANO · PARCH
- EBOLA · CHILLEDWITHFEAR
- COKES · HALLE · DRAMA · ERE
- OXEYE · MESS · SYNCS · LSD

## 19

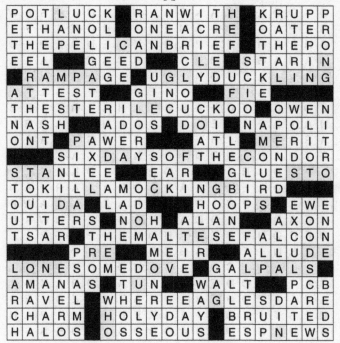

## 20

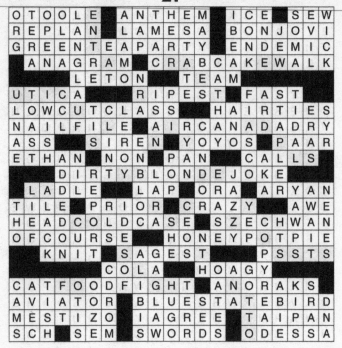

```
O T O O L E   A N T H E M   I C E   S E W
R E P L A N   L A M E S A   B O N J O V I
G R E E N T E A P A R T Y   E N D E M I C
  A N A G R A M   C R A B C A K E W A L K
      L E T O N     T E A M
U T I C A     R I P E S T   F A S T
L O W C U T C L A S S   H A I R T I E S
N A I L F I L E   A I R C A N A D A D R Y
A S S   S I R E N   Y O Y O S   P A A R
E T H A N   N O N   P A N   C A L L S
    D I R T Y B L O N D E J O K E
  L A D L E   L A P   O R A   A R Y A N
T I L E   P R I O R   C R A Z Y   A W E
H E A D C O L D C A S E   S Z E C H W A N
O F C O U R S E   H O N E Y P O T P I E
    K N I T   S A G E S T   P S S T S
      C O L A   H O A G Y
C A T F O O D F I G H T   A N O R A K S
A V I A T O R   B L U E S T A T E B I R D
M E S T I Z O   I A G R E E   T A I P A N
S C H   S E M   S W O R D S   O D E S S A
```

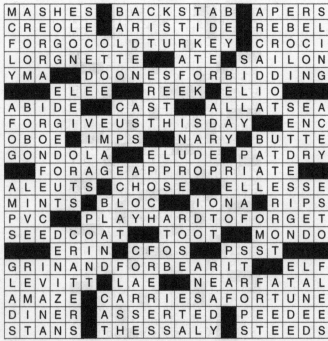

```
M A S H E S   B A C K S T A B   A P E R S
C R E O L E   A R I S T I D E   R E B E L
F O R G O C O L D T U R K E Y   C R O C I
L O R G N E T T E   A T E   S A I L O N
Y M A   D O O N E S F O R B I D D I N G
    E L E E   R E E K   E L I O
A B I D E   C A S T   A L L A T S E A
F O R G I V E U S T H I S D A Y   E N C
O B O E   I M P S   N A R Y   B U T T E
G O N D O L A   E L U D E   P A T D R Y
    F O R A G E A P P R O P R I A T E
A L E U T S   C H O S E   E L L E S S E
M I N T S   B L O C   I O N A   R I P S
P V C   P L A Y H A R D T O F O R G E T
S E E D C O A T   T O O T   M O N D O
    E R I N   C F O S   P S S T
G R I N A N D F O R B E A R I T   E L F
L E V I T T   L A E   N E A R F A T A L
A M A Z E   C A R R I E S A F O R T U N E
D I N E R   A S S E R T E D   P E E D E E
S T A N S   T H E S S A L Y   S T E E D S
```

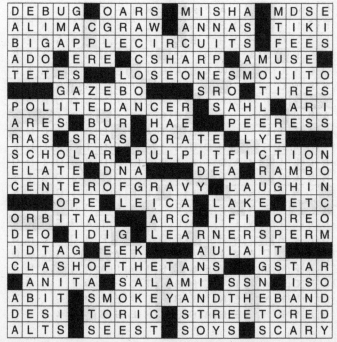

# 25

| | | | | | | | | | | | | | | | | | | | | |
|---|---|---|---|---|---|---|---|---|---|---|---|---|---|---|---|---|---|---|---|---|
| | S | T | R | A | P | | | B | A | R | G | A | I | N | | | S | L | O | P |
| | C | O | U | S | I | N | | A | G | E | L | I | M | I | T | | E | I | R | E |
| W | O | R | S | T | N | I | G | H | T | M | A | R | E | C | O | M | E | T | R | U |
| A | N | T | E | A | T | E | R | | | I | M | P | | K | N | O | T | T | | |
| T | E | E | S | | | C | A | L | F | | | I | N | E | E | D | H | E | L | P |
| | | | | T | H | E | S | O | U | T | H | P | O | L | | E | R | R | O | R |
| | S | A | M | O | A | | | S | E | A | B | E | D | | A | L | U | M | N | I |
| E | N | T | R | Y | L | E | V | E | L | J | O | | A | F | T | S | | A | D | Z |
| L | O | O | T | S | | A | E | R | | | | S | T | A | T | | A | T | O | E |
| M | G | M | | H | A | S | T | | D | I | S | C | | W | I | T | S | E | N | D |
| | | | B | O | T | T | O | M | O | F | T | H | E | C | L | A | S | | | |
| S | T | E | E | P | L | E | | I | T | S | Y | | L | E | A | N | | S | O | N |
| P | I | X | Y | | A | R | K | S | | | | V | E | T | | D | E | L | A | Y |
| A | N | O | | E | S | S | A | | A | B | J | E | C | T | P | O | V | E | R | T |
| R | E | T | I | N | T | | A | C | T | I | O | N | | | R | O | A | D | S | |
| T | A | I | N | T | | A | B | S | O | L | U | T | E | Z | E | R | | | | |
| A | R | C | H | R | I | V | A | L | | | R | I | T | Z | | | D | U | M | A |
| | | P | E | E | L | E | | E | O | N | | | A | T | T | H | E | T | O | P |
| T | H | E | R | E | S | N | O | W | H | E | R | E | T | O | G | O | B | U | T | U |
| A | R | T | I | | A | G | L | I | M | M | E | R | | P | I | E | R | R | E | |
| P | E | S | T | | | E | A | S | Y | O | N | E | | | F | R | A | N | S | |

# 26

| | | | | | | | | | | | | | | | | | | | | | |
|---|---|---|---|---|---|---|---|---|---|---|---|---|---|---|---|---|---|---|---|---|---|
| N | A | G | S | | | P | A | P | A | | S | K | I | R | T | | J | A | P | A | N |
| E | T | U | I | | S | O | R | E | S | | R | E | S | E | W | | I | R | A | B | U |
| L | O | N | G | S | H | O | R | T | S | | I | R | A | Q | I | | F | A | R | E | R |
| S | N | L | | C | A | L | O | R | I | C | | R | O | U | N | D | F | L | A | T | S |
| O | C | A | L | A | | | W | A | S | A | B | I | | E | K | E | S | | G | T | E |
| N | E | W | O | L | D | S | | | I | F | I | | I | S | L | S | | G | O | E | R |
| | | | S | P | O | O | F | S | | F | A | U | L | T | Y | S | O | U | N | D | S |
| A | R | S | | E | N | U | R | E | | E | S | T | E | S | | E | R | I | | | |
| L | I | T | T | L | E | L | O | T | S | | T | A | X | | D | R | Y | D | E | N | |
| T | B | A | R | S | | | N | O | U | R | I | | | T | U | T | | E | L | U | L |
| A | L | L | I | | B | A | D | F | A | I | R | G | O | O | D | S | | D | I | D | O |
| R | E | E | F | | I | R | S | | | S | E | E | N | O | | | J | O | S | I | E |
| | T | R | E | B | E | K | | A | L | I | | L | E | F | T | R | I | G | H | T | S |
| | | | C | A | N | | S | L | O | B | S | | A | A | R | O | N | | A | Y | S |
| L | A | S | T | I | N | I | T | I | A | L | S | | T | R | I | A | G | E | | | |
| O | L | L | A | | I | N | R | I | | E | G | G | | | P | R | O | C | O | N | S |
| O | B | I | | D | A | V | I | | A | S | T | L | E | Y | | | I | G | L | O | O |
| T | A | P | E | D | L | I | V | E | S | | S | I | M | I | A | N | S | | E | R | A |
| E | N | O | L | A | | T | I | T | H | E | | T | O | P | B | O | T | T | O | M | S |
| R | I | N | K | Y | | E | N | T | E | R | | C | T | E | A | M | | S | L | A | T |
| S | A | S | E | S | | E | G | A | D | S | | H | E | S | S | | | K | E | N | O |

| Q | U | A | K | E | R | S |   | R | I | N | G |   | B | E | L | L | S |   | S | F | P | D |
| E | N | V | E | L | O | P |   | I | R | A | E |   | I | N | O | I | L |   | T | R | U | E |
| D | E | A | D | A | S | A |   | N | A | I | L |   | P | O | W | E | R |   | L | O | C | K |
|   |   | S | L | A | Y |   | D | I | V | A |   |   |   |   |   |   |   |   | E | N | C | E |
| S | C | H |   |   |   |   | S | E | T |   | C | A | L | C |   |   |   |   | O | T | I | S |
| A | R | E |   | E | A | R | N |   | E | R | O |   | R | U | R | A | L |   |   |   |   |   |
| B | O | A |   | P | R | E | Y |   |   |   | E | R | A | T | O |   |   |   | U | S | N | A |
| E | S | T |   | A | C | D | C |   | O | U | T |   | G | A | M | E | S |   | S | T | E | M |
| R | T | E | S |   | L | S | T |   | C | R | O |   | S | T | I | N | E |   | S | E | X | Y |
| S | I | D | E |   | A | T | A | L | O | S | S |   |   | E | S | T | D |   | R | P | T | S |
| A | N | I | L |   | M | A | X | I | M | A | S |   |   |   |   |   |   |   |   |   |   |   |
| W | I | N | A |   | P | R | I | Z | E |   |   |   | P | R | I | S | M |   | W | A | N | E |
|   |   |   |   |   |   |   | H | O | L | D | T | H | E |   |   |   |   | O | P | E | N |
| B | O | P | S |   | N | A | D | A |   | A | T | I | S | S | U | E |   | E | P | I | C |
| A | L | O | T |   | A | V | E | R | T |   | J | O | E |   | T | N | T |   | S | E | G | A |
| C | L | O | Y |   | V | A | N | C | E |   | J | E | D |   | I | T | I | S |   | A | H | S |
| K | A | L | E |   | A | L | O | H | A |   |   |   |   |   | M | E | N | U |   | R | B | I |
|   | H | O | T | E | L |   | M | A | N |   | E | D | G | E |   |   |   |   |   | T | O | N |
| D | O | R | M |   | O | N | E | D |   | A | M | O |   |   |   |   |   |   |   | O | R | G |
| R | H | E | A |   |   |   |   |   | R | O | B | S |   | A | S | E | A |   |   |   |   |   |
| A | B | C | D |   | O | Z | A | W | A |   | T | R | A | P |   | S | P | I | D | E | R | S |
| F | O | U | R |   | S | E | D | A | N |   | H | A | I | R |   | H | A | R | D | H | I | T |
| T | Y | R | E |   | S | E | E | Y | A |   | A | L | L | Y |   | E | M | E | R | S | O | N |

| B | I | R | D | S |   | S | M | I | T | H | S |   | A | D | E |   | N | E | M | O |
| A | T | E | U | P |   | T | O | W | A | R | D |   | U | R | N |   | A | D | I | P |
| R | I | S | K | Y |   | O | N | E | T | H | I | N | K | A | T | A | T | I | M | E |
| A | S | I | A | N |   | A | T | R | A |   |   | A | S | T | H | M | A | T | I | C |
| K | I | N | K | O | F | T | H | E | R | O | A | D |   |   | R | I | L | E |   |   |
|   |   |   | I | V | E | S |   |   | X | S | A | N | D | O | S |   | D | I | D |   |
| G | U | S | S | E | T |   | M | I | M | E | O |   | E | A | N |   | C | O | D | E |
| U | N | A |   | L | A | D | Y | S | I | N | K | S | T | H | E | B | L | U | E | S |
| S | L | R | S |   | O | W | E | N |   |   | A | S | L |   | E | A | T | M | E |   |
| H | I | A | W | A | T | H | A |   | U | F | O | S |   | H | E | N |   |   |   |   |
|   | T | H | I | S | M | A | Y | S | T | I | N | K | A | L | I | T | T | L | E |   |
|   |   |   | N | T | S |   | E | E | N | Y |   | D | I | S | S | O | L | V | E |   |
| R | A | N | D | R |   | A | L | L |   | X | M | A | N |   | N | O | E | S |   |   |
| T | H | E | L | O | R | D | O | F | T | H | E | R | I | N | K | S |   | Y | R | S |
| E | A | V | E |   | A | I | N |   | E | A | S | E | R |   | N | E | E | D | T | O |
| S | T | E |   | L | I | N | E | A | R | A |   |   |   | S | O | N | Y |   |   |   |
|   |   | R | E | E | L |   |   | B | I | G | B | A | N | K | T | H | E | O | R | Y |
| P | A | M | D | A | W | B | E | R |   |   | O | H | I | O |   | O | H | G | E | E |
| A | W | I | N | K | A | N | D | A | P | R | A | Y | E | R |   | R | O | D | A | N |
| G | E | N | A |   | Y | A | O |   | D | E | T | E | C | T |   | A | L | E | R | T |
| O | D | D | S |   | S | I | M |   | T | O | S | S | E | S |   | S | E | N | S | E |

## 31

```
B E A T   A R C H   T S A R   S P O T O N
A T L E I S U R E   R A R A   H A D A G O
S A L T W A T E R T A F F Y   O P I N E D
A P N E A   G E N E V A   S Y R I N G E S
L E I   N E E D   N E R F   I T S
    G O N E R   R E L I E F P I T C H E R
I S H T A R   C O T   N A P E   L A N E
B A T H   P R O   O L D I E   R A S T A
E M E E R   R I M I N I   R E P E N T E D
T E R R A   E M I N E N T   E D G E R S
    P U P P E T S T R I N G S
S H A R P S   R E L E A S E   E A G E R
C A R E E N E D   R E L I N E   A B U S E
A T O L L   D O I N G   P O T   A N N A
R E M I   L I N T   S S T   H I T T E R
P R A C T I C A L J O K E   T O N E R
    O T T   L O R I   F O O L   I F S
S O U R P U S S   T A L L E R   A N G L E
I M P A I R   L I T T L E R E D W A G O N
B I T I N G   U L E E   M A R E S N E S T
S T O D G Y   R E D D   S L O W   U R S A
```

## 32

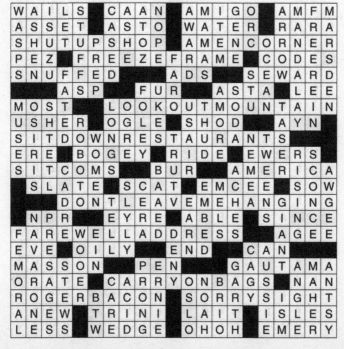

```
W A I L S   C A A N   A M I G O   A M F M
A S S E T   A S T O   W A T E R   R A R A
S H U T U P S H O P   A M E N C O R N E R
P E Z   F R E E Z E F R A M E   C O D E S
S N U F F E D   A D S   S E W A R D
    A S P   F U R   A S T A   L E E
M O S T   L O O K O U T M O U N T A I N
U S H E R   O G L E   S H O D   A Y N
S I T D O W N R E S T A U R A N T S
E R E   B O G E Y   R I D E   E W E R S
S I T C O M S   B U R   A M E R I C A
  S L A T E   S C A T   E M C E E   S O W
    D O N T L E A V E M E H A N G I N G
  N P R   E Y R E   A B L E   S I N C E
F A R E W E L L A D D R E S S   A G E E
E V E   O I L Y   E N D   C A N
M A S S O N   P E N   G A U T A M A
O R A T E   C A R R Y O N B A G S   N A N
R O G E R B A C O N   S O R R Y S I G H T
A N E W   T R I N I   L A I T   I S L E S
L E S S   W E D G E   O H O H   E M E R Y
```

**33**

**34**

**35**

HOLLOW · CLOD · ATTAINED
EROICA · FRODO · MOISTURE
COUNTSNO(I)SES · ANTIETAM
SEAHORSE · UTILS · CSI
COIN · LI(M)PSERVICE · FRET
RUNSTO · ISEE · DORA
ENG · RABBIT(P)EARS · PACES
ECU · IDEAS · EASE · KEA
PEPS · CHICKENFL(L)INGERS
WORKS · HONES · DEARIE
SOMEDAY · DIVOT · GENUSES
EVADED · SALIC · LEADS
TAKESONTHECH(A)IN · SFPD
ATE · SNEE · GRETA · ROE
TESLA · BROW(N)BEATEN · ERI
GINA · BEAU · ASSETS
IDOL · FACE(T)POWDER · EAST
ROO · ALLOY · YEARLONG
INDICATE · P(S)ALMREADERS
SHOWERED · AUNTS · SHINES
HONORERS · LETS · SUNTAN

**36**

JAB · OPALS · OLDAGE · ADDLE
USE · NORAH · COOLIT · LAUER
NIL · PLA(C)ESTOGOPEOPLETO
GALPAL · SPEAKSUP · GHETTO
POTOK · HUD · CLAY
THE(P)RINCESSANDTHE · FLU
HIPPO · OARS · KAUAI · MARAT
ARPEL · WMD · WITHR(E)LATIV(E)
WEED · THA · ZEN · FADESIN
SSR · SHOCKER · MAE · KRAKEN
THEWH(I)TESOFTHE(I)R
JAGUAR · ODA · HARVARD · TAN
INATREE · ION · OSS · SAGO
BESTOFL(U)CKTO · PIK · ATPAR
ESSEN · ISAAC · TELE · NADIA
STY · HEALTH(Y)WEALTH(Y)AND
BOIL · SEP · LIEIN
MOTOWN · DITSIEST · NUNCIO
WHE(R)ETHEWILDTHINGS · ERR
ANNAN · AMINOR · ODILE · RAY
HOSTS · GINKGO · WEBER · SEX

**37**

| A | C | E |   | A | S | C | A | P |   | C | O | R | A | L |   | N | O | A | H | S |
| M | R | X |   | S | M | A | R | T |   | A | R | E | T | E |   | O | P | R | A | H |
| B | O | X | S | C | O | R | E | S |   | N | I | S | E | I |   | T | E | T | R | A |
| L | O | O | P | H | O | L | E |   | R | A | S | C | A | L |   | O | N | E | A | L |
| E | N | N | E |   | C | A | L | L | E | D | O | U | T | A | T | F | I | R | S | T |
|   |   |   | W | A | H |   |   | I | N | A | N | E |   |   | A | T | T | Y | S |   |
|   | S | T | E | P |   | C | A | P | E |   |   | R | O | P | E |   |   |   |   |   |
| F | A | I | R | B | A | L | L |   | W | A | L | K | E | D | I | N | A | R | U | N |
| E | L | M | S |   | M | A | O |   | S | L | E | N | D | E | R |   | L | U | K | E |
| Z | E | E |   | P | I | N | O | N |   | I | C | E |   |   | C | O | B | R | A |   |
|   |   | S | W | I | N | G | F | O | R | T | H | E | F | E | N | C | E | S |   |   |
| S | P | L | A | T |   |   | S | E | T |   | L | I | L | A | C |   | I | N | K |   |
| O | D | O | R |   | E | N | F | I | E | L | D |   | E | I | N |   | S | T | A | G |
| B | A | T | T | I | N | G | O | R | D | E | R |   | F | O | U | L | T | I | P | S |
|   |   |   | D | O | O | R |   |   |   | Y | E | S | T |   | I | O | N | A |   |   |
|   | N | O | S | E | R |   | A | S | T | O | R |   |   | C | E | O |   |   |   |   |
| B | O | T | T | O | M | O | F | T | H | E | F | I | F | T | H |   | P | L | E | A |
| R | E | O | R | G |   | B | E | L | I | E | F |   | R | E | A | L | T | O | R | S |
| A | V | O | I | R |   | A | D | A | R | N |   | F | U | L | L | C | O | U | N | T |
| G | I | L | D | A |   | M | I | S | T | S |   | A | I | L | E | D |   | T | I | E |
| G | L | E | E | M |   | A | N | T | S | Y |   | S | T | A | T | S |   | S | E | R |

**38**

| W | I | N |   | D | O | W | N | S |   | A | D | A | P | T |   | C | S | I | S |
| A | N | A | S |   | A | W | A | I | T |   | V | O | T | R | E |   | R | A | N | K |
| R | U | I | N |   | T | E | S | S | A |   | O | R | T | O | N |   | A | L | O | U |
| D | I | V | I | D | E | D | H | I | G | H | W | A | Y |   | P | A | C | E | R |
| S | T | E | V | E |   |   | G | E | E |   | S | M | I | R | K | S |   |   |   |
|   |   | E | V | I | L |   | B | E | A | D | S |   | I | N | P | E | R | I | L |
| F | A | L | L | E | N | A | P | A | R | T |   | L | A | S | S |   | D | O | L | L |
| L | I | E |   | L | A | T | I | N | S |   | R | O | M | E |   | S | W | O | R | D |
| A | R | M | B | O | N | E | S |   | S | E | V | E | R |   | L | I | M | E | S |
| B | E | A | R | P | I | T |   | A | C | U | M | E | N |   | I | O | N |   |   |
|   | S | N | O |   | T | O | R | N | A | S | U | N | D | E | R |   | D | S | T |
|   | K | E | Y |   | H | A | R | A | S | S |   | R | E | T | O | T | A | L |   |
| H | I | D | E | R |   | G | O | T | O | N |   | E | M | P | O | W | E | R | S |
| I | S | I | N | G |   | I | D | O | L |   | T | O | R | I | E | S |   | A | S | A |
| G | A | R | P |   | E | G | A | L |   | B | A | N | A | N | A | S | P | L | I | T |
| H | O | T | R | O | L | L |   | E | B | O | L | A |   | E | T | U | I |   |   |
|   | B | O | R | G | I | A |   | O | A | K |   |   | P | C | L | A | B |   |   |
|   | T | I | M | E | R |   | F | R | A | C | T | U | R | E | D | S | K | U | L | L |
| W | I | K | I |   | E | A | T | A | T |   | O | D | E | T | O |   | E | N | D | E |
| A | V | E | S |   | C | U | R | I | E |   | M | O | T | T | O |   | R | N | A | S |
| Y | O | R | E |   | O | F | A | L | L |   | E | N | D | E | R |   | S | S | S |

## 39

| L | E | G | R | E | S | T | S | | O | C | A | S | E | Y | | F | A | T | A | L |
| A | W | E | A | T | H | E | R | | R | U | F | F | L | E | | A | G | O | G | O |
| L | E | T | T | H | E | T | I | M | E | S | R | O | L | L | | B | O | W | E | R |
| A | R | S | E | N | E | | | U | L | A | | E | L | B | E | | N | N | E | |
| | A | D | O | S | | D | E | S | C | R | Y | | O | R | E | I | D | A | | |
| L | O | G | | H | O | U | S | E | K | E | E | P | I | N | G | S | E | A | L | |
| P | A | R | A | S | | W | A | L | | A | R | O | U | S | E | S | | | | |
| S | H | I | P | L | O | L | L | I | P | O | P | | R | D | A | | | F | E | M |
| | U | P | T | O | N | | | O | N | S | E | T | | I | G | U | A | N | A | |
| | E | V | E | S | | M | R | T | | R | A | D | | A | K | R | O | N | | |
| Y | O | U | R | E | A | M | A | N | C | H | A | R | L | I | E | B | R | O | W | N |
| A | P | L | A | N | | U | T | E | | E | L | S | | A | L | F | A | | | |
| D | U | L | L | E | A | | O | M | E | G | A | | | H | E | I | R | S | | |
| A | S | A | | N | A | N | | N | O | N | E | W | S | I | S | N | E | W | S | |
| | | | D | A | S | B | O | O | T | | | V | I | A | | T | E | N | A | M |
| T | H | E | E | R | A | O | F | F | E | E | L | I | N | G | S | | | D | N | A |
| R | E | N | O | I | R | | T | R | A | I | T | S | | A | L | L | E | | | |
| I | T | S | | G | A | M | E | | S | T | E | | F | A | E | R | O | E | | |
| V | E | L | M | A | | I | M | I | N | T | O | S | O | M | E | T | H | I | N | G |
| E | R | E | C | T | | M | I | L | I | E | U | | C | O | S | T | A | N | Z | A |
| T | O | R | S | O | | I | N | S | E | R | T | | D | E | T | E | R | G | E | D |

## 40

| H | I | P | P | O | | S | T | E | M | | A | T | T | A | R | | D | A | L | I |
| A | L | A | I | N | | T | I | T | O | | B | A | H | A | I | | E | L | A | N |
| S | L | I | C | E | S | I | N | T | O | | E | B | E | R | T | | G | I | G | A |
| | | N | O | T | E | N | O | U | G | H | T | O | R | E | T | I | R | E | O | N |
| A | S | K | | O | A | K | | | E | T | U | I | | | D | E | N | S | E | |
| G | O | I | N | G | T | O | B | E | A | R | E | L | A | T | I | V | E | | | |
| E | L | L | I | O | T | | A | F | L | | D | I | L | A | T | E | | F | A | X |
| G | A | L | L | | L | C | D | T | V | S | | | T | I | L | | S | A | T | E |
| A | C | E | | S | E | A | L | | A | I | R | P | O | L | L | U | T | I | O | N |
| P | E | R | O | T | | L | O | W | | R | A | E | | | D | H | A | R | M | A |
| | | L | E | T | I | T | A | L | L | H | A | N | G | O | U | T | | | | |
| A | Z | A | L | E | A | | C | I | O | | T | A | O | | R | E | E | K | S | |
| F | I | N | A | L | L | Y | G | O | T | I | T | | D | U | M | A | | A | I | T |
| A | N | T | S | | C | I | R | | N | O | L | I | T | A | | I | S | M | E | |
| R | E | E | | R | E | P | U | T | E | | R | A | N | | F | A | C | T | O | R |
| | | R | E | D | E | F | I | N | E | T | H | E | M | I | S | S | I | O | N | |
| S | A | L | E | S | | F | L | A | W | | | O | O | P | | N | N | E | | |
| T | H | A | T | H | A | S | N | T | B | E | E | N | W | A | S | H | E | D | | |
| Y | E | T | I | | L | I | E | S | L | | A | M | I | N | O | A | C | I | D | S |
| L | A | I | N | | A | N | S | A | E | | S | E | R | E | | L | H | A | S | A |
| E | D | N | A | | N | E | S | T | S | | E | X | E | D | | T | O | N | T | O |

## 41

Puzzle 41

| P R O N G | R O N D O | L A P D | R P M S |
| R U M O R | O C E A N | I N R I | I R M A |
| O N E M O R E T I M E | M N E M O N I C S |
| E N E | E G O M A N I A | S M U G G L E |
| N E U | A G A S | S E E I T |
| J I F | E N G I N E M O U N T S | O U L U |
| A M I L L I O N | D E L L A | T E N N I S |
| P A N A S O N I C | D A P S | R E E V E |
| E D D Y | N O T T O M E N T I O N | M E M |
| D E I S T | S R T A | O M N I V O R E |
| N O O I L | L E X U S | A T E A T |
| M A G N E T I C | I S I S | S M I L E |
| A R N | D I V I N E M O T H E R | P O O L |
| D I E C I | E N O L | E A S E M E N T S |
| R A M O N A | E N I A C | L A T E D A T E |
| E L O N | N O M E N C L A T U R E | L O S |
| T R A L A | O C A S | I T T |
| V I D E O E D | I R O N M I K E | O I D |
| O N E M O M E N T | S T A T E S W O M E N |
| C O E N | I S I T | T O R I C | A T S E A |
| E N D S | A T T Y | S N A C K | S H O R N |

Puzzle 42

| A R R O W | R C V R | T B S P | C P A S |
| B O I S E | O H I O | K O R E A | L O L L |
| C A P R I | B E E R B U R I A L P O L K A |
| R E I G N O F T E R R I E R | I S L E T |
| C H E T | M O T I F | L E O N E |
| A B S | H I D E | E N M I T I E S |
| B O T A N I C A L G U A R D I A N S |
| U S A G E | S I E N N A | C I G | D O T |
| T H R A S H | K O D I A K M O M E N T |
| C I T I B A N K | D U E | N A S T Y |
| C O H N | M A G O O | G E R R Y | I D O L |
| A M A S S | R O O | E R A S A B L E |
| P A R T Y I N G G I F T | M A M M A L |
| T N T | R O E | I L D U C E | M A O R I |
| L I T T L E O R P H E A N A N N I E |
| R E S O N A T E | E L S E | A D D |
| O R I N G | C U O M O | C A L F |
| D O D G E | P A R K I N G M E T E O R S |
| M I L E S P E R G A L L E O N | G R O H L |
| A C E S | C A R E Y | A R O D | I G L O O |
| N A S T | S L E D | Y E N S | T E L E X |

Grid 43:

| A | R | T | S | ■ | L | E | A | F | L | I | K | E | ■ | ■ | T | S | G | A | R | P |
| N | E | H | I | ■ | L | E | N | A | O | L | I | N | ■ | S | H | E | L | T | E | R |
| G | A | E | L | I | C | W | A | R | N | I | N | G | ■ | H | A | V | A | R | T | I |
| E | L | I | O | T | ■ | ■ | ■ | E | G | A | D | ■ | A | R | T | E | S | I | A | N |
| R | A | S | ■ | C | L | A | S | S | I | C | A | C | T | I | O | N | S | U | I | T |
| E | L | L | ■ | H | U | G | O | ■ | ■ | ■ | L | I | E | N | ■ | ■ | M | L | S | ■ |
| D | E | E | D | ■ | R | U | S | T | I | C | B | U | C | K | E | T | S | ■ | ■ | ■ |
| ■ | ■ | O | S | A | K | A | ■ | A | B | O | M | B | ■ | ■ | A | L | C | A | N | ■ |
| U | P | F | O | R | ■ | U | N | S | E | T | ■ | L | A | I | L | A | A | L | I | ■ |
| S | U | M | ■ | S | C | A | N | N | E | D | ■ | K | I | N | G | L | Y | R | I | C |
| E | R | A | T | ■ | R | O | D | I | N | ■ | C | N | O | T | E | ■ | S | P | E | E |
| F | I | N | E | T | U | N | I | C | ■ | P | R | O | N | E | T | O | ■ | E | N | T |
| U | T | I | L | I | Z | E | D | ■ | B | E | E | T | S | ■ | ■ | P | A | N | S | Y |
| L | Y | C | E | E | ■ | ■ | I | R | E | S | T | ■ | Z | I | P | I | T | ■ | ■ | ■ |
| ■ | ■ | O | R | I | G | I | N | A | L | C | Y | N | I | C | ■ | L | E | V | I | ■ |
| S | O | O | ■ | ■ | W | I | S | C | ■ | ■ | ■ | O | T | O | E | ■ | R | A | M | ■ |
| T | O | P | I | C | O | F | T | H | E | M | O | R | N | I | N | G | ■ | A | R | P |
| A | L | I | M | E | N | T | S | ■ | C | E | R | A | ■ | ■ | G | O | N | N | A | ■ |
| M | A | N | M | A | D | E | ■ | G | R | E | A | T | L | Y | M | Y | S | T | I | C |
| P | L | E | A | S | E | D | ■ | P | U | T | T | O | S | E | A | ■ | L | I | S | T |
| S | A | D | D | E | R | ■ | ■ | A | S | S | E | N | T | T | O | ■ | O | C | H | S |

## 44

Grid 44:

| B | R | A | S | S | ■ | S | T | R | A | W | ■ | S | O | P | ■ | G | R | A | S | S |
| R | A | B | A | T | ■ | T | R | O | T | H | ■ | T | W | A | ■ | T | O | V | A | H |
| A | C | E | L | A | ■ | R | O | S | E | A | G | A | I | N | ■ | O | T | E | R | O |
| S | K | E | T | C | H | O | U | T | ■ | T | H | I | N | G | S | ■ | C | R | A | P |
| ■ | ■ | S | K | I | P | P | E | D | ■ | I | N | G | R | A | M | ■ | A | L | P | ■ |
| P | A | P | ■ | S | P | H | E | R | I | C | ■ | S | T | A | V | E | ■ | G | E | E |
| O | N | A | T | ■ | S | E | R | E | N | E | R | ■ | O | V | E | R | S | E | E | R |
| P | A | R | E | N | T | ■ | ■ | D | A | T | E | D | ■ | Y | A | L | L | ■ | ■ | ■ |
| S | T | A | M | B | E | R | G | ■ | H | U | N | C | H | ■ | S | O | A | R | E | D |
| T | O | D | ■ | C | R | O | O | K | ■ | S | I | T | O | N | ■ | T | W | I | N | E |
| A | L | I | T | ■ | S | T | I | E | S | ■ | N | E | V | I | L | ■ | S | P | E | W |
| R | I | G | H | T | ■ | S | N | I | T | S | ■ | N | E | N | E | S | ■ | P | R | Y |
| S | A | M | E | A | S | ■ | G | R | A | T | E | ■ | R | E | T | R | I | E | V | E |
| ■ | ■ | U | N | T | O | ■ | A | L | E | P | H | ■ | S | A | D | D | A | Y | ■ | ■ |
| J | O | H | N | G | A | L | T | ■ | E | A | S | E | F | U | L | ■ | S | I | T | E |
| U | N | E | ■ | L | Y | D | I | A | ■ | M | O | R | O | N | I | C | ■ | T | E | D |
| M | E | W | ■ | E | E | L | E | R | S | ■ | ■ | M | E | R | I | D | I | A | ■ | ■ |
| P | H | E | W | ■ | R | A | G | T | O | P | ■ | W | A | T | E | R | D | R | O | P |
| I | O | D | I | C | ■ | T | A | L | L | A | D | E | G | A | ■ | C | A | I | R | O |
| N | U | T | S | O | ■ | I | M | A | ■ | S | A | G | E | R | ■ | U | P | P | E | R |
| G | R | O | P | E | ■ | N | E | B | ■ | S | W | O | R | D | ■ | S | T | E | N | T |

```
C A B A L _ P A R C _ I D I D _ C O M E T
A L E R O _ A B E L _ N A V Y _ E L O P E
P L A Y W I T H M A T C H E S _ D I V A N
_ _ C A S S I O _ S E A L _ L E A V E _
J O H N _ L O R I S E S _ G E T R E A L _
A L B _ M E S S W I T H T E X A S _ M A G
C L A W A T _ _ I C H _ R O I L _ S U C H
O I L E D _ C I S _ _ S O D A _ P A S T E
B E L I E V E T H E H Y P E _ T O M C A T
_ _ R A I S E _ L O R E _ F I R E L I T
D O H _ D R A M _ P I U _ P A R T _ E D O
A M A T E U R _ R A S P _ O V E R T _ _
G I V E N S _ Q U I T Y O U R D A Y J O B
A G E N T _ D U B S _ _ R T E _ I R E N E
M O A T _ S O I L _ N B A _ _ S T A L I N
A S C _ Q U O T E M E O N T H I S _ L C D
_ H O T W I R E _ O W N G O A L _ A Y E S
_ _ W H E T S _ S C A M _ A D V E R B _
H U M O R _ T A L K T O S T R A N G E R S
A P A R T _ E S A U _ T H E O _ D U A N E
G I N N Y _ P I M P _ S E E N _ S E N A T
```

```
M A W R _ W A D I _ _ S C A M _ _ I R A N
E U R O _ E G A D _ D I A N A _ S T O L E
G R E A T D A Z E _ E M P T Y Z E S T E R
A A N D W _ _ S A W B I T _ S O L A C E D
_ _ _ H I K E _ S H A L O M _ N F L _ _
A L P A C I N O _ A S A R U L E _ L A H R
M A I Z E L O B S T E R _ D I S A G R E E
A T T A _ T R E A T S _ M C M _ T O E I N
S T O R K _ M Y T H _ R E A P _ T O N N E
S E N D E R _ S E E J U S T I C E D O Z E
_ _ _ I O U _ H A M _ _ D I M _ _ _ _
H I G H L I G H T E R P E Z _ A P P E A R
E N R O L _ L E V Y _ R E E L _ T O N G A
A L A M O _ I A S _ C O L L E T _ O L A V
R E V E R S E R _ F R A S I E R C R A Z E
S T E M _ A S S U R E S _ G R O U P I E S
_ _ A M Y _ T R E A T Y _ Y U L E _ _
M A S K I N G _ G E T S I N _ _ P O S S E
E M P E R O R Z E R O _ K I D Z A P P E R
S M O R E _ A S O U R _ E T U I _ L A V A
H O T S _ M A N N _ _ S E E P _ E Y E S
```

```
T R A C E   P I C K O F F     P A C M A N
H U R L S   T R U E F A C T   A C H E B E
U N C U T   A R T I F I C I A L H E A R T
S E T T E R S   T E L   A M I E   L I S
    I C E E   O W E R   L R O N   E T D
A R C H   C I V I L   A A A S   N E I G H
R E C   T O M A S   I L K   P A L M E R
M D I   A R U L E   G U E S S E R   E D S
A F R A I D S O   C O M E Q U I C K
D O C I L E   F A I R   R U E   A L B
A R L O   R I F F S   M I A T A   P O O L
  D E L   M I R   V E E R   L O U V R E
    I T S A C I N C H   E I G H T E E N
N F L   R A C E C A R   B I D E N   T D S
P R O P E L   A S S   E N E R O   R O E
R E I N K   A I N T   P E C A N   A I M S
    E S C   O R C A   T O S H   O C T A
A W L   E R E I   A O L   K N O W N A S
D I A M O N D N E C K L A C E   D O G G Y
E L N I N O   G A M E O V E R   A R L E S
N L E A S T   T E N S I O N   S K E E T
```

```
T A S S   B A G   D A M U P   R E A P S
A R T E   A G O   H E L E N A   U L T R A
X M A S T R E E   O P E N I N G N O T E S
S E N T M E S S A G E   D O S   I M S
A N D E S   W R E N   E D G R I M L E Y
L I S T   Q U I T   D A Y O   K N E A D
E A T   R U S T Y   S I D E   I T T
  O N E I S H   N O R I S K   H O S E D
A D R E M   R O M A N   E N S U E   E L Y
S E E S A W   U N I T S   T U R F   R A N
I N A T I E   T O A H A L T   S A L V I A
A S S   N E W S   D E L I A   A M I E N S
G E O   S P E A R   S A N K A   I N S E T
O R N O T   E Y E L I D   E M P L O Y
    P O P   I C E T   R A S P Y   O A S
  S H E B A   N O N U   A G O G   L U N A
P E A C E S I G N   A D Z E   C A R O M
L T S   S T D   T U R N O N A D I M E
A S S W E E T A S P I E   I D E A L G A S
Y A L I E   A V I S O S   U A E   E H L E
S T E I N   G E T I N   S Y D   S T Y X
```

## 51

| S | A | M | E | H | E | R | E | ■ | O | P | A | Q | U | E | ■ | P | A | I | L | S |
| T | R | A | V | E | L | E | D | ■ | M | E | D | U | S | A | ■ | E | L | L | I | E |
| A | N | G | E | L | M | A | N | A | G | E | M | E | N | T | ■ | N | I | T | T | I |
| G | O | I | N | ■ | S | P | A | R | ■ | R | I | B | ■ | S | E | N | O | R | A | S |
| ■ | ■ | ■ | T | E | T | E | ■ | M | A | S | T | E | R | ■ | G | A | T | O | ■ | ■ |
| S | H | A | U | N | ■ | D | O | R | M | ■ | S | C | A | L | Y | M | O | V | I | E |
| S | A | L | A | D | A | ■ | N | E | A | P | ■ | P | I | P | E | ■ | A | M | A | ■ |
| T | H | E | L | I | G | H | T | S | T | U | F | F | ■ | M | T | S | ■ | T | E | S |
| S | A | X | ■ | C | A | W | ■ | T | I | N | L | I | K | E | ■ | J | O | L | T | ■ |
| ■ | ■ | D | O | T | Y | ■ | ■ | C | O | S | I | ■ | H | A | I | R | D | O | ■ | ■ |
| P | I | L | A | T | E | S | O | F | T | H | E | C | A | R | I | B | B | E | A | N |
| A | G | E | N | T | S | ■ | V | I | A | L | ■ | E | N | D | S | ■ | ■ | ■ | ■ | ■ |
| Y | U | N | G | ■ | P | I | E | D | I | S | H | ■ | C | G | I | ■ | M | S | G | ■ |
| C | A | N | ■ | T | W | O | ■ | F | A | N | T | A | S | T | I | C | F | O | U | L |
| U | N | O | ■ | V | O | L | E | ■ | E | Y | R | E | ■ | S | A | L | O | M | E | ■ |
| T | A | X | I | D | R | I | V | E | L | ■ | E | M | A | J | ■ | T | E | R | S | E |
| ■ | L | O | I | S | ■ | A | R | I | O | S | I | ■ | A | B | E | T | ■ | ■ | ■ | ■ |
| F | I | E | N | N | E | S | ■ | O | E | R | ■ | N | A | C | L | ■ | C | H | A | P |
| E | D | W | I | N | ■ | W | E | D | D | I | N | G | C | L | A | S | H | E | R | S |
| S | E | I | Z | E | ■ | A | R | E | T | O | O | ■ | H | Y | S | T | E | R | I | A |
| T | A | S | E | R | ■ | M | A | S | O | N | S | ■ | S | N | E | E | R | S | A | T |

## 52

| F | A | M | E | R | ■ | M | E | W | L | ■ | A | D | A | P | T | ■ | B | U | L | L |
| I | N | O | N | E | ■ | O | C | H | O | ■ | L | I | M | O | U | S | I | N | E | S |
| L | I | T | U | P | ■ | U | H | O | H | ■ | U | P | T | O | N | O | G | O | O | D |
| L | M | O | R | E | ■ | N | O | M | A | A | M | ■ | L | A | P | D | ■ | ■ | ■ | ■ |
| ■ | A | R | E | N | D | T | ■ | E | N | G | I | N | E | ■ | S | H | U | T | U | P |
| E | T | H | ■ | T | E | R | A | ■ | E | N | A | C | T | ■ | O | M | O | R | E | ■ |
| L | I | O | N | ■ | C | U | T | U | P | ■ | U | M | O | R | E | ■ | M | A | G | E |
| M | O | M | A | ■ | I | S | O | B | A | R | ■ | I | T | O | N | ■ | Y | S | E | R |
| O | N | E | U | P | ■ | H | M | O | R | E | ■ | B | A | L | T | I | ■ | T | O | E |
| ■ | ■ | R | E | S | ■ | L | I | S | T | ■ | G | L | O | M | ■ | E | N | D | ■ | ■ |
| ■ | B | U | T | W | A | I | T | T | H | E | R | E | S | M | O | R | E | ■ | ■ | ■ |
| A | L | A | ■ | C | A | P | N | ■ | Y | A | L | E | ■ | B | R | A | ■ | ■ | ■ | ■ |
| S | O | N | ■ | O | R | L | O | N | ■ | P | L | A | I | T | ■ | E | G | B | D | F |
| S | U | N | G | ■ | T | O | R | O | ■ | E | M | I | N | E | M | ■ | O | R | E | O |
| A | V | E | O | ■ | H | M | O | R | E | ■ | E | M | O | R | E | ■ | N | O | S | E |
| I | R | R | E | G | ■ | B | U | T | N | O | ■ | T | R | A | M | ■ | K | T | S | ■ |
| L | E | S | S | I | S | ■ | T | H | A | T | S | A | ■ | O | N | A | G | E | R | ■ |
| ■ | ■ | L | A | M | P | ■ | B | O | O | M | E | R | ■ | C | L | I | O | S | ■ | ■ |
| P | A | R | A | N | O | R | M | A | L | ■ | L | O | K | I | ■ | K | E | N | Y | A |
| A | P | O | S | T | R | O | P | H | E | ■ | A | R | E | S | ■ | L | A | T | E | X |
| D | E | B | T | ■ | E | D | G | A | R | ■ | R | E | S | T | ■ | E | M | O | R | E |

## 53

```
BOCA   PAPA   COMP   MAGPIE
BRAM   OVEN   OWIE   ACORNS
GO$NGLONG   PENNYSTO¢KS
UNHEROIC   ZANINESS   CIE
NOOSE   DIZZY   MALE   JENS
    NIA   SLIT   ENL   SAP
AGHAST   SPOSA   TELECOM
PLACEBO   IPASS   ROCKIER
SANS   ABIT   CHOC   ORANGE
EDD   FLOS   FRILLS   ESTAS
    DOLLAR$AND¢ENTS
NOBIS   SAYSME   FROS   BAD
FROSTS   CECE   PFFT   PORE
LETMEUP   SANTA   SWORNIN
    STARDOM   LTYRS   ONEDAY
    OYS   PAN   KICK   SSR
POMS   MANY   CESAR   PSALM
URL   MARIMBAS   POWERTIE
TI¢KERTAPES   SUNKCO$TS
TONIER   CHAT   ILER   ONEA
SNEAKY   SOME   CARP   MGRS
```

## 54

```
JINX   PARC   AGHAST   HENS
AMOK   AMOR   MEAGER   EVIL
WADEINTHEWATTEAU   RITE
AXE   RIO   DEJA   OMELETTE
    PERCOCET   TELS   AWAIT
UNOS   ONBOARD   VIE
TISTHECEZANNE   PENGUIN
ANI   ONADARE   DET   ANNE
HOTSPOTS   TEEUP   LUGAR
    MASC   BOODLES   AGENT
ASSOC   HELLODALI   CURES
SHAKA   AQUAMAN   CITI
CALEB   BUENA   POLANSKI
ALMA   SUI   NOBALLS   PEN
PLANETS   QUESERASEURAT
    DYE   MUSTSEE   FINS
SHAME   NAME   ISEASYON
PAKISTAN   RAFT   LIE   KIA
ITER   WITHFLYINGKAHLOS
THEO   ISRAEL   NOAH   BENT
SAMS   THAMES   GRES   ORSO
```

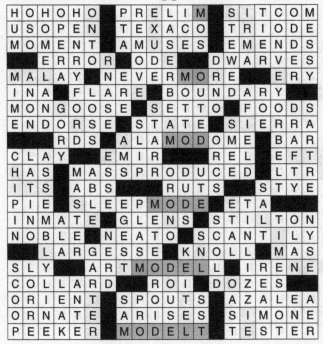

## 55

Puzzle 55:

| H | O | H | O | H | O | ■ | P | R | E | L | I | M | ■ | S | I | T | C | O | M |
| U | S | O | P | E | N | ■ | T | E | X | A | C | O | ■ | T | R | I | O | D | E |
| M | O | M | E | N | T | ■ | A | M | U | S | E | S | ■ | E | M | E | N | D | S |
| ■ | ■ | E | R | R | O | R | ■ | O | D | E | ■ | ■ | D | W | A | R | V | E | S |
| M | A | L | A | Y | ■ | N | E | V | E | R | M | O | R | E | ■ | ■ | E | R | Y |
| I | N | A | ■ | F | L | A | R | E | ■ | B | O | U | N | D | A | R | Y | ■ | ■ |
| M | O | N | G | O | O | S | E | ■ | S | E | T | T | O | ■ | F | O | O | D | S |
| E | N | D | O | R | S | E | ■ | S | T | A | T | E | ■ | S | I | E | R | R | A |
| ■ | ■ | R | D | S | ■ | A | L | A | M | O | D | O | M | E | ■ | B | A | R | ■ |
| C | L | A | Y | ■ | E | M | I | R | ■ | ■ | R | E | L | ■ | E | F | T | ■ | ■ |
| H | A | S | ■ | M | A | S | S | P | R | O | D | U | C | E | D | ■ | L | T | R |
| I | T | S | ■ | A | B | S | ■ | ■ | R | U | T | S | ■ | S | T | Y | E | ■ | ■ |
| P | I | E | ■ | S | L | E | E | P | M | O | D | E | ■ | E | T | A | ■ | ■ | ■ |
| I | N | M | A | T | E | ■ | G | L | E | N | S | ■ | S | T | I | L | T | O | N |
| N | O | B | L | E | ■ | N | E | A | T | O | ■ | S | C | A | N | T | I | L | Y |
| ■ | ■ | L | A | R | G | E | S | S | E | ■ | K | N | O | L | L | ■ | M | A | S |
| S | L | Y | ■ | A | R | T | M | O | D | E | L | L | ■ | I | R | E | N | E | ■ |
| C | O | L | L | A | R | D | ■ | ■ | R | O | I | ■ | D | O | Z | E | S | ■ | ■ |
| O | R | I | E | N | T | ■ | S | P | O | U | T | S | ■ | A | Z | A | L | E | A |
| O | R | N | A | T | E | ■ | A | R | I | S | E | S | ■ | S | I | M | O | N | E |
| P | E | E | K | E | R | ■ | M | O | D | E | L | T | ■ | T | E | S | T | E | R |

Puzzle 56:

| P | A | C | E | S | ■ | A | F | T | S | ■ | L | I | L | T | ■ | ■ | K | E | P | I |
| U | B | O | L | T | ■ | G | A | U | L | ■ | A | S | I | A | ■ | D | I | C | E | S |
| R | A | R | E | R | ■ | A | R | B | O | R | I | S | T | S | ■ | I | N | T | R | A |
| R | A | N | G | E | ■ | K | E | E | P | S | C | U | T | T | I | N | G | O | U | T |
| ■ | E | Y | E | S | H | A | D | E | S | ■ | E | L | I | T | E | S | ■ | ■ | ■ | ■ |
| F | D | R | ■ | T | E | A | S | ■ | ■ | A | R | E | N | A | ■ | I | M | P | S | ■ |
| J | U | S | T | W | E | N | T | D | O | W | N | ■ | G | L | A | Z | E | R | S | ■ |
| O | B | T | A | I | N | ■ | U | N | E | V | E | N | ■ | T | E | N | O | R | ■ | ■ |
| R | O | O | M | S | ■ | H | A | S | S | T | I | L | L | G | O | T | B | U | G | S |
| D | I | N | ■ | E | B | E | R | T | ■ | S | L | O | W | L | A | N | E | ■ | ■ | ■ |
| ■ | S | E | W | ■ | A | X | E | ■ | ■ | E | A | T | ■ | D | A | H | ■ | ■ | ■ | ■ |
| ■ | A | D | R | E | N | A | L | S | ■ | A | S | S | Y | R | ■ | T | A | J | ■ | ■ |
| F | A | I | L | E | D | S | O | M | E | T | E | S | T | S | ■ | H | E | A | V | E |
| R | U | B | L | E | ■ | T | O | N | N | E | S | ■ | ■ | M | U | L | D | E | R | ■ |
| A | D | E | P | T | A | T | ■ | I | S | O | N | T | H | E | B | L | I | N | K | ■ |
| N | I | T | A | ■ | L | A | T | I | N | ■ | H | U | L | A | ■ | S | T | Y | ■ | ■ |
| ■ | ■ | P | I | P | P | I | N | ■ | E | C | C | E | N | T | R | I | C | ■ | ■ | ■ |
| D | E | V | E | L | O | P | E | D | A | S | H | O | R | T | ■ | B | R | O | O | M |
| O | Z | A | R | K | ■ | I | D | E | N | T | I | C | A | L | ■ | P | O | U | R | S |
| T | R | I | E | S | ■ | N | Y | E | T | ■ | D | O | M | E | ■ | I | N | N | E | R |
| S | A | N | D | ■ | G | E | D | S | ■ | E | A | S | Y | ■ | E | S | T | O | P | ■ |

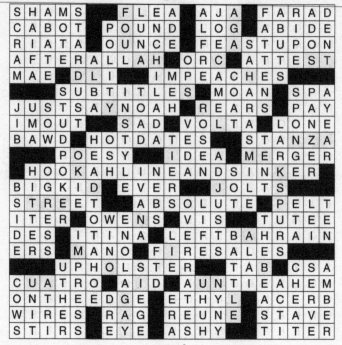

Grid 57:

| S | H | A | M | S |   |   | F | L | E | A |   | A | J | A |   | F | A | R | A | D |
| C | A | B | O | T |   | P | O | U | N | D |   | L | O | G |   | A | B | I | D | E |
| R | I | A | T | A |   | O | U | N | C | E |   | F | E | A | S | T | U | P | O | N |
| A | F | T | E | R | A | L | L | A | H |   | O | R | C |   | A | T | T | E | S | T |
| M | A | E |   | D | L | I |   |   | I | M | P | E | A | C | H | E | S |   |   |   |
|   |   |   | S | U | B | T | I | T | L | E | S |   | M | O | A | N |   | S | P | A |
| J | U | S | T | S | A | Y | N | O | A | H |   | R | E | A | R | S |   | P | A | Y |
| I | M | O | U | T |   |   | S | A | D |   | V | O | L | T | A |   | L | O | N | E |
| B | A | W | D |   | H | O | T | D | A | T | E | S |   |   | S | T | A | N | Z | A |
|   |   |   | P | O | E | S | Y |   |   | I | D | E | A |   | M | E | R | G | E | R |
|   | H | O | O | K | A | H | L | I | N | E | A | N | D | S | I | N | K | E | R |   |
| B | I | G | K | I | D |   | E | V | E | R |   | J | O | L | T | S |   |   |   |   |
| S | T | R | E | E | T |   |   | A | B | S | O | L | U | T | E |   | P | E | L | T |
| I | T | E | R |   | O | W | E | N | S |   | V | I | S |   |   | T | U | T | E | E |
| D | E | S |   | I | T | I | N | A |   | L | E | F | T | B | A | H | R | A | I | N |
| E | R | S |   | M | A | N | O |   | F | I | R | E | S | A | L | E | S |   |   |   |
|   |   |   | U | P | H | O | L | S | T | E | R |   |   | T | A | B |   | C | S | A |
| C | U | A | T | R | O |   | A | I | D |   | A | U | N | T | I | E | A | H | E | M |
| O | N | T | H | E | E | D | G | E |   | E | T | H | Y | L |   | A | C | E | R | B |
| W | I | R | E | S |   | R | A | G |   | R | E | U | N | E |   | S | T | A | V | E |
| S | T | I | R | S |   | E | Y | E |   | A | S | H | Y |   |   | T | I | T | E | R |

## 58

Grid 58:

| T | E | L | E | P | H | O | N | E |   | B | A | R |   | C | L | O | T | H | E | S |
| I | N | I | T | I | A | L | E | D |   | R | U | E |   | R | A | V | I | O | L | I |
| C | H | A | S | T | I | S | E | D |   | A | T | L |   | U | N | E | N | D | E | D |
| K | A | I |   | R | O | S | Y |   | C | O | I | N | S |   | R | E | S | E | E |   |
| E | L | S |   | I | S | N | O |   | R | E | P | E | A | T | E | D |   |   |   |   |
| T | O | E | A | T |   | N | A | N |   | I | F | F | I | E | R |   | C | A | F |   |
|   |   |   | D | O | G | G |   | R | A | I | L |   | T | E | R | I | G | A | R | R |
| O | F | M | E |   | R | I | C | O |   | N | O | P | A | R |   | V | E | R | G | E |
| F | O | E | S |   | A | L | O | U | E | T | T | E |   |   | D | E | S | R | E | E |
| F | U | N | T |   | B | R | O | N | T | E |   | R | I | S | E | S |   | I | N | T |
| E | R | N | E |   | B | O | R | D | E | R | L | I | N | E | S |   | M | E | T | H |
| N | C | O |   | S | A | Y | S | T |   | B | I | M | I | N | I |   | A | S | I | R |
| S | O | N | T | A | G |   |   | H | O | R | S | E | C | A | R |   | N | O | N | O |
| I | L | I | E | D |   | B | E | E | N | E |   | T | E | T | E |   | G | N | A | W |
| V | O | T | E | D | F | O | R |   | I | D | L | E |   | E | S | S | E |   |   |   |
| E | R | E |   | L | I | B | I | D | O |   | A | R | R |   |   | G | R | I | N | D |
|   |   |   | E | N | S | C | O | N | C | E |   | E | T | A | T |   | D | O | O |   |
| P | I | C | A | S |   | L | A | U | D | E |   | S | T | U | B |   | I | T | T |   |
| I | M | A | L | O | N | E |   | S | O | D |   | F | I | N | A | L | E | D | I | T |
| P | A | P | E | R | E | D |   | E | M | E |   | P | R | E | C | I | P | I | C | E |
| E | X | P | R | E | S | S |   | R | E | D |   | D | E | D | I | C | A | T | E | D |

## 59

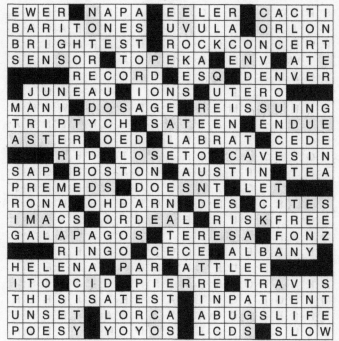

| E | W | E | R | | N | A | P | A | | E | E | L | E | R | | C | A | C | T | I |
| B | A | R | I | T | O | N | E | S | | U | V | U | L | A | | O | R | L | O | N |
| B | R | I | G | H | T | E | S | T | | R | O | C | K | C | O | N | C | E | R | T |
| S | E | N | S | O | R | | T | O | P | E | K | A | | E | N | V | | A | T | E |
| | | | R | E | C | O | R | D | | E | S | Q | | D | E | N | V | E | R | |
| | J | U | N | E | A | U | | I | O | N | S | | U | T | E | R | O | | | |
| M | A | N | I | | D | O | S | A | G | E | | R | E | I | S | S | U | I | N | G |
| T | R | I | P | T | Y | C | H | | S | A | T | E | E | N | | E | N | D | U | E |
| A | S | T | E | R | | O | E | D | | L | A | B | R | A | T | | C | E | D | E |
| | | R | I | D | | L | O | S | E | T | O | | C | A | V | E | S | I | N | |
| S | A | P | | B | O | S | T | O | N | | A | U | S | T | I | N | | T | E | A |
| P | R | E | M | E | D | S | | D | O | E | S | N | T | | L | E | T | | | |
| R | O | N | A | | O | H | D | A | R | N | | D | E | S | | C | I | T | E | S |
| I | M | A | C | S | | O | R | D | E | A | L | | R | I | S | K | F | R | E | E |
| G | A | L | A | P | A | G | O | S | | T | E | R | E | S | A | | F | O | N | Z |
| | | R | I | N | G | O | | C | E | C | E | | A | L | B | A | N | Y | | |
| H | E | L | E | N | A | | P | A | R | | A | T | T | L | E | E | | | | |
| I | T | O | | C | I | D | | P | I | E | R | R | E | | T | R | A | V | I | S |
| T | H | I | S | I | S | A | T | E | S | T | | I | N | P | A | T | I | E | N | T |
| U | N | S | E | T | | L | O | R | C | A | | A | B | U | G | S | L | I | F | E |
| P | O | E | S | Y | | Y | O | Y | O | S | | L | C | D | S | | S | L | O | W |

## 60

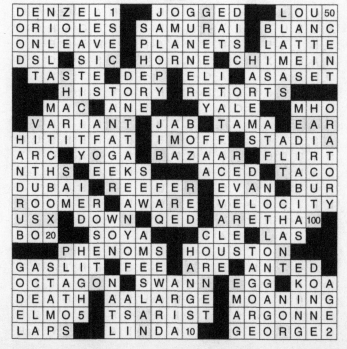

| D | E | N | Z | E | L | 1 | | J | O | G | G | E | D | | L | O | U | 50 |
| O | R | I | O | L | E | S | | S | A | M | U | R | A | I | | B | L | A | N | C |
| O | N | L | E | A | V | E | | P | L | A | N | E | T | S | | L | A | T | T | E |
| D | S | L | | S | I | C | | H | O | R | N | E | | C | H | I | M | E | I | N |
| | T | A | S | T | E | | D | E | P | | E | L | I | | A | S | A | S | E | T |
| | | H | I | S | T | O | R | Y | | R | E | T | O | R | T | S | | | | |
| | M | A | C | | A | N | E | | | Y | A | L | E | | | M | H | O | | |
| V | A | R | I | A | N | T | | J | A | B | | T | A | M | A | | E | A | R | |
| H | I | T | I | T | F | A | T | | I | M | O | F | F | | S | T | A | D | I | A |
| A | R | C | | Y | O | G | A | | B | A | Z | A | A | R | | F | L | I | R | T |
| N | T | H | S | | E | E | K | S | | A | C | E | D | | T | A | C | O | | |
| D | U | B | A | I | | R | E | E | F | E | R | | E | V | A | N | | B | U | R |
| R | O | O | M | E | R | | A | W | A | R | E | | V | E | L | O | C | I | T | Y |
| U | S | X | | D | O | W | N | | Q | E | D | | A | R | E | T | H | A | 100 | |
| B | O | 20 | | S | O | Y | A | | | C | L | E | | L | A | S | | | | |
| | | P | H | E | N | O | M | S | | H | O | U | S | T | O | N | | | | |
| G | A | S | L | I | T | | F | E | E | | A | R | E | | A | N | T | E | D | |
| O | C | T | A | G | O | N | | S | W | A | N | N | | E | G | G | | K | O | A |
| D | E | A | T | H | | A | A | L | A | R | G | E | | M | O | A | N | I | N | G |
| E | L | M | O | 5 | | T | S | A | R | I | S | T | | A | R | G | O | N | N | E |
| L | A | P | S | | L | I | N | D | A | 10 | | G | E | O | R | G | E | 2 | |

**61**

```
S P A Y   T A L C   M C A T S   S E P I A
I L I A   O H I O   R I C O H   E A R L S
P A R K A V E N U E C O U G A R Q U E S T
  T W I X   M A R S H   P A L A U   S A O
S E A M E N   I S I T   E L M E R S
C A V A L I E R C A P R I D I P L O M A T
H U E   G M A   Y S E R     S W A M I
    A L H I R T   A M O U R   E N Y A
B O B C A T R A B B I T A C C O R D
R O L E X   A R A   T A L E   A B S
I N T R E P I D R A M C H A L L E N G E R
M A S   S O M A   S O O     B U R N T
    S T O R M T R O O P E R S O N A T A
A Q U I   H E N C E   S H A N K S
M U N R O   B I T O   U Z I   A T F
C E L E B R I T Y G O L F D E F E N D E R
  O N S I D E   N E M O   F L I M S Y
A K A   C O I N S   T E R S E   A X I S
M I D G E T O U T B A C K E X P L O R E R
P R E E N   C R A M P   E R A S   N E R F
S I D L E   Y E T I S   D E M I   S D A K
```

**62**

```
H O G   A I L S   T H E M   R A H   C F O
A L L U P S E T   R O B E   P R O S H O P
S E I Z E H E R S A L A D   I M T H E R E
R A D I X   R E I L L Y   S A U C E R
O N E S E T   A G E E   S H A R I   K I A
O N O   S O C K H E R P L A Y E R   H G T
M A N S   L O S T   A L U M N A   B E N E
    L A D Y   B T U S   C B E R
  S C A L Y   A T L   S H U T H E R B U G
S T O P G O   C H U M   P L S   A G O N Y
E A U   R U B H E R C H I C K E N   A I M
A R N I E   I O S   S O L E   A B O R T S
L E T H E R B O M B   O E R   T A R D Y
  H O N E   I R E D   J A G S
S T E P   G R A T I A   B I E B   O P A L
T O R   L I C K H E R B O T T L E   H B O
A P P   I M A C S   T E T S   E N T I R E
B L A I N E   C H A C H A   D A L E S
B I R D I N G   J U M P H E R C A B L E S
E N T E N T E   I K E A   R E A L S I Z E
D E S   G S T   G E N L   E A R L   P E R
```

## 63

The Braille letters spell FEEL THE LOVE.

## 64

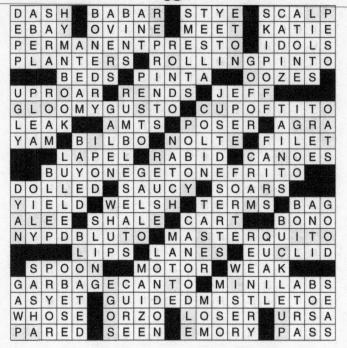

| A | S | A | T | E | A | M |   | T | O | E | C | A | P | S |   | S | T | A | M | P | E | D |
| I | N | V | O | I | C | E |   | A | T | M | C | A | R | D |   | D | O | W | O | R | S | E |
| M | A | I | N | S | T | R | E | E | T | A | C | R | O | S | S | A | M | E | R | I | C | A |
| S | T | A | S |   | E | V | A |   | A | G | L | E | T |   | E | K | E |   | I | M | O | F |
| A | C | T | O | N |   | R | A | W |   |   | E | S | L |   |   | S | T | A | R | T |
| T | H | E | F | I | R | S | T | M | A | J | O | R | M | E | M | O | R | I | A | L | T | O |
|   |   |   | S | A | M | O | A |   | A | N | E |   | W | A | N | E | D |
| O | N | E | S | I | Z | E |   | T | U | N | E | D | I | N |   | A | D | S | P | A | C | E |
| L | O | D | I |   | R | W | Y |   | N | E | I | L | S |   | M | I | O |   | E | G | O | N |
| L | O | T | S | A |   | S | O | F | I | A |   | I | N | K | E | R |   | B | R | I | N | Y |
| A | N | V | I | L |   | N | E | O | N |   | O | O | O | H |   | N | I | N | J | A |
|   | G | U | T |   | E | N | E |   | N | T | H |   | S | P | A |
| C | A | S | T | A | N | E | T | S |   | L | O | W | V | I | S | I | O | N |
| A | R | I | A |   | I | S | R |   | A | C | H |   | G | E | T |   | E | L | I | O |
| T | H | E | S | I | X | T | E | E | N | T | H | U | S | P | R | E | S | I | D | E | N | T |
| E | A | V | E | D |   | S | L | A | T | E | T | I | L | E |   | D | A | N | K | E |
| S | T | E | R | O | L | S |   | L | I | E |   | C | R | U |   | I | L | L | N | E | S | S |
|   | L | I | N | C | O | L | N |   | H | I | G | H | W | A | Y |
| H | E | A | D |   | N | O | U |   |   |   | O | O | P |   | N | C | A | A |
| I | N | D | R | A | G |   | A | P | P | L | I | E | D | T | O |   | E | B | O | O | K | S |
| T | S | A | O | C | O | T | T | S | A | O | C | M | O | R | F | S | L | E | V | A | R | T |
| C | U | T | I | E |   | O | R | A | N | G | E | T | R | E | E | S |   | V | A | L | O | R |
| H | E | E | D | S |   | M | O | T | T | S |   | S | A | N | D | S |   | Y | E | S | N | O |

| P | C | B | O | A | R | D |   | A | T | C | A | M | P |   | S | A | L | A | D | S |
| C | O | U | L | T | E | R |   | N | E | U | T | E | R |   | E | N | A | M | E | L |
| T | H | R | E | E | C | A | R | G | A | R | A | G | E |   | M | O | N | I | C | A |
|   | E | G | O |   | W | O | E | S |   |   | W | R | I | N | G | D | R | Y |
| P | R | E | L | I | M |   | P | R | E | P |   | O | W | E |   |   | S | E | E |
| L | E | S | E | M | A | J | E | S | T | E |   | P | I | X | E | L | A | T | E | D |
| Y | R | S |   | M | C | A |   | Y | E | E |   | X | I | S |
|   |   | L | O | E | W | E |   | C | O | N | C | R | E | T | E | P | U | M | P |
| S | W | A | R | D |   | L | S | A | T | S |   | E | L | O |   | S | P | E | E |
| A | W | A | I | T |   | S | M | O | R | E |   | S | T | O | L | I |   | H | A | S |
| F | A | I | R | A | M | O | U | N | T |   | H | A | R | A | S | S | M | E | N | T |
| T | N | T |   | L | A | N | N | Y |   | M | A | T | I | N |   | A | I | R | E | S |
| R | E | E | K |   | H | I | D |   | H | I | R | E | E |   | B | O | N | E | R |
| A | E | R | I | A | L | C | O | M | B | A | T |   | S | N | E | A | K |
|   |   | E | Y | E |   | O | O | O |   |   | F | R | O |   | C | S | I |
| O | N | A | V | E | R | A | G | E |   | W | I | D | E | L | Y | K | N | O | W | N |
| Y | E | S |   |   | B | U | S |   | S | M | E | E |   | L | I | A | N | E | S |
| S | P | A | C | E | J | A | M |   | B | A | L | E |   | P | G | A |
| T | A | M | A | L | E |   | B | A | L | L | E | T | S | L | I | P | P | E | R | S |
| E | L | A | P | S | E |   | O | H | Y | E | A | H |   | A | D | M | I | R | A | L |
| R | I | N | S | E | R |   | S | L | E | E | T | S |   | L | O | S | E | S | T | O |

**69**

```
O B A M A █ T H A W █ M O T T O █ C L A P
P A R I S █ O O N A █ E N R O N █ L A I R
E M N S H E H R D S █ R E I N E █ E R L E
L A O S █ X E N A █ G R A P E L E A V E S
█ █ █ J C O L E █ B O I L S █ I X N A Y S
E N G A R D E █ B O D E S █ B T U S █ █ █
C O M P O U N F R C U R █ C A R R █ T S E
G L E A N S █ I A C T █ D A T E B O O K S
█ A N N I █ I N S E C R E T █ █ S P R I T
█ █ █ E L L E █ H E K A T E █ E S M E █ █
O C H N S S S T E R █ L E M O N D R O P S
C L A Y █ D A U B E D █ A D E N █ █ █ █ █
H A R P O █ N A V Y Y A R D █ I T E M █ █
R U M D B I L E Y █ N A L A █ T E E M E D
E S S █ E D Y S █ B A N A N A S P L I T S
█ █ O R L E █ T U S K S █ S H E L L A C █
S E A D O O █ O U S T S █ S T I R S █ █ █
O X O D N V E R S I Y █ A L A R █ A N N A
L A R S █ E R A S E █ F R U I T F L I E S
O C T O █ T I L L S █ T E R R █ L I B R A
S T A N █ O N S E T █ C A P E █ A E S O P
```

**70**

```
S A B E N A █ R E S I S T S █ A M A T I S
C R A N E S █ I N U T E R O █ S A V A N T
H I Y O S I L V E R A W A Y █ P R I N C E
U A L █ S A B E █ F L E X █ R E T A K E N
S N O B █ N O N A C I D █ A E R A T I N G
S E R U M █ █ L I A █ U M P S █ E N S E █
█ █ █ L E S S F A T █ I N B R E D █ G E L
T H E B A L C O N Y I S C L O S E D █ █ █
E A P █ D O O R S █ D O L E S █ C O T A N
A S A S █ T O T █ C I N E █ C A J O L E █
T H T H T H T H T H A T S A L L F O L K S
R E H A B S █ █ H O M O █ L A A █ S T A T
O S A G E █ O T E R I █ A P I N G █ E L L
█ █ S A Y G O O D N I G H T G R A C I E █
M U S █ M E L O N S █ P L A Y S U P █ █ █
I L E S █ S A T E █ F O E █ █ B E A C H
R A T T A I L S █ B A D T R I P █ X E R O
A L B E R T A █ B A R N █ A V E O █ N O I
G U A R D S █ A N D M A Y G O D B L E S S
E M I N E M █ M A G E N T A █ A L E A S T
S E L E N E █ T I E R O D S █ L A S S E S
```

## 71

| M | O | C | H | A | | C | R | O | W | E | | C | A | R | B | | H | A | I | L |
| A | A | R | O | N | | O | K | R | A | S | | A | B | A | A | | A | G | R | A |
| C | H | A | T | E | A | U | O | I | L | S | | M | E | D | I | A | B | I | A | S |
| S | U | N | L | A | M | P | | R | O | U | E | A | I | R | L | I | N | E | S | |
| | | E | R | A | | T | H | U | | N | O | T | I | N | I | T | | | | |
| E | L | B | A | | B | O | A | S | T | S | | | S | C | A | L | I | A | | |
| G | O | A | D | S | | U | N | I | | H | E | N | N | A | | I | T | E | R | S |
| O | O | H | | U | N | D | E | R | S | E | A | O | U | I | J | A | | I | O | S |
| S | P | A | R | R | E | D | | P | O | S | T | G | A | M | E | | B | A | B | A |
| | | I | S | E | E | | M | I | L | O | | N | E | W | S | R | O | O | M | |
| | S | O | V | S | | F | I | N | D | P | E | A | C | E | | T | A | U | T | |
| S | T | E | P | T | U | R | N | | R | U | D | E | | T | A | C | T | | | |
| L | A | U | D | | S | A | N | D | B | A | R | S | | D | I | R | E | C | T | V |
| A | T | V | | M | A | U | I | O | E | N | O | P | H | I | L | E | | O | W | E |
| V | E | R | S | A | | D | E | L | C | O | | E | E | E | | D | E | M | O | N |
| S | N | E | A | K | S | | | A | S | G | A | R | D | | | R | E | S | T | |
| | | G | E | T | R | E | A | L | | E | K | E | | S | H | U | | | | |
| A | D | I | E | U | O | A | R | S | M | A | N | | | C | H | E | D | D | A | R |
| D | O | N | T | P | A | N | I | C | | P | R | A | G | U | E | A | I | O | L | I |
| A | N | N | E | | T | A | C | O | | S | E | W | O | N | | T | T | O | P | S |
| M | E | S | A | | S | T | A | T | | E | S | S | A | Y | | H | E | S | S | E |

## 72

| M | A | C | Y | S | | F | A | L | S | E | | A | K | O | N | | D | A | B |
| A | D | A | S | H | | B | A | H | A | M | A | | D | E | R | I | S | I | V | E |
| H | E | L | L | O | M | A | R | Y | L | O | U | | D | Y | S | T | O | P | I | A |
| E | L | L | | R | E | D | M | E | A | T | | W | I | F | E | | U | P | O | N |
| R | E | T | I | T | L | E | | S | W | E | E | T | C | A | R | O | L | I | N | E |
| | | O | C | T | O | | | R | O | T | C | | U | S | N | | | | | |
| C | O | M | E | O | N | E | I | L | E | E | N | | T | I | T | | G | P | A | |
| A | P | I | A | N | | N | B | A | T | V | | C | O | S | | A | O | U | T | |
| M | A | N | X | | O | N | E | E | Y | E | | S | A | R | A | S | M | I | L | E |
| P | H | D | | G | N | U | | M | R | P | I | M | | B | A | I | L | E | E | |
| | | J | U | L | I | E | D | O | Y | A | L | O | V | E | M | E | | | | |
| A | Y | E | A | Y | E | | R | U | N | T | S | | O | L | E | | P | S | I | |
| S | E | X | Y | S | A | D | I | E | | I | T | A | L | I | A | | B | L | O | T |
| H | A | T | S | | V | O | N | | M | E | T | A | L | | C | O | A | L | S | |
| E | R | R | | R | E | G | | H | E | L | P | M | E | R | H | O | N | D | A | |
| | | A | E | C | | E | T | T | U | | | | E | A | S | T | | | | |
| W | A | L | K | A | W | A | Y | R | E | N | E | E | | B | R | I | T | C | O | M |
| A | L | A | I | | A | T | R | A | | E | L | L | I | M | A | N | | E | L | A |
| F | E | R | N | A | N | D | O | | L | A | Y | D | O | W | N | S | A | L | L | Y |
| T | U | G | G | E | D | O | N | | O | L | S | E | N | S | | A | L | L | I | E |
| S | T | E | | R | A | G | E | | P | E | E | R | S | | W | I | S | E | R | |

## 73

Grid 73 (across rows):

BBS · DIP · TPAIN · ETHANOL
EEW · ENA · AETNA · SUITORS
RAE · NIL · BEING · PREENED
GREATDIVIDE · WINS
MENTALNOTE · SHOES · EWES
AREOLE · THEREAND · AGAIN
NSYNC · SEA · OAST · THATSO
ABES · HUMP · WHALE
SMORES · MASS · DOE · RDA
CHOPIN · FINE · CONCLAVES
NUTTED · ENG · COW · LABORS
BLOSSOMED · BONN · OCELOT
CAR · VID · TONE · SCREEN
PAPER · BOOK · MAKO
LOOSER · LAWS · DIX · SODOM
BROKE · MOUNTAIN · ESPANA
SALS · WOODS · LOSSLEADER
WARP · BACKINBLACK
NIAGARA · OPINE · KIA · ILE
IDCARDS · LOGOS · ENL · SUR
POETESS · DIANE · SOL · TBS

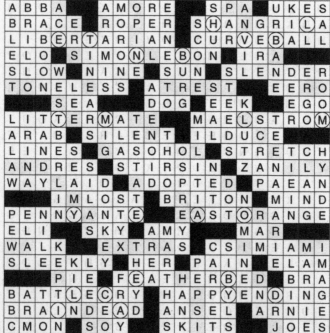

## 74

Grid 74 (across rows):

ABBA · AMORE · SPA · UKES
BRACE · ROPER · SHANGRILA
LIBERTARIAN · CURVEBALL
ELO · SIMONLEBON · IRA
SLOW · NINE · SUN · SLENDER
TONELESS · ATREST · EERO
SEA · DOG · EEK · EGO
LITTERMATE · MAELSTROM
ARAB · SILENT · ILDUCE
LINES · GASOHOL · STRETCH
ANDRES · STIRSIN · ZANILY
WAYLAID · ADOPTED · PAEAN
IMLOST · BRITON · MIND
PENNYANTE · EASTORANGE
ELI · SKY · AMY · MAR
WALK · EXTRAS · CSIMIAMI
SLEEKLY · HER · PAIN · ELAM
PIE · FEATHERBED · BRA
BATTLECRY · HAPPYENDING
BRAINDEAD · ANSEL · ARNIE
CMON · SOY · SKITS · JOES

```
C C C C C   I S U P   A U E L   T T T T T
C R O A T   T O U R   L U A U   L E T H E
C E L T S   C L U E   T U R K   C A T E R
C S I S   H O U S E R U L E   C T R S
C C C C C   U U U U U   N O T M E
    A S P C A   M R I   J U K E S
J A U N T I E R   E O S   U N I C Y C L E
A L F   E L I A S   M S N B C   P A L
B I O N I C L E G   T O O K A T A X I
    O N E A   A G A I N   R E L O
T O P S C O R E   A S S   E N D O R S E D
I N L E A F   N A S T I E R   O H E N R Y
L E A R N T   E L P R A D O   F A R I N A
D A Y S   H E R B S   H I D E F   O D E D
A L E   A E I O U   T E A T S   E S S
    D I V A N   M C R A E   C H I R R
  T H R I C E   T H I R D   H E R O E S
M A O I S T   T R A G E D Y   T I N M A N
A M O S   I D E A S   N O O S E   D A T E
Z E K E   O U N C E   T W Y L A   O R B S
E D Y S   N O O K   N O R M   S K Y S
```